D0207614

OXFORD STUDIES IN THE HISTORY OF PHILOSOPHY

VOLUME II

Studies in
Seventeenth-Century
European Philosophy

Studies in Seventeenth-Century European Philosophy

Edited by

M. A. STEWART

CLARENDON PRESS · OXFORD

1997

Oxford University Press, Great Clarendon Street, Oxford OX2 6DP

Oxford New York
Athens Auckland Bangkok Bogota Bombay
Buenos Aires Calcutta Cape Town Dar es Salaam
Delhi Florence Hong Kong Istanbul Karachi
Kuala Lumpur Madras Madrid Melbourne
Mexico City Nairobi Paris Singapore
Taipei Tokyo Toronto Warsaw
and associated companies in
Berlin Ibadan

Oxford is a trade mark of Oxford University Press

Published in the United States
by Oxford University Press Inc., New York

© *in this collection Oxford University Press 1997*

All rights reserved. No part of this publication may be reproduced,
stored in a retrieval system, or transmitted, in any form or by any means,
without the prior permission in writing of Oxford University Press.
Within the UK, exceptions are allowed in respect of any fair dealing for the
purpose of research or private study, or criticism or review, as permitted
under the Copyright, Designs and Patents Act, 1988, or in the case of
reprographic reproduction in accordance with the terms of the licences
issued by the Copyright Licensing Agency. Enquiries concerning
reproduction outside these terms and in other countries should be
sent to the Rights Department, Oxford University Press,
at the address above

British Library Cataloguing in Publication Data
Data available

Library of Congress Cataloging in Publication Data
Data available
ISBN 0–19–823940–8

1 3 5 7 9 10 8 6 4 2

Typeset by Cambrian Typesetters, Frimley, Surrey
Printed in Great Britain on acid-free paper by
Bookcraft (Bath) Ltd
Midsomer Norton, Somerset

OXFORD STUDIES IN THE HISTORY OF PHILOSOPHY

EDITOR

M. A. Stewart
Department of Philosophy, University of Lancaster
Furness College, Lancaster LA1 4YG

ADVISORY BOARD

David Berman, *Trinity College, Dublin*
John Dunn, *King's College, Cambridge*
Daniel Garber, *University of Chicago*
David Fate Norton, *McGill University*
Michael J. Petry, *Erasmus University, Rotterdam*

PREFACE

This volume conforms to the same general conception of the history of philosophy as the first publication in the series and offers something of the same characteristic blend of historical and analytical commentary. The new collection has been selected from submissions received in response to two separate commissions over a period of several years. One was a call for papers in the broad area of seventeenth-century philosophy, the second for papers on philosophical activity in the Low Countries in the early modern period. Some of the earliest contributions that were accepted for publication have already been widely cited elsewhere in the secondary literature. The main constraint on bringing them to publication has been the need to create a thematically homogeneous selection. This has been made possible by building the present collection round the work of Descartes, Leibniz, and Bayle. All three drew upon a deep knowledge of classical philosophical traditions and alike contributed and reacted extensively to intellectual developments across Europe in their time—including, as several of our contributors show, specific developments in the Netherlands. A companion volume on *English philosophy in the age of Locke* is in preparation.

Stephen Menn and Tad M. Schmaltz explore significant aspects of Descartes's rejection of scholasticism. Menn shows that Descartes's debt to Augustine, first detected by Arnauld, goes a good deal deeper than has been supposed. His Augustinian metaphysics gives him the space within which to develop a non-Aristotelian physics consistent with the new theory of matter; but it is of particular significance for his account of judgement, an aspect of a more general theory of voluntary action devised with a clear eye to its theological ramifications. Schmaltz looks at Cartesian psychology from another perspective, examining preconceptions about the scholastic theory of sensation that lie behind Descartes's controversy with the Dutch professor, Regius. While the controversy throws light on Descartes's own theory of -signs, Schmaltz contends that it was distorted by his imperfect understanding of scholasticism.

Turning to later Cartesianism, Steven Nadler re-examines the nature of occasionalism. He takes up a suggestion by Thomas Lennon that the occasionalist programme was never primarily intended to circumvent the problems of mind-body dualism, and shows that there was in fact no mind-body problem, distinct from the problem of interaction as it exists even for body-body relations, in this tradition. For Malebranche, for instance, no finite substance, whether body or mind, can be the source of a necessary connection with anything else—something that God alone can achieve by being infinite. For the Flemish Geulincx, nothing can be a cause that does not have the knowledge to ensure its effect. Problems about causation and creation surface again, from a neoplatonist perspective, in Stuart Brown's survey of the work and career of the Brabant thinker F. M. van Helmont. Though not principally a philosophical writer, van Helmont was an active link within and between groups of philosophical, medical, and cabbalistical scholars in Germany, England, and the Netherlands. His speculations on the origin of matter attracted interest and different responses from Conway, More, Locke, and Leibniz, and are one likely influence on Leibniz's monadology.

Two contributors deal directly with Leibniz's work in relation to the new science. Christia Mercer argues that Leibniz's early thought is marked by a rejection not of Aristotle but of the non-Greek Aristotelianism of later scholasticism, and is to be understood as his embracing the eclecticism of the "reformed" philosophy which sought to harmonize an authentic Aristotle with the new mechanism. Thus Mercer, like Menn, sees the move towards mechanism as a decisive factor in the relationship of her sources to scholasticism. She argues the case by reference to the debate over substantial forms and the individuation of matter. Catherine Wilson shows how the same interests carry through to Leibniz's later work in the age of the microscope, and suggests another influence on the development of his monadology—the discovery of micro-organisms. The preformationist theories of Malebranche, as well as the experimental work of the Dutch microscopists, have an important place in this story.

Bayle's work is the subject of our two concluding papers. Thomas Lennon starts from Bayle's ambivalent conception of human nature, and uses the thinking-matter controversy to illustrate his view of the infirmity of reason, justifying support for toleration on all speculative questions; but Bayle also believed in a natural propensity to discord and therefore a need for authoritarian government. Though there are affinities between Bayle's view of conscience in theological matters and Locke's, there was probably no direct influence, but both may have been reacting to the work of Jurieu. Lennon's Bayle remains close to his Calvinist roots, but in David Wootton's estimation these were abandoned. To what degree could religious faith coexist with adventurous moral thinking? Wootton reopens the question of how to understand Bayle's literary technique, and suggests that the fondness for titillating detail that Bayle himself characterized as "obscenities" may be a sign that he challenged not only received mores but also, in the circumstances of the times, their religious foundations.

Reviewers of the first volume in this series uniformly queried the suitableness of including book reviews, and these have now been abandoned after consultation and agreement with the Press. Our apologies are due to those who prepared some early reviews for this volume.

The principal adviser for this collection was Daniel Garber, to whom I am grateful for his guidance when the volume was in the original planning stage. I also acknowledge the benefit of advice from Stuart Brown, Desmond Clarke, Jean-Paul Pittion, George MacDonald Ross, Catherine Wilson, Roger Woolhouse, and John Wright. Ruth Evelyn Savage was editorial assistant. My own editorial work was completed while I was a visiting fellow in the Research School of Social Sciences at the Australian National University.

CONTENTS

I

DESCARTES, AUGUSTINE, AND THE STATUS OF FAITH

STEPHEN MENN

1. INTRODUCTION

Ever since the Augustinian theologian Antoine Arnauld wrote the 'Fourth set of Objections' to the *Meditations*, scholars have been struck by the resemblances between Descartes's philosophy and that of St Augustine. "It first occurs to me to marvel [*mirari*]", says Arnauld, "that the most eminent man [Descartes] has established as the first principle of his whole philosophy the same thing that was established by the divine Augustine, a man of the most acute intellect and entirely admirable [*mirandus*] not only in theological but also in philosophical matters" (AT vii. 197–8);[1] for both Descartes in the *Meditations* and Augustine in the dialogue *De libero arbitrio* (*On free will*) begin their reconstructions of knowledge with the indubitable knowledge of oneself as a thinking thing. Nor do the resemblances stop there. Descartes begins where Augustine begins, with the doctrine of the soul, and proceeds as Augustine proceeds, to the doctrine of God; in so doing, he works out a whole metaphysics along the lines of *De libero arbitrio*. Descartes, like Augustine and unlike Aristotle and St Thomas, works out his concepts of the soul and God without reference to what the senses report about the physical universe. Thus, the soul is conceived essentially as a mind or thinking thing, only incidentally as what animates a body; God is conceived essentially as the source of truth to the mind, only incidentally as the governor of the physical world. The laws of nature are God's free decrees, not intellectual necessities which he must follow; the human mind, too, is superior in its freedom to the causal order of nature, though its power over bodies is limited. On all of these

© Stephen Menn 1997

[1] References to Descartes's works, and to the Objections to the *Meditations*, are to *Oeuvres de Descartes*, ed. C. Adam and P. Tannery (11 vols, Paris 1974–83), henceforth cited as 'AT' followed by volume and page numbers. Translations from Descartes and other authors are mine; in general, I have preferred to translate literally.

topics Descartes agrees with Augustine and disagrees with Aristotle; and on all of them he differs, at least in the stress he places on the different conceptions, from St Thomas.[2]

Descartes and Arnauld were both opponents of the scholastic philosophy, which in all of its varieties attempted to carry out St Thomas's project of harmonizing the Augustinian doctrine of God and the soul with the Aristotelian doctrine of body as a composite of matter and form. Descartes's philosophy sharply separates the Augustinian metaphysics from the Aristotelian physics: while the second, third, and fourth Meditations offer a metaphysics largely drawn from Augustine, the fifth and sixth offer an analysis of body as matter alone, which is directly opposed to the Aristotelian conception. Indeed, we know that one of Descartes's principal aims in writing the *Meditations* was to present the Augustinian metaphysics he shared with the scholastics in such a way as to establish the foundations of a mechanistic and thus anti-Aristotelian physics. As he writes to Mersenne, "I think I have put in many other things [besides the metaphysical assertions explicitly proved in the different Meditations]; and I will tell you, between ourselves, that these six Meditations contain all the foundations of my Physics. But please do not say so, for those who favour Aristotle might make more difficulties about approving of them; and I hope that those who will read them will accustom themselves insensibly to my principles, and recognize their truth, before perceiving that they destroy those of Aristotle" (AT iii. 297–8).

Arnauld's opposition to scholasticism was primarily theological, based on a total loyalty to St Augustine: together with a broad current of Reformation and Counter-Reformation thought, he regarded the scholastic attempt to reconcile Augustine with Aristotle as a betrayal that preserved the form of Augustine's assertions while denying the substance of his conceptions. When Arnauld admires Augustine "not only in theological but also in philosophical matters", he is implicitly promoting Augustine as a rival to Aristotle, and urging a philosophy which would base itself integrally on Augustine's

---

[2] These conceptions of God and the soul are present throughout, in both Augustine and Descartes, and may be discovered in any work. The idea of an intellectual knowledge of God and the soul divorced from sensation is developed particularly in Augustine's *Confessions*, Bk VII, and in his *Soliloquies*; it is the dominant theme of Descartes's *Meditations*. For the picture of the human soul as essentially thinking, see Augustine's discussion of the soul in preparation for his proof of God in *De libero arbitrio*, Bk II, but especially his analysis of its faculties in *De trinitate*, Bks IX–X; and Descartes's second Meditation. For the doctrine of God as the source of truth, and the highest object of thought, see *De libero arbitrio*, Bk II, and Descartes's third Meditation. The conception of the will is not as clearly developed in a single place, but for the human will see *De libero arbitrio*, Bk III, and Descartes's fourth Meditation. The freedom and sovereignty of the divine will are everywhere where Augustine discusses the physics of creation, as in the *Confessions*, Bks XI–XIII. Descartes thinks that God acts freely even in establishing what are apparently necessary truths: see AT vii. 431–2.

conceptions, instead of accepting Augustine's theological conclusions on authority and then turning to Aristotle for a philosophical explication. This is what he thinks he has found in the *Meditations*. While remaining the leader of the Jansenist party in the Church and the defender of strict Augustinian theology, Arnauld came to adopt the Cartesian philosophy, and after Descartes's death became one of its chief spokesmen.[3]

Thus from the first publication of the *Meditations* on, there has been a tendency to interpret Descartes as presenting an Augustinian philosophy; but at the same time there has often been a suspicion that, despite the *philosophical* parallels, the *religious* implications of Descartes's project run counter to Augustine's intention of giving an understanding of the Christian faith. Descartes himself says little about the religious implications of his work: he observes a strict separation between the disciplines of philosophy and revealed theology, and he makes it clear on many occasions that his business is only with the former. This is in itself not radical or surprising, since the distinction between the two disciplines, although ignored by St Augustine, had been observed by the scholastics since the days of St Thomas; but since Descartes intends a radical reform of traditional philosophy, based on doubting everything that can be doubted and reconstructing the indubitable, it is natural to ask whether traditional theology will remain unshaken.

Arnauld appends to his philosophical Objections a section "on those things which might delay the theologians", in which, besides noting some areas of detail where Descartes's philosophy might run the risk of conflict with Catholic orthodoxy, he raises the issue of the scope of methodological doubt. "Another thing I would like our Author to indicate is that, when he asserts that we should not assent to anything except what we clearly and distinctly know, he is concerned only with those things which pertain to learning and fall under the scope of the understanding, and not with those which pertain to faith and to the conduct of life; and thus that he is condemning the rashness of the opinionated, not the persuasion of those who prudently believe" (AT vii. 215–16). And yet Arnauld seems oddly unconcerned about this potential challenge to faith; he is rather more worried about how to reconcile the doctrine of body as extension with the mystery of transubstantiation. He is sure that his proposed clarification expresses Descartes's real intention, and he is content with Descartes's policy of separating philosophy and theology; he is merely concerned that Descartes should not give the irreligious a chance to misinterpret his words. Arnauld offers Descartes a quotation from Augustine's treatise *De utilitate credendi* (*On the usefulness of believing*) on the distinction between belief and opinion, which would provide

[3] This history has been admirably sketched by Henri Gouhier in his *Cartésianisme et augustinisme au XVIIe siècle* (Paris 1978).

justification for a sceptical attack on opinion while preserving the immunity of faith, and submits the matter to Descartes's own best judgement. Descartes in his Reply seems equally unconcerned, and accepts Arnauld's explanation *in toto*:

That I always made an exception for those things which pertain to faith and to the conduct of life . . . is shown by the whole context of what I wrote; and I also expressly explained it in the Reply to the Second Objections, number 5; and I also gave advance notice of it in the Synopsis; so that in this way I may declare how much credit I give to the most eminent man's [Arnauld's] judgement, and how much I have accepted his advice. (AT vii. 247–8)

Despite Arnauld's endorsement, and his Augustinian justification of Descartes's position, debate continues about the religious implications of Descartes's philosophical project, and about what light this sheds on his apparent affinity with the thought of St Augustine. No serious scholar doubts that Descartes was personally a devout Catholic; but the question remains whether the logic of his thought, with its apparent indifference to the concerns of faith, does not reveal a different spirit from that of St Augustine.

This is the conclusion of Étienne Gilson, who has pursued the investigation of Descartes's sources perhaps more extensively than any other scholar. Gilson recognizes that Descartes's metaphysics resembles Augustine's at many points, and that the resemblance is too close to be coincidental: he admits both a direct and an indirect influence of Augustine on Descartes. But Gilson asserts that Descartes's attempt to work out a philosophy independent of theology is contrary to the Augustinian spirit. According to Gilson, Descartes's only real constructive concern was with the mathematization of physics; in attempting to demonstrate the presupposition of this project, that body consists in extension alone, Descartes realized "that he needed a metaphysics, and even a metaphysics of the distinction between soul and body". Since by his mathematical method he had "abandoned Thomist empiricism", he had to find a metaphysics from some other source, and "that of St Augustine was there, ready to be accepted", being generally in the air in the early seventeenth century: "surrounded by Augustinians, Descartes needed no more than a brief conversation to see opening before him the road to a metaphysics by which his method could pass".[4]

In this way, according to Gilson, Descartes's "method condemned him to follow in metaphysics the road of St Augustine";[5] but he took up only that part of Augustine's metaphysics which could be proved by the mathematical

[4] E. Gilson, *Études sur le rôle de la pensée médiévale dans la formation du système cartésien*, 5th edn (Paris 1984), 200–201.

[5] Gilson, *The future of Augustinian metaphysics*, reprinted in *A Gilson reader*, ed. A. Pegis (Garden City, NY 1957), 86.

method, and thus missed the essence of Augustine's thought, which is its religious inspiration. Gilson says, "The problem of the relations of reason and faith is not one that can be considered as incidental when we are trying to situate a doctrine in relation to that of St Augustine; on the contrary, the idea of a *sapientia christiana*, specifically opposed to the Greek and purely rational notion of a *natural philosophy*, constitutes the very point of departure of the doctrine. To deny the sufficiency of reason is as essential a function of Augustinianism as to deny the sufficiency of nature, and the possibility of a philosophy developing itself validly without worrying about the data of revelation is the radical negation of St Augustine's *De utilitate credendi*, of his whole doctrine, indeed of his whole experience. But if Descartes is opposed to St Augustine on this central and decisive point of Augustinianism, how could he be an Augustinian?"[6]

On this view, then, Descartes represents a modern and entirely un-Augustinian current of thought; in developing a philosophy separate from theology, says Gilson, he is "pursuing radically anti-Augustinian ends". Descartes is simply scavenging pieces of Augustinian doctrine to patch the internal difficulties of his physics; the real meaning of Augustine's thought is not preserved. Gilson goes so far as to say that "it follows . . . that even when the two philosophies employ the same concepts and arrange them in the same order, they do not mean the same things".[7]

In what follows, I shall be arguing against Gilson's conclusion. It is certainly true that Descartes's primary purpose in taking up Augustine's metaphysics is to use it to derive a physics opposed to Aristotelian or Thomist empiricism; but it does not automatically follow either that Descartes is altering the meaning of Augustine's thought or that he is betraying Augustine's religious intentions. The key question is whether Augustine's thought can be built up into a scientific system without destroying its essential character. It is all too plain why Gilson wants to argue that it cannot: as a neo-Thomist confronting Augustinianism as a still-living tendency in Christian philosophy, he wishes to preserve it from the "temptation" of Cartesianism which would turn it into a systematic rival to Thomism.[8] Gilson approves of Augustinianism as a discipline of religious devotion; but as a philosophy he finds it, and wishes to keep it, unscientific and incomplete. Thomism, for him, is the only systematic Christian philosophy, and it can construct its philosophy in relative independence of the data of revelation; but when Augustinianism does this in an attempt to set itself up as a science, it has abandoned its calling and can only corrupt scientific philosophy.

I shall not address the question of the nature of Augustinianism and of

---

[6] Gilson, *Études*, 289–90.   [7] Gilson, *Future*, 92–3.   [8] Ibid., 85 *et passim*.

Descartes's use of it in its fullest scope. But I shall argue that Descartes is borrowing from Augustine precisely at the point where Gilson sees his greatest divergence from the saint, in his conception of the role of reason in philosophy and consequently of the relations between reason and faith. I shall examine how Descartes makes the Augustinian metaphysics function in specifying and justifying the method he intends to use in the reconstruction of the sciences, and show how he accomplishes this by the particular way he presents this metaphysics in the *Meditations*. I shall argue that Descartes is not distorting or dismembering Augustine's metaphysics, but is taking it as he finds it and deriving the consequences for scientific method. In particular, it will follow that Descartes's position on faith and reason is a natural outgrowth of Augustinian principles, and that it is fully consistent with Augustine's original intentions. This is what Arnauld, a man intimately familiar with the writings and ways of thought of St Augustine, saw in Descartes, and it explains the calmness of his response to Descartes's apparent challenge to faith. By spelling out Descartes's Augustinian reasons for his position on faith and reason, I hope to vindicate Arnauld's interpretation of Descartes and Augustine against Gilson's.

II. THEODICY AND METHOD

The key to Descartes's plan of using Augustine's metaphysics to justify his scientific method will be found in the fourth Meditation. This Meditation is entitled 'Of the true and the false', but its content is psychological rather than logical: it presents a theory of the human activity of judgement which explains the origin and the conditions of error in judgement, and therefore allows Descartes to formulate a method for judging without running the risk of error. Now, the theory of action Descartes presents in the fourth Meditation is entirely traditional: it is Augustine's theory, and it is accepted by the whole tradition of Christian philosophy after him. The real innovation and the real work of the fourth Meditation come in situating the activity of judgement in terms of this general theory of action. In this section, I shall examine Descartes's use of this Augustinian theory of action in formulating his theory of judgement, and show that the application of this general theory of action to the case of judgement allows him to derive conclusions, both about human freedom in judgement and about a divine guarantee of certain special judgements, which are essential if his scientific method is to succeed.

Augustine develops a comprehensive theory of human and divine action in *De libero arbitrio*. He is doing so in response to the problem of the origin of evil, and indeed in some manuscripts the dialogue bears the title, 'Whence evil?'. It opens with the question, "Tell me, I beg you, whether God is not the author of evil?" (*DLA*, I. i. I);[9] Augustine believes that God is *not* the author of moral evil or evil-doing, although he may be the author of natural evils dispensed as a just punishment for sin. But, not contented with mere *believing*, he wishes to *understand* how it can be that "all things which are, are from one God, and yet that God is not the author of sins", although sins do exist. "For", he says, "it disturbs the mind how, if sins are from those souls which God created, and these souls are from God, the sins should not be referred by a small step to God" (*DLA*, I. ii. 4). In order to gain the understanding which the mind thus troubled desires, Augustine first proves that God exists and is the source of all good and no evil things, and then argues that God has produced something good, not something evil, in giving human beings the power of free will which they can put to either good or evil use. Augustine must argue that the evil results of human choice do not contradict God's beneficence: to do this he works out a whole theory of divine and human responsibility, by which he can distinguish between the perfections that a world created by a beneficent God must have, and the greater perfections that such a world may lack. He will argue that the world is good enough: that it does have the appropriate kind of goodness, even though it may not prima facie seem to, and that its lack of the higher kind of goodness is not a difficulty for understanding the beneficence of God.

Descartes, in the fourth Meditation, is applying Augustine's theory of human and divine action to solve a problem that had arisen in the first Meditation. The argument of the *Meditations* as a whole is that God and the soul are better known than bodies: the first Meditation proves this in a negative way by arguing that we can have no certainty about the world until we know that God does not deceive us. Descartes says in the first Meditation that it would not suffice to learn that there was no creator powerful enough to deceive us: the less powerful my creator is thought to be, "it will be that much more likely that I am so imperfect as to be always deceived" (AT vii. 21). The remaining hope, to establish the possibility of knowledge, is to show that we are creatures of a God who is all-powerful but also all-beneficent, and therefore does not choose to deceive us. But even if this can be shown, it may not resolve the difficulties about certainty, for "if it is contrary to his goodness to have created me such that I should always be deceived, for the same reason it would also seem to be foreign to him to permit me to be deceived even occasionally; but this cannot be said" (ibid.).

Descartes's problem here is analogous to Augustine's, of which indeed it is a special case. He wishes to prove that human beings are creatures of an

---

[9] Augustine's works will be cited by the book, chapter, and paragraph numbers (where these exist) which are found in the Benedictine edition (reprinted in Migne's *Patrologia latina* and elsewhere), and which are preserved in most modern editions. The title of *De libero arbitrio* will be abbreviated as '*DLA*'.

omnipotent God who produces nothing that is not good, while admitting that human beings act in an evil way in passing erroneous judgements. To understand how these can be true simultaneously, Descartes, like Augustine, must work out a theory of divine and human responsibility, so that he can judge what degrees of perfection can and cannot be asserted of God's creatures. He does this, simply, by following Augustine: in the second and third Meditations he develops a proof for the existence and perfection of God which closely resembles the proof of *De libero arbitrio*, and then turns in the fourth Meditation to examine the consequences for the perfection of human beings as works of God. Here he takes over Augustine's theory of free will as a divine gift and its human use for good or evil, but he applies it exclusively to understanding the human activity of *judging* rightly or wrongly.

In interpreting the fourth Meditation, we must be careful to distinguish between the problems which Descartes explicitly takes up and the points he is really trying to make. Explicitly, he is trying to reconcile the perfection of God with the fact of human error; but in reality, as soon as the problem has been posed in this way, the solution is an automatic application of Augustine's theory. What Descartes is really trying to do is to put forward an understanding of judgement in terms of the Augustinian theory of action; and this leads him to a theory of judgement which differs from the then current accounts in ways which provide crucial justifications for his scientific method. On the one hand, this leads him to assert the *freedom* of judgement: if God cannot be blamed for errors in our judgement, that judgement must be under our own total control, so that we can methodically alter our habits of judgement, radically if necessary. On the other hand, Descartes will also be able to derive a *guarantee* that, if we follow the proper method, our judgements will be true: although God need not have made us infallible, he must have made us such that, if we use our will as he intends, we will not go wrong. Descartes's project in the fourth Meditation is to use the Augustinian theory of action to derive these consequences, and to determine which judgements do indeed bear the divine guarantee.

The fourth Meditation begins with a cheery assessment of the consequences of the third Meditation proof for the existence and perfection of God: "Already I seem to see a way by which, from this contemplation of the true God, 'in whom', indeed, 'all treasures of the sciences and of wisdom are hid', one might arrive at a knowledge of other things" (AT vii. 53).[10] The God of the third Meditation is contrasted with the deceiving God of the first as the

---

[10] The quotation is from Colossians 2: 3, in the Latin of the Vulgate, except that the singular *scientiae* (knowledge) has been transformed into the plural *scientiarum* (the sciences), and placed before instead of after wisdom: Descartes is going to make good the pious sentiment of St Paul, and show how we can actually come to a true system of the sciences, building up to wisdom, from the knowledge we have of God.

"true" God, not only in the sense that he really exists, but also because his perfection implies that he is the source of truth and not of falsity. "For I know that it cannot happen that he should ever deceive me: for in every fraud or deception some imperfection is found; and although the *power* to deceive seems to be some evidence of ingenuity or power, beyond a doubt the *will* to deceive bears witness of either malice or weakness, and therefore cannot be found in God" (ibid.). This veracity of my creator seems to offer a guarantee of knowledge: for "I observe that there is in me a certain faculty of judging, which I have certainly received from God, as I have all the other things that are in me" (AT vii. 53–4), and since God does not wish to deceive me, he will not have given me a faculty for making mistakes, but a faculty for judging rightly.

Here Descartes raises the point he had already made in the first Meditation: this seems to prove too much. I plainly do fall into error: even if this is an abuse of my faculty of judging, the error would still seem to be derived, ultimately, from God. This is the problem of *De libero arbitrio*. Descartes responds by developing, stage by stage, the solution of the dialogue, and in so doing sets out his theory of the act of judgement and of the conditions under which its truth is guaranteed.

He first offers an incomplete solution to the problem, based on an inadequate understanding of judgement; he then points out the insufficiency of this solution, and offers a correction which shows how judgement is properly to be understood. He begins by observing a way in which he could deviate from the truth without God's having to endow him with a special faculty for that purpose. He perceives "not only a real and positive idea of God, or of a supremely perfect being, but also a certain negative idea of nothing, or of what is supremely absent from all perfection" (AT vii. 54). We ourselves are somewhere in between God and nothingness: God has created us out of nothing and granted us some perfections, while withholding others: our imperfections result, not from a positive act of God, but simply from the original nothingness or lack of all perfections from which we were drawn, inasmuch as God has not given us the full measure of perfections which he himself possesses. And this is the explanation of error, which is "not something real which depends on God, but simply a defect; nor do I need, in order to err, some faculty given by God for this purpose, but it happens that I err from the fact that the faculty of judging the truth which I have from him is not infinite in me" (ibid.).

Descartes here is taking up a traditional explanation of creaturely imperfections, which Augustine had applied to account for the wrong actions of created natures. Thus Augustine says, "Since that motion of turning away [from eternal to temporal goods], which we declare to be sin, is a defective motion, and every defect is of nothing, see to what it pertains, and do not doubt that it does not pertain to God" (*DLA*, II. xx. 54). Even more closely, when Descartes says that he errs "not inasmuch as I have been created by the supreme being . . . but inasmuch as I also somehow participate in nothing or in non-being" (AT vii. 54), we may compare Augustine's expression in *De natura boni* (*On the nature of the good*), that corruptible natures have whatever perfections they have "for this reason, that it is God by whom they have been made; but they are not immutable for this reason, that it is nothing out of which they have been made" (*De natura boni*, x).

Both Descartes and Augustine accept this as true, but neither accepts it as an adequate account of moral or cognitive error. As Descartes immediately says, "nevertheless, this is not yet altogether satisfactory" (AT vii. 54). For Augustine, this analysis in terms of God and nothingness explains the imperfection which is a common condition for all created natures, not sin, a special condition into which some of these created natures have fallen of their own will and from which, with the help of God, they can again emerge. Descartes's programme depends on distinguishing between error as voluntary sin and involuntary finitude. It is certainly our creaturely finitude which makes error *possible*; nothing Descartes can do will abolish this condition of finitude, but if error is something beyond this finitude and can be brought under the control of the will, he has a hope of eliminating the habit of error. But if Augustine is right, error *must* be voluntary, since it is not merely a lack of divine perfection, but a positive evil which cannot be part of a nature as constituted by God.

The key premise is that error is a positive evil and not a mere creaturely imperfection. Descartes thinks that this is obvious on inspection; the only problem is to give an adequate formulation of the antithesis. Descartes uses a common scholastic distinction drawn from Aristotle: "error is not a pure negation, but a privation or lack of some knowledge which somehow *ought* to be in me" (AT vii. 55). Descartes's gloss on the term refers back to Aristotle's definition: "we say that one of the things which is capable of some possession is *deprived* of it when the possession is not present at all in what it is natural for it to be present in, and when it is natural", so that blindness will be a privation, while not-seeing is a pure negation.[11] But it is not entirely clear how error fits under this definition.

The pure negation of knowledge is not error, but ignorance. This is a concomitant of being made out of nothing. God has given me, among other perfections, certain items of knowledge; he has not given me knowledge of other things, and I am consequently ignorant about them. But this does not imply that I am in error about them. I can fall into error only when I myself act, by passing judgement on matters about which I am ignorant, so that I am guessing and am liable to guess wrong.

This distinction between the negativity of ignorance and the positive evil of

---

[11] Aristotle, *Categories*, 12a 28–31.

error is drawn essentially from the Augustinian theory of action, despite Descartes's use of scholastic terminology. Descartes takes his concept and his definition from two different traditions, and consequently the definition does not fit perfectly. We may say that a judgement is the sort of thing that *ought* to be true, and that therefore an absence of truth in a judgement is a privation, while an absence of truth not located in a judgement is a mere negation. But this is a rather indirect way of capturing the difference between error and ignorance: the major difference is that error involves *action*. Descartes's strategy here is to use an analysis in the scholastic style as a point of entry for a doctrine of judgement which follows Augustine, and which is significantly different from the scholastic theory.

Further on in the fourth Meditation, Descartes sets out his theory of judgement in precise terms. He does so, ostensibly, to answer the question of where the privation of error comes from, if it does not come from God. He follows Augustine in saying that such a defect must come from ourselves; and he follows him further in explicating this process in terms of the faculty of will or free will.[12] Free will, for Augustine, is a gift which human beings and angels have received from God; it is good because it enables rational creatures to achieve their proper perfection by voluntarily adhering to the chief and eternal good, which is God. Unlike the eternal good itself, however, the good of free will has a capacity for abuse: the will can "turn away" from God and "turn towards" something which God has created, something not positively evil but good in a lesser degree. When the will takes created goods as an occasion for turning away from God, this free act of the will is the origin of moral evil; it is also what exposes us to the possibility of suffering natural evil, since we have bound our happiness up with something we can lose against our will. Now, one consequence of this account of the origin of evil is that it allows us to understand how evil can exist in God's creation without God's having created anything positively evil. But it also allows us to control this evil, to the extent that it proceeds from ourselves. I have already quoted from Augustine: "Since that motion of turning away, which we declare to be sin, is a defective motion, and every defect is of nothing, see to what it pertains, and do not doubt that it does not pertain to God" (*DLA*, II. xx. 54). But this would be true even of a pure negation; the crucial consequence of the observation that sin is, in Descartes's language, a privation, lies in what immediately follows: "Which defect, however, since it is voluntary, is placed within our power. For if you are afraid of it, you ought not to will it, and if you do not will it, it will not be. What therefore is safer than to be in that life where what you do not want cannot befall you?" (ibid.).

Descartes follows this account of the origin of evil in the will with a

---

[12] Descartes, like Augustine, alternates between the terms '*voluntas*' (will) and '*liberum arbitrium*' (free will); he generally treats them as synonyms.

consequent optimism about bringing evil under control. This leads him to say that judgement is an act of the will. This must be the case, if our judgement is to be methodically reformed; but it commits Descartes to a faculty psychology contradicting the scholastic account. Augustine had invented the terminology of the faculty of will; the scholastics accepted it on his authority, and integrated it rather uneasily into the Aristotelian scheme of vegetative, sensitive, and rational faculties. But the scholastics based their *logic* purely on Aristotle, and they explained *judgement*, without reference to the will, as an act of the faculty of intellect. Descartes's theory of judgement is in some respects based on the scholastic account; but he modifies it crucially by reassigning the act of judgement from the intellect to the will, and thus making it subject to moral responsibility.

For the scholastics, the intellect has three genera of operations: a first act of "simple apprehension" or the "formation of a quiddity", in which the intellect grasps some essence without making any assertion capable of truth or falsity; a second operation of judgement or "the intellect composing and dividing", which truly or falsely combines the concept of a subject with the concept of a predicate; and a third operation of reasoning from given judgements to their consequences.[13] Descartes accepts the crucial distinction between simple apprehension and judgement, but his integration of logic into the theory of action alters his conceptions both of judgement and of simple apprehension. In the third Meditation, he offers the following division of his thoughts:

Some of these are as it were images of things, to which alone the name 'idea' properly belongs: as when I think of a man, or a chimaera, or heaven, or an angel, or God. But others have other forms beside this: as when I will, when I fear, when I affirm, when I deny, I still always apprehend some thing as the subject of my thought, but I also embrace in my thought something more than the likeness of that thing; and of these some are called volitions or affections, while others are called judgements. (AT vii. 37)

In grouping judgements together with other states of the will, and contradistinguishing all of these from simple apprehension, Descartes is following a principle of division independent of the traditional Aristotelian classification by faculties. The primary division, for Descartes, is between

---

[13] This is the consensus position of late scholasticism; the stages of its development are complex and obscure. A classic text for the distinction between the first two acts is Thomas Aquinas, *De veritate*, qu. 1, art. 5. Descartes's contemporary John of St Thomas uses the division of the three acts of the intellect to yield the ground-plan of his formal logic, *Cursus philosophicus Thomisticus* (Taurini 1930), i. 5. Although the scholastics always insist that judgement is formally an act of the intellect rather than of the will, they do allow that it can be causally influenced by the will, usually indirectly, through the formation of habits, rather than by the will's directly producing an act of assent, as in Descartes. The scholastics never treat judgement as the kind of free action to which the theodicy of *De libero arbitrio* could be applied.

active and passive states in the soul. He conceives the intellect as a "faculty of knowing [*cognoscendi*]", through which "I merely perceive ideas about which I can pass judgement, nor is any error properly so-called found in it thus precisely regarded" (AT vii. 56). The "activity" of intellect is simply the passive reception of such knowledge as God has chosen to give us in constructing our nature: it involves no creaturely action which could be right or wrong, and its absence is not error but the pure negation of ignorance. Judgements and volitions, on the other hand, which Descartes groups together as acts of the will, suppose a prior reception of knowledge, and constitute an action in response to it which can be right or wrong. Only within this genus of voluntary activities of the soul does Descartes distinguish between judgements and what would more usually be considered states of the will.

Thus Descartes restricts the faculty of intellect to simple apprehension or intellectual perception of essences; and he calls this intellectual perception *knowledge*. Here he uses the general word '*cognitio*', which means knowledge or acquaintance with things; but he regards *scientia*, which is strictly scientific knowledge of truths, as a species of this intellectual perception distinguished by the degree of its certainty, and not as a separate genus of intellectual act. "All *scientia* is a certain and evident *cognitio*" (AT x. 362),[14] and thus in particular it is a *cognitio*: scientific knowledge never consists in an act of judgement, but simply in the intuitive understanding of some essence. Reasoning is not to be understood as a third act by which the intellect proceeds from prior to consequent judgements, but as an intellectual perception that the premises entail the conclusion; it is therefore simply a variety of the first and only operation of the intellect.

Judgements are not contained in intellectual acts, on this view, but they are closely bound up with them. Judgements, and volitions as well, are responses by the will when something "is put forward by the intellect to affirm or deny, or to pursue or flee" (AT vii. 57); thus judgement will take the logical form of affirming as actual an idea put forward by the intellect as a mere possibility. This picture of judgement as assent to an idea, rather than as connecting two ideas together, is not Aristotelian: it derives ultimately from ancient Stoicism, and Descartes has picked it up from intermediate sources, probably Cicero and Augustine, both of whom accept this picture from the Stoics and both of whom were major influences on Descartes. He does not fill in the detailed implications of this picture for formal logic. He says that "the foremost and most frequent error" found in judgements "consists in my judging that ideas which are in me are similar or conformable to certain things placed outside me" (AT vii. 37), and indeed it seems that he regards

---

[14] This quotation is from the *Regulae*, which is not always reliable as a guide to Descartes's mature doctrine; but he reaffirms the same view in the second Replies, AT vii. 141.

this as the *only* possible type of error, and thus as the only type of content in a judgement that could be true or false; but nowhere does he attempt systematically to reduce all judgements to this form. Perhaps his view is that even in such propositions as "Snow is white" I have a complex idea *of the proposition*, of what it would be for it to be true, and that when I affirm the proposition I am affirming that there is a reality corresponding to that idea. This analysis is awkward, but it has the virtue of stressing that what constitutes a judgement is not the combination of two terms, but the voluntary attitude of affirmation.

Although the theory of judgement as voluntary assent was Stoic before it was Augustinian, Descartes places this theory of judgement in the context of a very un-Stoic Augustinian metaphysics, which leads him to a stronger view than the Stoics' of our freedom in judgement, and a narrower view than the Stoics' of what ideas we should and must assent to.

Following Augustine (rather than the Stoics), Descartes traces all our free activity, including all our judgements, to the faculty of will. Will or free will, says Descartes, "consists just in this, that we can either do or not do the same thing (that is, affirm it or deny it, pursue it or flee it); or rather that we are so disposed to what is proposed to us by the intellect for affirming or denying, or for pursuing or fleeing, that we feel ourselves to be determined to it by no external force" (AT vii. 57). Descartes adds this clarification in order to show that "I do not have to be drawn both ways in order to be free", and that "neither divine grace nor natural knowledge ever diminishes freedom, but they rather increase and strengthen it" (AT vii. 57–8). When the idea presented by the intellect is clearly perceived to be true, or when its truth is supernaturally guaranteed by divine grace, the will always affirms the truth of the idea; but it does so spontaneously, without any external constraint, and can therefore still be said to be free.

However, these situations arise only where the "light in the intellect" is so clear that for the mind not to assent would be contrary to its nature. In every other case, we have liberty of indifference, and not merely of spontaneity. Where the intellect presents an idea that is neither clearly perceived to be true nor clearly perceived to be false, the will is not determined by anything beyond itself, and may equally choose to assent to the idea, to deny it and assent to its opposite, or to abstain from passing judgement.

So far, Descartes's analysis of our freedom in judgement is not far from the Stoics'. But the Stoics think that sensory impressions (when formed under favourable circumstances) are clear, and that our nature inevitably leads us to assent to them. For Descartes, by contrast, the mind's "nature" is purely intellectual, and leads us to assent to an idea only if the idea has a clear objective content that rationally requires assent; whereas sensory impressions have no clear objective content, and do not rationally require anything. The practice of the first Meditation shows that it was not a necessity of our nature, but only a habit of our wills, that led us to assent to sensations: so this practice reveals a freedom of the will in judgement much more radical than the Stoics (or most other philosophers) had thought. Descartes stresses that this liberty of indifference does not extend "only to those things about which the intellect knows nothing at all, but generally to all those which are not known sufficiently clearly by it: for however much probable conjectures draw me in one direction, the bare knowledge that they are just conjectures, and not certain and indubitable reasons, suffices to push my assent in the opposite direction" (AT vii. 59). This liberty of indifference in unclear ideas accounts both for our fall into error and for our possible redemption from it. This Augustinian view of the origin of error contrasts with humanist views, popular in Descartes's day, which attribute the moral fall to a prior deficiency in judgement. Descartes does the reverse: if I judge badly, it is not because I have received a defective faculty of judgement, but because I freely abuse the gift of free will in judging the truth of ideas.

Augustine asserts, and Descartes agrees, that when we have said that an evil will is the cause of all evils, we cannot ask further what is the cause of this willing: we will what we will simply because we will to. But Augustine does try to give a weaker sort of explanation for our habit of willing wrongly: we are born into a double condition of ignorance, which makes it possible for us to mistake the false for the true, and difficulty, which makes it hard for us to resist the passions of the body even when they promote error. The state of ignorance and difficulty is not a cause of moral or cognitive error, and it does not excuse the will; but it makes it "natural" for the will to lead us into error.

This conception has roots in older philosophy, but Augustine has made it a peculiarly theological doctrine, the consequence of the sin of Adam. Descartes, without making mention of the theological background one way or the other, adopts from Augustine this conception of the childish state which leads to error. Thus he describes in the sixth Replies the causes which had led him into error: "I had first, from infancy on, passed various judgements about physical things, inasmuch as they contributed to the preservation of the life I was beginning; and I afterwards retained these same opinions which I had then conceived about these things. And since the mind at that age used the organs of the body less correctly, and being more firmly attached to them did not think without them, it perceived things only confusedly. . . . And since I had never then freed myself from these prejudices in the rest of my life, there was nothing at all that I knew distinctly enough" (AT vii. 441). Thus we are born into a condition of ignorance, where we do not have clear knowledge of the different objects of our perceptions; and we are subject to the great passions which nature has given for our biological survival. We voluntarily submit to these passions, and affirm the ideas which they suggest to us (for example, this fire is painful to me); but, in our ignorance and haste, we accidentally assent as well to other ideas which we have not clearly distinguished from these (pain is objectively in the fire), and thus begin a habit of erroneous assent. If this is so, we can break this habit of assent only by reassessing all that we have accepted since our childhood, distinguishing what is clear from what is not, and restricting our assent to the clear perceptions.

The doctrines of the human will, and of the goodness of all that comes from God, imply that this is possible. If God is not the source of anything defective, then we can err only in *acting*, not in receiving what God gives us; further, God must have created us in such a way that, although we *can* err through the misuse of our free will, we *need* not. God is responsible for the invincible habits of action which he has built into our nature, and if he had not given us a way of avoiding error, error would be an invincible habit, and God would be responsible for it. But, as Descartes observes, we are constituted in such a way that we always assent to whatever we clearly perceive; it follows that the reality we discover and assent to in our clear perceptions is not a product of our own action, but something we receive from God: "every clear and distinct perception is doubtless *something*, and therefore it cannot be from nothing, but necessarily has God for author— God, I say, that most perfect being, to whom it is repugnant to be deceptive—and therefore it is doubtless true" (AT vii. 62). We have extended our judgements beyond these things which we clearly perceive, and have therefore slipped into the habit of error. But we know that God has made us able to withhold our assent from all but the truths we have received from him, and thus to escape from error. If, when we truly try our best to doubt something, we still assent to it, it must be true and we need not regret our assent. If, on the other hand, we are capable of doubting something, then it is insufficiently clear, and it is an abuse of free will to assent to it. God's intention for us is that we comprehensively withdraw our assent from all the doubtful things we once assented to: and this is what Descartes has been teaching us how to do in the *Meditations*.

This conclusion allows Descartes to redeem the promise made at the beginning of the fourth Meditation: "already I seem to see a way by which, from this contemplation of the true God, . . . one might arrive at a knowledge of other things" (AT vii. 53). The obvious possibility of error posed a challenge to this prospect, but now that Descartes has shown that error comes only from our deviating from or adding to what God has given us, he can again use our divine creation as a guarantee in searching for truth about other things; if it is as yet unclear how much positive truth he will find, at least he will avoid error.

Descartes intends the fourth Meditation to give a metaphysical justification and a metaphysical context for his scientific method. The method of clear and distinct ideas is not put forward simply as one method among others, perhaps safer or more efficient; rather, it is the only means of establishing "the habit of not erring", in which "the greatest and pre-eminent perfection of man consists" (AT vii. 62). It is by following the Cartesian method that we properly fulfil our role within God's universe. Here, as usual, Descartes is following an idea from Augustine's *De libero arbitrio*, and adapting it to the justification of his method. Descartes and Augustine both admit that, though God has made us perfect in the sense of not having positive imperfections, he has not made us as perfect as he could have. Both use the same response to show that this is consistent with the goodness and power of God. It is agreed that our free will, although capable of being abused, is necessary for us to be as perfect as we are, and God could not have improved us by denying us the freedom we need to sin; but, as God has given us sufficient light not to err on clear ideas, and grace not to err in inspired acts, so he could have brought it about, without impairing our freedom, that we would never err at all: "namely, if he had put into my understanding a clear and distinct perception of all things about which I would ever deliberate; or even if he had impressed upon my memory, so firmly that I could never forget it, that I should never judge about any thing which I did not clearly and distinctly understand" (AT vii. 61). But, say Augustine and Descartes, it is not an objection against God's goodness that he has not made me perfect in this way, unless he has made *none* of his creatures so perfect.

Augustine, dealing with the question of why God created natures liable to sin, writes as follows:

It is not true reason but envious weakness when you think that something ought to have been made better, and wish that nothing else inferior had been made, as if after looking at heaven you wished that the earth had not been made—quite unjustly. You would rightly find fault if you saw that heaven had been omitted and only earth had been made, for you would say that it should have been made the way you think heaven could be. As therefore you see that that to whose image you wished the earth to be conformed has also been made, but that it is called not earth but heaven, I believe that since you have not been defrauded of the better thing for something inferior to be made and for the earth to exist, you should not be envious. (*DLA*, III. v. 13)

What corresponds to heaven in this simile is the angelic nature, which God has created in such a way that he knows it will not fall into sin: the angels are better than us, and the world would be deficient if there were no angels; but since there are angels (as we can prove, in a pinch, a priori from God's goodness), and the world is more perfect for having both the angelic and human natures, our complaint can only be that we ourselves are not angels— and this, Augustine suggests, is merely a personal grudge, not an argument against God's goodness. The world is better for having in it natures with the weakness that makes them liable to sin, but this does not mean that it is better for these weaker natures actually to sin: on the contrary, sin is a positive defect which damages the cosmic order, but which God cannot entirely eliminate without also eliminating the diversity of natures. As human

beings liable to sin, we serve a different function in the cosmic order from
that of the angels; we fulfil it properly when, with the aid of God, we resist
temptation and do not commit actual sin.

Thus far Augustine. Descartes, although he speaks more briefly, makes at
least by allusion all the same points, and applies them to the problem of error
in judgement.

I easily understand that I would have been more perfect than I now am, considered as
a particular whole, if I had been made in such a way by God. But I cannot therefore
deny that it is somehow a greater perfection in the entirety of things that some of its
parts are not immune from error, and others are, than if they were all completely
alike. And I have no right to complain that God wanted me to play that role in the
world, which is not the foremost and most perfect of all. (AT vii. 61)

Descartes, it seems, will play his role well if, despite the weakness of his
nature, he succeeds in avoiding error. Although he cannot avoid error, as
perhaps the angels do, by knowing everything he should ever be concerned to
know, yet he has found in the course of the *Meditations* that the other way is
open: although God has not firmly impressed on Descartes's memory (as
perhaps he has on the angels') the maxim that tells him to suspend judgement
on unclear ideas, none the less he has given Descartes the ability to recognize
this maxim and to persevere in trying to follow it, despite his inborn
condition of susceptibility to error. "Although I discover such an infirmity in
myself that I cannot always cling concentratedly to one and the same *cognitio*,
I can, however, by attentive and frequently repeated meditation, bring it
about that I remember it as often as practice demands, and thus that I should
acquire a habit of not erring" (AT vii. 62). The discipline of meditation will
teach us to distinguish what we perceive clearly from what we perceive only
obscurely, and to restrict our assent to the former; for Descartes, as we have
seen, this is not merely the road to science, but the perfection of human
nature, by which it overcomes its disabilities and assimilates itself, as far as
possible, to the angels.

III. THE STATUS OF FAITH

From the point we have now reached, we can begin to address the issues
raised by Gilson about Descartes's relation to Augustinianism. We may speak
with some confidence of a positive sense in which Descartes is an
Augustinian. He has not simply borrowed a few ornamental doctrines, as
Gilson suggests; the whole structure of his philosophy depends on his
methodological adaptation of Augustine's doctrine of the divine and human
natures and their activities. But the question remains: has Descartes, in
adapting Augustine's metaphysics to support his scientific method, abandoned

Augustine's original intention to confirm the Christian faith? What has become of faith under the new directions for judgement?

To answer this question, we must first describe the system of thought that Descartes derives from his method, and then determine the status of faith in relation to such a system.

The fundamental property of the science produced by Descartes's method is that it consists of *clear ideas*. This means, in the first place, that it consists of ideas rather than of judgements: for scientific knowledge, like all knowledge, consists for Descartes in an act of the intellect rather than of the will. Judgement does not constitute knowledge, but follows spontaneously on the possession of knowledge which is clear and distinct. And it is this which characterizes *scientific* knowledge: "every *scientia* is a certain and evident *cognitio*" (AT x. 362), and these are precisely the clear and distinct ideas, since just such perceptions are supported by the guarantee of the non-deceiving God. The conclusion of the fourth Meditation is that we ought to assent only to these ideas, and Descartes therefore undertakes to separate the clear from the obscure perceptions. The benefit of the fourth Meditation is just that it yields this programme: "for I shall attain [the truth] indeed, if I only attend sufficiently to all the things which I perfectly understand, and segregate them from the rest, which I apprehend more confusedly and obscurely. To this matter I will diligently devote myself from now on" (AT vii. 62).

In the fifth Meditation, Descartes begins to practise this method explicitly, and thus sets out to isolate his clear ideas in a systematic fashion. He discovers, in particular, that he has clear ideas of extension and its modes; and in each case he recognizes that what he clearly perceives is something true, and therefore really existing, independently of his mind. Descartes builds up his scientific system in an orderly way, at each stage accepting into it only those ideas whose content he clearly perceives; each such act of intellectual perception renders further and more complex conceptions clear in their turn, and contributes to a comprehensive system of clear perceptions of reality, of which Euclidean geometry is an exemplary part. As we expand the domain of our scientific knowledge, the method permits us to pass more and more judgements and enables us to justify them with formal arguments; but these judgements and these arguments are merely the observable by-products of a science essentially constituted by simple apprehension.

Such is the scientific system which Descartes derives from the divine guarantee of the truth of clear perceptions, and the divine gift of the power not to assent to things which we do not clearly perceive. Given this description of the scientific system, it will not be difficult to show how Descartes's application of Augustinian principles leads him to his characteristic position on the relation of faith to science. If we do this, we can vindicate, against Gilson, the claim that Descartes's philosophy, including

his doctrine of faith and reason, is a consistent outgrowth of Augustinianism.

We must verify three main points about Descartes's position on faith and
reason. Firstly, we must show that the principles of St Augustine,
systematically applied to scientific method as they are in the fourth
Meditation, lead to an exclusion of the truths of the faith from the
philosophical or scientific system. This will make it clear that Descartes has
not abandoned his Augustinian principles for some alien motivation in
coming to this conclusion. Secondly, we must show that the application of
these principles does not exclude the possibility of faith in revealed religion
outside the bounds of the scientific system; and thirdly, that this non-
philosophical faith is in fact *required* by the internal necessities of the
philosophical programme. Thus, Descartes is not the agent of a sort of
suicide of Augustinianism, in which its principles would lead to a destruction
of its highest goal. The place of revealed religion, so far from being destroyed
by the work of reason, will be confirmed by it; it will simply be *distinguished*
from the philosophical project, and in a way that is not foreign to Augustine
himself.

From our survey of the form of the system resulting from the method of
the fourth Meditation, it is clear that faith could not be a part of such a
system. Faith, whether in revealed religion or in anything else, is an act of the
will, and we have seen that no act of the will can be part of this system: it
consists exclusively in the passive perception of objectively real ideas. That
faith is an act of the will rather than of the understanding seems clear: for
faith is a species of judgement, of assent to something which puts forward a
claim to be true; and we have seen that according to Descartes all judgements
are acts of the will. But faith is more *obviously* an act of will than some other
sorts of judgement; for in cases where the will assents to ideas which are
clearly and distinctly perceived to be true, the active function of the will
(though genuinely active and spontaneous) follows automatically on the
passive function of the understanding. It would hardly be worth Descartes's
time to distinguish the operations of the will and the intellect in these cases, if
these were the only cases; but the distinction is of crucial importance in the
case of those things which we perceive only obscurely and confusedly, and so
Descartes is careful to mark it in general. Faith, however, is an act of the will
in the stronger sense: it is not consequent on knowledge and does not depend
on an idea which is intrinsically clear and therefore certain; on the contrary, it
is an assent to something obscure in itself, in which some but not others
concur. Thus even in the early *Regulae*, before he has worked out his mature
psychology of will and intellect, Descartes singles out faith as an act of the
will: the rejection of any assent on the part of the *ingenium* to things which it
has not clearly intuited or deduced "does not at all prevent us from believing
that those things which are divinely revealed are more certain than all

knowledge [*cognitio*], for whatever faith in them is about things that are obscure, is not an action of the *ingenium*, but of the will" (AT x. 370). He has not yet made the subtle point that the will is involved even in assenting to clear perceptions; but it already seems obvious to him that faith is an act of the will, going beyond anything that is perceived, and that this in some way removes it from the scope of the method.

But if faith is an act whereby the will assents to something which remains obscure to the understanding, and if (as Descartes has said many times), we ought not to assent to anything unclear, then it would seem that we ought never to *believe* anything, as opposed to knowing it with certainty; that Descartes would recommend against faith in anything, whether in divine revelation or in anything else that we do not clearly and distinctly perceive to be true. Perhaps he can escape this consequence by saying, as he does in the fourth Meditation, that divine grace as well as natural knowledge can irresistibly incline us to assent to the ideas which we consider. But if this is the case, then the faith which divine grace induces in us would seem to be just like our assent to scientific knowledge and equally worthy of being included in a scientific system: the fact that, as an act of judgement, it is not formally identical with an act of understanding should not exclude it from the practice of scientific research, any more than it excludes any other judgement. Thus when we see that Descartes does not, in fact, involve revealed doctrines in his scientific research or writing, we could only explain this by supposing that he has some personal prejudice against including them—arising, say, from a desire to avoid theological controversy, or from some secret disbelief.

In fact, however, a closer investigation of Descartes's conception of the action of grace will show how grace can justify faith without justifying its inclusion in the scientific system. Descartes sets out his position most clearly in the passage which he calls to Arnauld's attention, in responding to the Second Objectors' concern about the status of faith under his method. The Objectors write:

Fifthly, if the will never strays or sins when it follows a clear and distinct *cognitio* of its mind, and exposes itself to danger when it pursues a conception of the intellect which is very far from clear and distinct, then see what follows from this: namely, that a Turk, or anyone else, not only does not sin in not embracing the Christian religion, but also sins if he does embrace it, since he does not clearly or distinctly know its truth. Indeed, if this rule of yours is true, the will will hardly be permitted to embrace anything, since we know hardly anything with that clarity and distinctness which you require for a certainty vulnerable to no doubt. See, therefore, that when you desire to protect the truth, you do not prove too much, and overturn rather than build up. (AT vii. 126–7)

Descartes replies that it is obvious that the will exposes itself to danger by following an unclear perception. This is not a controversial point among either philosophers or theologians: everyone agrees that we are safer when we understand something more clearly before we assent to it, "and that they sin who pass a judgement without knowing its cause" (AT vii. 147).

It is obvious that pursuing something obscure is dangerous, and the Second Objectors could not have brought any positive reasons against this claim. But they are plainly worried about its consequences: these seem to be at least irreligious, and possibly suicidal, if the will is to be forbidden to make those probable judgements needed for the preservation of life. Descartes seeks to reassure the Objectors by showing what really does and what really does not follow from this doctrine about what things the will should embrace.

Since he is not saying anything beyond what all philosophers and theologians have said, Descartes does not think that he is in any more trouble than they are; so he comes to the common defence, using what he apparently takes to be the standard line of reply. There is no force to the objection about embracing the faith: "for although faith is said to be about obscure things, yet that on account of which [*propter quod*] we embrace it is not obscure, but brighter than any natural light" (ibid.). For, says Descartes, we require clarity only in the *ratio formalis* which moves the will to assent, and not in "the matter or the thing itself to which we assent" (ibid.); and in the case of someone moved by supernatural grace to assent to the truth of Christianity, the *ratio formalis* on account of which he assents "consists in a certain internal light, such that when we are supernaturally illumined with it by God, we are confident that those things which are put forward for us to believe have been revealed by him and that it surely cannot be that he would lie, which is more certain than any natural light and often also more evident on account of the light of grace" (AT vii. 148).

The "cause" or justification which can provide a clear *ratio formalis* for a judgement can thus be of either of two types: "one is from the natural light, the other from divine grace" (ibid.). There is therefore nothing wrong with assenting to something which is obscure in itself, when one is led to confidence in it by divine grace. I do not discover any reason for assent in examining the proposition itself, but I do in perceiving it in a certain relationship to God (whatever precisely that is supposed to feel like when it happens). This does not seem to be in principle any different from my assent to a proposition which I read in the newspaper ('NIXON RESIGNS'), which does not seem evident merely from considering the ideas of Nixon and of resignation, but which I come to believe through considering the relationships between the newspaper, myself (would they lie to me?), and the proposition (could they be mistaken?)—except, of course, that the newspaper story is less certain than the natural light of reason, while divine revelation is more so.

Descartes gives an example, even in the case of the natural light, where we can have a clear *ratio* for assenting to something which is itself obscure; but the discrepancy between the clarities of the reason and the subject matter would seem to be inessential in the case of the natural light and to become important only in the case of faith. The natural example is "when I judge that *obscurity* should be removed from our concepts"; for the subject matter of the sentence is "obscurity itself" (AT vii. 147). The obscurity of the subject in this example is inessential because the *ratio* for assenting to the proposition derives from a clear perception which I have concerning the relationships between the different terms proposed for my judgement, even if it is not a perception of the *subject* of the judgement: it can become one through a rearrangement of the sentence. In the case of assent to matters of faith, however, no such rearrangement is possible, because the certainty is not derived from anything within the objects of the judgement; it is derived from a particular grace of God shown to the individual who is to assent, and this will vary from one individual to another (and perhaps from one time to another as well), so that the *ratio formalis* moving the will in this case cannot be ultimately equivalent to or derived from any feature of the things judged, without reference to the person judging and to God.

Choosing our words carefully, we may say that the certainty coming from divine grace is a *subjective* certainty, while the certainty coming from the natural light is an *objective* certainty. There is, of course, no hint here of modern anti-realism: the *truth* of propositions accepted by faith is an objective truth; that is, it comes from the things judged really being as they are judged to be. What is *not* objective, *not* derived from a corresponding property of the object, in the case of propositions maintained by faith, is the *certainty* of the judgement. We may say that whenever a person has no doubt about something which he affirms, he has a subjective certainty of its truth. Descartes thinks that if this person is *right* not to doubt, then his subjective certainty must have come to him from God (otherwise it is self-manufactured). But God could have given it in either of two ways: in the case of the natural light, the subjective certainty is given *mediately*, via the clarity with which God endows the objects of our perception, and thus the certainty of the subjective act, like its truth, will come from something corresponding in the object; whereas in the case of divine grace, God is creating the subjective certainty *immediately* in the soul, by an extraordinary causality bypassing the causality of created natures.

It should now be clear why the truths of faith, although their certainty (like that of our clear perceptions) comes to us by a divine illumination, cannot be incorporated into the scientific system. The scientific system is composed of ideas which we clearly and distinctly perceive, and which we therefore know with certainty to be true. The truths of faith, however, are not of this sort: they concern things which we can only obscurely perceive, and which we therefore do not *know* to be true, although owing to the grace of God we may *believe* them. If, out of a misplaced enthusiasm, we tried to mix them in with our clear ideas, this would not in any way contribute to scientific progress, since this progress takes place only through the development of more and more clear perceptions, none of which can be supported on a foundation which is itself only obscurely perceived. Indeed, this procedure could very rapidly lead us into philosophical and theological error, if it tempts us to assume that obscure ideas are clear. If, say, God inspires me to believe that he consists in a trinity of persons comprising a single essence, and if I convince myself that I clearly understand this to be true and try to build up a science out of it, I shall have to invent some general notion of a divine person and show that the properties of divine persons in general clearly imply that there must be three of them; but since I do not in fact clearly perceive this, I shall be inventing obscure propositions, which as soon as I go beyond the revealed doctrine will be just as likely to be false as to be true. This will damage my philosophy, and may also lead me into a heretical theology—which may get me into trouble, whether with the Inquisition or with God at the last judgment. As Descartes remarks in the *Discourse*, "the road [to heaven] is as open to the most ignorant as to the most learned" (AT vi. 8), and we can only become more likely to miss it by pretending to understand things which are beyond our capacities.

This explains why, for Descartes, the truths of faith and the truths of reason must be kept in separate compartments: it is a natural consequence of his doctrine of knowledge as the evident perception of clear ideas. To believe something, even something which turns out to be true, because I wrongly think that I clearly perceive it, is to be opinionated: this is what Descartes has been combating from the beginning, and is the opposite of the right use of the will needed for philosophy. Indeed, if the Turk of the second set of Objections "embraces [the revealed doctrines of Christianity], although they are obscure to him, having been led to [accept] them by some false reasoning", he will "not therefore be a believer [*fidelis*, one of the faithful], but rather he will be sinning in not using his reason rightly. Nor do I think that any orthodox theologian has ever felt otherwise about these matters" (AT vii. 148). Thus faith in revealed religion is distinguished from opinion based on obscure intellectual perceptions; it belongs in a different category of acts of will and has a different problem of justification. The Augustinian theory of grace which Descartes accepts gives him one way of showing that a judgement of faith in revealed religion may be legitimate outside the bounds of the scientific system, while retaining his insistence that the system of clear ideas remains unaffected by any such act of judgement.

Our third point remains to be addressed. Descartes's principles of method make faith possible outside, and only outside, the scientific system; but it is not clear that they make it *necessary* even there. The doctrine of faith has the look of being an extraneous addition to the Cartesian method, compatible with but not required by Descartes's basic principles; if this is so, the method will in itself be neutral to the question of a non-philosophical faith.

In fact, however, this is not the case. Descartes does not think that his method would be a coherent whole without a place reserved for faith, and he proceeds to show the Objectors how it requires some variety of faith. The Objectors had been concerned about the practical implications of the method, not only for religion but also for the maintenance of life. Descartes replies, addressing both concerns, by distinguishing between theoretical and practical judgements.

Besides, I wish you to recall here that I have very carefully distinguished, with regard to those things which it is permitted to embrace, between the practice of life [*usus vitae*] and the contemplation of truth [*contemplatio veritatis*]. For as far as the practice of life is concerned, I am so far from thinking that we should assent to nothing except things clearly perceived, that on the contrary I do not think that we should always wait even for *likely*[15] things, but that sometimes we must choose one out of many things entirely unknown, and hold it no less firmly after it is chosen (as long as we can give no reasons for the opposite choice), than if it had been chosen on account of very clear reasons, as I have explained on page 26 of the *Discourse on the method*. But where we are concerned only with the contemplation of truth, who has ever denied that we should hold back our assent from things which are obscure and not distinctly enough perceived? But that I have dealt with this alone in my *Meditations*, the thing itself bears witness, and I have also declared it in express words at the end of the first Meditation, in saying that I could not give way too much here to distrust [*diffidentia*, the opposite of *fides*], since I was concerning myself not with doing things, but only with knowing them. (AT vii. 149)

Descartes correctly refers the Objectors back to Part Three of the *Discourse*, and to the statement of the project of the *Meditations*, for this distinction between practical and speculative concerns. In those places he had been forced to draw this distinction, and to accept different standards of evidence for speculative and practical judgements, in order to begin the project of the reconstruction of his beliefs: he must accept, for practical purposes, many things which he does not *know* to be true, if he is to survive long enough for any certainty to emerge from his doubt.

Now it is clear that this constitutes Descartes's appropriate reply to the last part of the Objection—"if this rule of yours is true, the will will hardly be permitted to embrace anything, since we know hardly anything with that clarity and distinctness which you require for a certainty vulnerable to no doubt" (AT vii. 126)—and that he intends this clarification of his method to show that it does not lead to the potentially suicidal implications which might have been imagined. It is at first sight less clear what follows for the religious implications: does Descartes intend to refer the assent to divinely revealed truths to "the contemplation of truth", or to "the practice of life"? Is this practical justification of assent under conditions of uncertainty intended (*inter*

---

[15] My stress.

alia) to justify religious faith, or does he wish to justify faith on a "speculative" basis, as a step towards contemplation of the truth?

We have seen that Descartes does *not* regard faith in divine revelation as a step toward scientific knowledge, because it is not a *cognitio*, nor immediately connected with one; and it would seem (e.g. from the passage from the first Meditation which we have just seen him citing in this connection) that he identifies knowledge (*cognitio*) with the "contemplation of truth". So we might conjecture that Descartes is thinking of religious faith as part of the "practice of life", and that the justification of acting without clear knowledge (or even verisimilitude) would be equally a justification of faith. Fortunately, Descartes confirms this conjecture in discussing Arnauld's concerns about the religious implications of the method; and by turning to this passage of the fourth Replies, we will be able to clear up the unclarities about Descartes's doctrine of faith which remain from the second Replies.

I have already referred to Descartes's reply to Arnauld: "That in the fourth Meditation I discussed only 'the error which is committed in the judgement [*dijudicatione*] of true and false, not that which occurs in the pursuit of good and evil', and that I always made an exception for 'those things which pertain to faith and to the conduct of life' when I asserted that 'we ought not to assent to anything except what we clearly know [*cognoscamus*]', is shown by the whole context of what I wrote; and I also expressly explained it in the Reply to the Second Objections, in number 5; and I also gave advance notice of it in the Synopsis" (AT vii. 247–8).

Descartes explains that he is restating all this now "in order to declare how much I yield [*tribuam*] to this most eminent man's judgement and how acceptable to me are his counsels" (AT vii. 248)—rather than to criticize Arnauld for repeating a point that had already been established. For Arnauld had first urged Descartes to declare that in the fourth Meditation he was concerning himself only with truth and falsehood, not with good and evil, and then immediately gone on to the second point which Descartes takes up, namely, "that when he asserts that we ought not to assent to anything except what we clearly and distinctly know, he is dealing just with those things which aim at learning, and fall under [the scope of] understanding [*ad disciplinas spectant & sub intelligentiam cadunt*], but not with those which pertain to faith and to the conduct of life [*ad fidem pertinent, & ad vitam agendam*], so that he is condemning the rashness of the opinionated, not the persuasion of those who prudently believe" (AT vii. 216). Descartes is agreeing, and pointing out that he had already said this in the passage we have considered from the second Replies. Arnauld's "*quae ad disciplinas spectant & sub intelligentiam cadunt*" are, in Descartes, those things which the will is permitted to embrace for the *contemplatio veritatis*; Arnauld's "*quae ad fidem pertinent & ad vitam agendam*" are those things which the will is permitted to embrace for the *usus vitae*. This is what Descartes is confirming in signalling his acceptance of Arnauld's concerns, and it helps us in interpreting the passage from the second Replies. For it is clear that, for both Arnauld and Descartes, the things which pertain to faith, though they may not be strictly *identical* with those which pertain to the practice or conduct of life, at least fall under the same category with them, and are immune to methodological doubt for the same reason.

According to Arnauld, Descartes is condemning "the rashness of the opinionated, not the persuasion of those who prudently believe". Those who believe, then, may do so *prudently*; that is, their belief is justified by its place in the conduct of life, rather than by any quality which the believer perceives in the ideas to which he assents. Faith or confidence in divine revelation is prudent for the same reason that the faith or confidence that one's food is not poisoned is prudent. We do not *know*, we do not certainly and evidently perceive, that our food is not poisoned—we certainly cannot prove this during the six-day course of Meditations, since we do not even prove the existence of body until the last day—and yet it is prudent to eat between Meditations, and this presupposes a confidence *for all practical purposes* that food procured in a normal manner will not kill us. And this is indeed Descartes's practice, as he explains it in Part Three of the *Discourse* in giving his provisional code of morals. Now, there is no need to go into the justification of the whole scheme of the provisional morals here; we are interested only in noting how religious faith fits into the scheme, and thus how it is justified by its place in the conduct of life. In Part Three of the *Discourse*, the truths of the faith are "set apart" from the process of the destruction of "all the rest of my opinions" (AT vi. 28), along with the maxims of the provisional morals. And indeed, remaining in the faith is already included in the first maxim of the code, where "keeping constantly the religion in which, by the grace of God, I have been instructed since childhood" (AT vi. 23) was a condition for the choice of the best opinions to be guided by in all spheres of outward activity, until the reconstruction of knowledge was complete. No especial reason is given for this, beyond the general necessity of choosing rules for life which would enable him to live as happily as he could until he could replace these opinions with certain knowledge. But it is clear enough that the confidence in revealed truths is analogous to confidence in other sorts of truth needed for living as happily as possible; just as belief in the nutritive value of food is necessary for my physical health, so belief in the saving value of divine grace is necessary for my spiritual health, for my general well-being whether in this world or the next. This would have been Descartes's belief prior to his philosophical reflection. He does not *know* that this is so, but he is not yet in a position to be ruled by knowledge alone; and *starting from this belief*, his conclusion will naturally be to retain it, along with his belief in food, during the meditative process.

This gives, in broad outline, Descartes's justification for the necessity of faith as an act of will, in the interim before knowledge can replace it. It is clear that some kind of faith will have to be preserved during the process of reconstruction; it may not be a logical necessity that this should include a religious as well as a medical component, but surely this is more plausible than the contrary possibility. No justification of *opinion*, in the narrower sense in which Arnauld intends that term, is included; opinion would be an attempt to pass judgement on things one does not know, in so far as they *sub intelligentiam cadunt*, that is, for the speculative purposes of the advancement of knowledge, which can in fact only be hindered by such accretions. It is in this sense that the *temeritas opinantium* is rightly condemned by the fourth Meditation, while the persuasion of believers remains immune to the censure.

At this conclusion, it will perhaps be said: Yes, this would appear to be Descartes's doctrine of faith, as it follows from his understanding of his philosophical project; and yes, this would account for the attitude towards faith which he does indeed take up in his philosophical or scientific writings. But all the same, there is something unsatisfactory about it, if this is supposed to bring him into line with the Augustinian tradition of Christian philosophy: surely this grudging acceptance of the necessity of faith as an interim measure is something far less than the religious aspirations of the philosophers and theologians of the age of faith, and especially of St Augustine and his followers.

This is an understandable way of looking at Descartes, but it is a distortion. In fact, Descartes's doctrine of faith is indistinguishable from Augustine's. Virtually identical descriptions of knowledge and faith and the attitude we must take towards them will be found in both authors. We incline to read them differently, because prejudices about the men and their times suggest to us that Descartes concedes a place to faith grudgingly, while Augustine does so with all his heart. But by brushing aside these prejudices and analysing the relevant texts, we see that their doctrines of faith are the same, and necessarily the same, since Descartes is led to his doctrine of faith by his adoption of the Augustinian doctrine of the free exercise of will in judgement.

We may briefly recall how Augustine came to his acceptance of a necessary place for religious faith, bringing out the main points of his position to see just how close to it Descartes remains. When Augustine was a Manichee, he refused to allow a place for faith in religious questions, and hoped to achieve a rationally grounded *knowledge* of God, the world, and the soul through the Manichaean *gnosis*, without having to commit himself to anything he had not rationally determined to be true. After his conversation with Faustus, he came to see that the Manichees did not offer any genuine knowledge, but demanded an implicit faith all the more "blind" for being unrecognized.

Upon coming into contact with Ambrose and the other Catholics at Milan, and deciding that orthodox Christianity was not (as he had earlier supposed) contrary to reason, he also re-evaluated its demand for faith in things yet unknown, which earlier he had ridiculed:

Already preferring the Catholic doctrine, I thought that it did more modestly and less deceptively to propose that what was not demonstrated should be believed (whether it had been [demonstrated], but not to some person, or whether it had not been [demonstrated] at all), than with a rash promise of knowledge [*scientia*] to laugh at credulity [as did the Manichees], and then afterwards to command that so many most fabulous and absurd things, which could not be demonstrated, should be believed. [Then I considered] . . . that I believed innumerable things which I had not seen, nor had I been present when they happened, like so many things in the history of nations, so many things about places and cities which I had not seen, so many things which I believed from friends and doctors and other people; if these things were not believed, we would get nothing at all done in this life. Finally, I considered how unshakenly firm I held by faith what parents I was born of, which I could not have known except by believing what I heard. In this way you [God] persuaded me that not those who believed your books, which you have established with so much authority in almost all nations, but those who did not believe them, should be censured; nor should I listen if they said, "how do you know that those books have been delivered to the human race by the spirit of the one true and most truthful God?". (*Confessions*, VI. v. 7)

Thus, for Augustine as for Descartes, some truths are to be accepted on faith, because it is a practical necessity, if we are to be able to do anything at all, to believe things which we do not yet know and which perhaps we can never know, or never in this life. For Augustine as for Descartes, faith extends, on the same principle, to many everyday things, things which "no one of sound mind has ever seriously doubted" (AT vii. 16); by reflecting on our faith in these things, we can see that faith in the Bible is more plausible than its contrary. But for Augustine as for Descartes, the search for truth does not stop here: we are not to be *satisfied* with the degree of certainty we have been forced to accept, but are to press on towards knowledge. Faith is a half-way house towards knowledge, given where "we are too weak to find the truth by pure reason" (*Confessions*, VI. v. 8), guiding and protecting us until we can discover by reason the truths which we have all along believed by faith. Augustine is everywhere insistent that we must attain to "understanding", to "proof", or to "knowledge", at which point faith will no longer be necessary; his disagreement with those who would have knowledge immediately is a disagreement only about the *means* to knowledge.

This and nothing else is the justification for religious faith in the Augustinian tradition of Christian philosophy—however much its devotion to faith may have been amplified by the nostalgia of later times. This is the tradition to which Descartes stands heir, and he would appear to have preserved it faithfully. Descartes's entire project depends on his adoption of the Augustinian theory of passive knowledge and voluntary belief, and the attitude towards religion is the immediate consequence. It is true that Descartes does not "blend" faith and reason, but we have seen the justification for this in his scientific project, and it is not an essential difference from Augustine. For Augustine, faith stands in the same relation to knowledge as chicory does to coffee: it is a more readily available but less attractive substitute. If he sometimes "blends" them in the same work—well, we do the same with coffee and chicory, if we have some amount of coffee but not enough to go around. This does not mean that faith and reason lose their separate origins and their separate natures for Augustine, any more than they do for Descartes. For Augustine's purpose in his writing—deepening the religious knowledge of believers—it is convenient to blend them, to discuss them together; but this is not binding on Descartes when he uses the same principles for different purposes, and he is not in any way betraying Augustine when he confines his discussion of pragmatic and religious faith mainly to the third Part of the *Discourse*.

It is clear that, by the time Descartes wrote the *Meditations*, he was not a stranger to the Augustinian doctrine of belief, of knowledge, and of the opinion which falsely claims to be knowledge but in fact demands blind faith. It is something which he presupposes, not something which he needs to be told. In this light it is easy to understand Descartes's reaction to Arnauld, when Arnauld proposes the considerations which we have already discussed about faith and the conduct of life. Arnauld attaches to the passage I have cited a long extract from Augustine's anti-Manichaean treatise *De utilitate credendi*, which systematizes the conclusions described in our chapter from the *Confessions*, distinguishing belief, knowledge, and opinion, and condemning opinion while justifying belief as a step on the road to knowledge:

There are three things which, though very close together, are most worthy of distinction in the minds of men: to understand, to believe, and to opine.

He *understands*, who comprehends something by certain reason. He *believes*, who, moved by some weighty authority, judges something to be true even though he does not comprehend it by certain reason. He *opines*, who thinks that he knows what he does not know.

To *opine* is for two reasons very shameful: if someone has persuaded himself that he already knows something, he cannot learn when it becomes possible to learn it; and also, in itself rashness is not a sign of a well-ordered soul.

What we understand, therefore, we owe to *reason*; what we believe, to *authority*; what we opine, to *error*. These things have been said that we may understand that we, in holding by faith even to those things which we have not yet comprehended, are innocent of the rashness of the opinionated.

For those who say that we should believe nothing, except what we know, are afraid of this word 'opinion', which is said to be most shameful and wretched. But if someone diligently considers how much difference there is between thinking that one knows and understanding that one does not know, he may believe, moved by some authority, and so surely avoid the sins both of error and of inhumanity and pride. (AT vii. 216–17)[16]

Arnauld proposes this triple distinction and recommendation of belief—the intellectual core of the treatise *De utilitate credendi*, the very treatise that Gilson had chosen to exemplify the Augustinian spirit which Descartes in his view contradicts—to show why Descartes is condemning only the rashness of the opinionated and not the persuasion of believers; he urges Descartes to accept this clarification of his meaning. As we have seen, Descartes accepts it, almost without comment. He knows it already, and feels that he has also *said* it already: whether or not he already knew the particular passage to which Arnauld refers, he certainly knows the idea which it contains, which he could easily have found in our chapter from the *Confessions* or in any of an almost infinite number of parallel passages in St Augustine.

Descartes seems to feel that what Arnauld wished to clarify was already clear enough; but he prints and endorses Arnauld's statements, and in addition makes the corrections which Arnauld suggests in the text of the *Meditations*, to guard against possible misinterpretations. He accepts the clarifications, as Arnauld had intended, not because he himself did not understand that his doctrine was in conformity with Augustinian orthodoxy, but because his readers might not. Arnauld and Descartes are concerned for the naive reader unversed in the Christian philosophical tradition and in the writings of St Augustine, for it is only such a person who is in danger of being led astray by the *Meditations*. For the present day, when Descartes has been assumed into the philosophical canon and Augustine has fallen out, these comments of the second and fourth exchanges of Objections and Replies provide a useful means for relating Descartes to the intellectual tradition in which he stands, and explicating more fully his doctrine of faith and reason.

Department of Philosophy
McGill University

[16] Although this passage is introduced with the phrase "as Blessed Augustine wisely advises, *De utilitate credendi*, chapter 15", and although it is printed in roman type to distinguish it from the surrounding text of Arnauld (which is in italics), it is not precisely a quotation, nor is it from chapter 15 of that work. It is from chapter 11, and it is a series of passages stitched together, with the intervening matter (less immediately relevant to Arnauld's point) deleted. In the edition of the *Corpus scriptorum ecclesiasticorum latinorum*, xxv (Vindobonae 1891), the first paragraph is from p. 31, lines 23–5; the third from p. 32, lines 13–16; the fourth from p. 32, lines 22–4; and the fifth from p. 33, lines 20–26. I cannot locate a precise origin for the second paragraph, but it gives an accurate summary of how Augustine is distinguishing the terms in question. This indicates that Arnauld was treating the texts of Augustine in a rather familiar manner; but he is not in any way modifying or distorting Augustine's thought, merely selecting the texts so as to make the point in a small compass while remaining as close as possible to the original words. (Arnauld is not to be blamed for the wrong chapter reference, which was supplied by Mersenne (AT iii. 359). Perhaps Mersenne was also responsible for printing the whole text, including a paragraph of Arnauld summarizing Augustine, as if it were a continuous quotation from Augustine.)

DESCARTES ON INNATE IDEAS, SENSATION, AND SCHOLASTICISM: THE RESPONSE TO REGIUS

TAD M. SCHMALTZ

Toward the end of his life, Descartes claimed, in response to the apostate Henricus Regius (Henri de Roy), that "there is nothing in our ideas which is not innate to the mind". This claim in *Notae in programma quoddam*[1] is followed by the assertion that even sensory ideas must be so innate. This nativist view of sensation is among the most baffling of Descartes's doctrines, and it has not gone without scrutiny.[2] Commentators have often attempted to assess the *Notes* simply by providing analyses of what Descartes could have meant by the terms we translate as 'innate' and 'sensory idea'. While this has yielded some interesting results, it is not sufficient. Descartes offered his nativist account of sensation as part of a reaction to views proposed by his contemporaries, and this account is not considered properly when abstracted from the wider context of this reaction. Indeed, such abstraction forces the

---

© Tad M. Schmaltz 1997

[1] Hereafter referred to as *Notes*. In citations from Descartes's works I use the following abbreviations for the works and editions stated: '*RI*' for the pre-1630 *Regulae ad directionem ingenii*; '*LM*' for *Le Monde* and '*TH*' for *Traité de l'homme* (both written 1633); '*Diop.*' for *La Dioptrique* and '*DM*' for *Discours de la méthode* (both published 1637); '*Med.*' for *Meditationes de prima philosophia* and '*RO*' for 'Responsiones authoris ad objectiones' (both 1642); '*PP*' for *Principia philosophiae* (Latin edn, 1644), citing part and section numbers; and '*PA*' for *Les Passions de l'âme* (1649), citing part and section numbers. I refer to *Oeuvres de Descartes*, ed. C. Adam and P. Tannery (11 vols, Paris 1974–83), as 'AT', followed by volume and page numbers. The translations provided here are my own.

[2] The discussions cited in this essay include R. M. Adams, 'Where do our ideas come from?—Descartes *vs.* Locke', in *Innate ideas*, ed. S. P. Stich (Berkeley 1975), 71–87, at 75–8; R. McRae, 'Innate ideas', in *Cartesian studies*, ed. R. J. Butler (Oxford 1972), 32–54, at 51–3; J. W. Yolton, *Perceptual acquaintance from Descartes to Reid* (Minneapolis 1984), 19, 22; F. van de Pitte, 'Descartes' innate ideas', *Kant-studien* 76 (1985), 363–84; and M. D. Wilson, 'Descartes on the origin of sensation', *Philosophical topics* 19 (1991), 293–323. Adams comes closest to the interpretative approach that I recommend, though he is less critical of Descartes's reaction to the schoolmen than am I.

interpreter to miss the important ways in which the response to Regius derives from Descartes's other discussions of sensation. I thus attempt to consider these remarks in historical perspective in order to provide an assessment of his discussion of sensation in general, as well as of his particular response to Regius.

In section I, I consider the context of the argument in the *Notes* for the innate sensory faculty of mind. I begin by offering my own analyses of the relevant terms, proposing that Descartes took sensory ideas to be innate in the special sense of being produced by a faculty of mind. I further provide an interpretation of his account of sensory ideas. After addressing the charge that the argument in this work is not worthy of serious consideration because its conclusion is inconsistent with doctrines vital for Descartes, I move on to discuss various elements of the argument. Descartes initially offered the innate sensory faculty as an alternative to a naive transmission view that he attributed—unjustifiably—to the schoolmen of his day. While this may not be the only time that Descartes failed to comprehend the view of his opponents, it is a striking example of this sort of failure. In his more mature writings, though, he indicated that his differences with the schoolmen stem from his rejection of the scholastic doctrine that sensations resemble the qualities of bodies. He took this rejection of resemblance to reveal, moreover, that a new account of the sensory role of mind is required. I discuss his rejection of resemblance and its purported implications, and contend that the response to Regius is best seen as part of a comprehensive reaction to the scholastic view of sensation.

Having so explicated the argument of the *Notes*, I turn in section II to consider its strength. I compare Descartes's position that sensation involves mental activity with the scholastic account of sensation and conclude that, though he could have provided a strong response to the schoolmen, such a response would undermine the argument of the *Notes*. I then discuss the objection, common to Regius and Locke, that sensory ideas are not innate to mind but are produced by external objects. Once again Descartes could have offered a strong response, but the materials for such a response are not found in the *Notes*. The reason for this is that he was preoccupied with his misguided view of the scholastic account of sensation. In the end, Descartes's response to Regius suffers from the same sort of disregard of context that has prevented a proper understanding of the response itself.

I. THE ARGUMENT OF THE 'NOTES'

Let us turn, then, to the remarks in the *Notes*. The target of these remarks, Regius, was once the primary exponent of the new Cartesian philosophy at the University of Utrecht. He fell out of favour with Descartes after publication of his *Fundamenta physices* in 1646.[3] Descartes complained in the preface to the French edition of the *Principles of philosophy* that in the *Fundamenta* his former disciple erred in denying "certain truths of metaphysics on which the whole of physics must be based" (AT ix-2. 20). Regius responded by publishing anonymously a pamphlet entitled 'An account of the human mind, or rational soul, where it is explained what it is, and what it can be', in which he outlined his position on the nature and knowledge of mind and body. The 1648 *Notes* is Descartes's point-by-point response to the twenty-one theses offered in that pamphlet.[4]

Regius declared in the twelfth thesis that the mind is devoid of "ideas, or notions, or axioms that are innate", and concluded in the thirteenth that "all common notions that are engraved in the mind have their origin in observation of things, or in verbal instruction" (AT viii-2. 345). This latter contention is similar to the claim of Locke that all materials of knowledge come "from *Experience*: In that, all our Knowledge is founded; and from that it ultimately derives it self" (*Essay*, II. i. 2). The position of both writers is that nothing can be known except that which is supplied to the mind by experience.[5]

One reason why the *Notes* is so valuable is that it provides the most complete Cartesian rejoinder to this sort of Lockean position. Descartes took exception, in particular, to what he understood to be the implication of Regius's remarks; namely, that "the faculty of thought is not able to accomplish anything by itself, could never perceive or think anything except what it receives [*accipit*] from observation or tradition, that is, from the senses".[6] It is worth citing Descartes's response at some length before we consider its various elements. He began by claiming that

whoever correctly considers how far our senses extend, and what it is precisely that is able to reach [*pervenire*] to our faculty of thought from them, must admit that in no case do they exhibit to us ideas of things just as we form them in thought. So much so,

---

[3] Regius (1589–1679) held a chair in medicine at the University of Utrecht. For further discussion of Descartes's tempestuous relations with Regius, see G. Rodis-Lewis's introduction to her edition of Descartes, *Lettres à Regius et Rémarques sur l'explication de l'esprit humain* (Paris 1959), 7–19. Cf. P. Dibon, 'Notes bibliographiques sur les cartésiens hollandais', in *Descartes et le cartésianisme hollandais*, ed. E. J. Dijksterhuis and others (Paris 1950), 280–87; T. Verbeek, *La Quérelle d'Utrecht* (Paris 1988), 38–47; id., 'Le Contexte historique des *Notae in programma quoddam*', in *Descartes et Regius*, ed. T. Verbeek (Amsterdam 1993), 1–33.

[4] In this work, Descartes responded also to some of the objections to his system provided in *Consideratio theologica*, a pamphlet published by a theologian at Utrecht, Jacobus Revius

[5] In *Essay* II. i. 4, Locke allowed that reflection on the operations of the understanding is a source of ideas, as well as sense experience of external objects. In theses 16, 17, 18, 20, and 21 of his pamphlet, Regius discussed various kinds of mental operations (AT viii-2. 345–6). Evidently he believed that "observation of things" includes observation of these operations.

[6] As argued in the previous note, Regius suggested in his pamphlet that "observation or tradition" involves more than the reception of material from the outer senses. I follow the *Notes*, however, in focusing on the case of outer sense perception.

that nothing is in our ideas which is not innate to the mind, or to the faculty of thinking [*nihil sit in nostris ideis, quod menti, sive cogitandi facultati, non fuerit innatum*], except only those circumstances that pertain to experience: such as that we judge that these or those ideas, which we now have present to our thought, are referred to certain things placed outside us. (AT viii-2. 359)

The material for judgements relating to experience does not consist of ideas sent (*immiserunt*) "to our mind through the sense organs"; rather, the sense organs send something that "gives occasion" (*dedit occasionem*) to the mind to "form [the ideas] at this time rather than another, by means of a faculty innate to it" (*ad ipsas, per innatum sibi facultatem, hoc tempore potius quam alio, efformandas*). Descartes explained that "nothing approaches [*accedit*] to our mind from external objects through the sense organs, except certain motions". Citing remarks in the 1637 *Dioptrics*, he asserted that the figures arising from bodily motions "are not conceived by us just as they are in the sense organs", and concluded from this that "the ideas of motions and figures themselves are innate to us. And so much the more must the ideas of pain, colours, sounds, and the like be innate, so that our mind is able, on the occasion of certain corporeal motions [*occasione quorundam motuum corporeorum*], to exhibit them to itself; for they have no likeness [*similitudinem*] to corporeal motions" (AT viii-2. 359).

(a) *The mental faculty and sensory ideas*

An initial formulation of Descartes's position in these passages is as follows: The motions in the brain which give rise to sensory ideas are not exact replicas of these ideas. Given this lack of resemblance, mental ideas cannot be identified with such motions and cannot arise directly from these motions. Sensory ideas, therefore, must be formed by an inborn faculty of the mind. These ideas need not be innate in the sense of being always present to mind, given Descartes's claim to Regius that sometimes innate ideas exist only in a mental faculty, and "to exist in a faculty is not to exist actually [*actu*], but merely potentially [*potentia*], since the name 'faculty' denotes nothing but a potential [*potentiam*]" (AT viii-2. 61).[7] The nature of this potential existence in the mind may seem unclear, for '*potentia*' can denote potential (as opposed to actual) existence as well as potency or power. But I believe that Descartes intended both senses of the term. Not only do sensory ideas have a potential existence in the mind; they are also present in the mind in the sense that the mind from the start has had a faculty that can form them.[8] Descartes

---

[7] A similar reconstruction of the argument is presented in Adams, 75–8, and in Wilson.

[8] The claim that Descartes took the innate mental faculty to involve a power to form sensory ideas is supported somewhat by the fact that he had spoken in the early *Regulae* of the mind as a *vis* that applies itself to corporeal images when sensing or imagining (AT x. 415). Moreover,

emphasized this aspect of innateness when he responded to Hobbes that an idea is innate when "we have within ourselves the faculty of eliciting [*eliciendi*] the idea" (AT vii. 189). The view of the *Notes* is that sensory ideas are innate to mind because the mind has always had not merely the potential to possess these ideas but also a faculty that can elicit or form them.[9]

The nature of the sensory ideas that Descartes took to be formed by mind can best be understood in light of three distinctions. The first is between ideas as bodily and as mental. Descartes often affirmed that sensation is possible only for a human being constituted by the union of distinct mental and bodily substances.[10] In pre-1640 discussions of sensation, but also in works composed after that date, he suggested that sensory ideas pertain to the bodily part of the human being when he identified these ideas with corporeal figures in the brain.[11] Yet in a shift anticipated in his early works, but more pronounced in post-1640 writings, he indicated that such ideas pertain rather to the mental part of the human being when he noted that the term 'idea' denotes a mode of thought, i.e. a modification of a thinking substance.[12] In his Responses to the Second Objections, for instance, Descartes claimed that images in the brain are ideas only "in so far as they inform that mind attending to [*conversam*] that part of the brain" (AT vii. 161). On this view, the forms of mind which arise from mental consideration of the brain are distinct from the parts of the brain to which the mind attends.[13] This

---

Louis de la Forge believed that he was adhering to the doctrine of the *Notes* when he held that innate ideas are contained in a power (*puissance*) of mind that is active (*Traité de l'esprit de l'homme*, in La Forge, *Oeuvres philosophiques*, ed. P. Clair (Paris 1974), 181). Contrary to McRae, 52–3, I see no reason to take La Forge's interpretation to be in error on this point.

[9] In *Descartes' philosophy of science* (Manchester 1982), D. M. Clarke interprets Descartes as drawing from the rejection of resemblance the conclusion that "those ideas which are provoked by and correlated with extra-mental stimuli are innate in the sense of being irreducible to the type of reality which triggers them in the mind" (p. 50). I take this conclusion to overlook the significance of the claim to Regius that the mind has a faculty that *forms* sensory ideas.

[10] See *TH*: AT xi. 143–4; *Med.* VI: AT vii. 81; *PP* I. 48, II. 2–3: AT viii-1. 23, 41–2; the 1642 letter to Regius at AT iii. 493; the 1643 letters to Elisabeth at AT iii. 665, 690–94; and the 1649 letter to More at AT v. 402. The position of the *Notes* is that the union is a conjunction of distinct substances (AT viii-2. 351). Such a position differs from the suggestion in Descartes's 1643 correspondence with Elisabeth that the union creates a single entity with its own attribute and modes. See T. M. Schmaltz, 'Descartes and Malebranche on mind and mind-body union', *Philosophical review* 101 (1992), 281–325, for a more detailed discussion of the account of mind-body union offered in this correspondence and in related works. In the present essay, I emphasize those texts most suggestive of the account of the union in the *Notes*.

[11] See *RI* XII, XIV: AT x. 414, 441; *TH*: AT xi. 176–7; *DM*: AT vi. 55. For an example of this use of the term 'idea' in later works, see *PA* II. 120, 136: AT xi. 417, 429. E. and F. S. Michael discuss the historical background of this sort of understanding of ideas in 'Corporeal ideas in seventeenth-century psychology', *Journal of the history of ideas* 50 (1989), 31–48.

[12] For examples of anticipation, see Descartes's reference in *Le Monde* to "the [sensory] ideas we have in our mind" (AT xi. 3); and also his claim in the *Discourse* that "I could not deny that the ideas [of corporeal things] were truly in my mind" (AT vi. 35).

[13] See also *RO* III, V: AT vii. 181, 392–3; two 1641 letters to Mersenne at AT iii. 361, 392–3; and *PP* I. 9: AT viii-1. 7.

distinction between the bodily and mental aspects of sensation is reflected in
the view of the *Notes* that sensory ideas are produced in the mind when the
operation of a mental faculty is triggered by the presence of motions in the
brain.

In the Preface to his *Meditations,* Descartes introduced a second
distinction, claiming that an idea "can be taken materially, as an operation of
the intellect", or "alternatively, it can be taken objectively, as the thing
represented by the operation itself" (AT vii. 8). When taken materially, an
idea is simply a mental act, but this idea also can represent various objects.
Viewed objectively, an idea is the aspect of a mental act which directs the
mind to particular objects. Descartes emphasized this objective aspect when
he stated in Meditation III that all ideas are "as if images of things" (*tanquam
rerum imagines*), and that "when I will, when I fear, when I affirm, when I
deny, I always indeed apprehend something as the subject of my thought"
(AT vii. 37). The objective reality of ideas involves the presentation to mind
of a subject of thought.[14] The account of sensation in the *Notes* does not
advert to the concept of objective reality. None the less, Descartes suggested
that sensory ideas have a sort of content that does not resemble the bodily
motions that approach the mind. He was concerned in this text not with ideas
as mental operations but rather with the content of these ideas. Admittedly,
there is some controversy over whether he is entitled to hold that sensory
ideas have such content. He stressed that bodies must be characterized in
terms of extension. This doctrine does seem to commit him to the view that
sensory ideas of features not so characterizable, ideas such as those of colour
and sound, cannot represent features of bodies and therefore cannot possess
any sort of representational content. I shall address this matter below, but I
would indicate that the response to Regius does not sharply distinguish the
production of ideas of figure and motion from the production of ideas of
colour and sound. Descartes emphasized there that all these ideas must be
produced by a faculty of mind, and for the same reason.

Finally, there is a third distinction germane to the remarks to Regius.
Descartes wrote to Arnauld in 1648 that sensation involves two elements:
direct and reflex thought. Direct thoughts are akin to "the first and simple
thoughts of childhood . . . for instance, the pain they feel when some wind
distends their intestines or the pleasure they feel when nourished by sweet
blood". An example of reflex thought, on the other hand, is "when an adult
feels something and simultaneously perceives that he has not felt it before".
Descartes noted that such reflection must be attributed "to the intellect

---

[14] For discussion of Descartes's doctrine of ideas, see V. C. Chappell, 'The theory of ideas',
in *Essays on Descartes' Meditations*, ed. A. O. Rorty (Berkeley 1986), 177–98; W. Sellars,
'Berkeley and Descartes', in *Studies in perception*, ed. P. Machamer and R. Turnbull (Columbus,
Oh. 1978), 259–311.

alone, in spite of its being so linked to sensation that the two occur together and appear to be indistinguishable from each other" (AT v. 221). He had also suggested, in a letter to Arnauld earlier that year, that reflective thought includes sensory experience connected conceptually with previous experiences (AT v. 192).[15] In light of these remarks, sensory ideas can be considered either as percepts (the particular forms of direct sensory thoughts) or as concepts (the universal forms by means of which these direct thoughts are classified). The first appears to be what Descartes had in mind when discussing sensory ideas produced by mind in the *Notes*, for he was concerned with what is given immediately in sensation, prior to further determination by will and intellect. In any case, he did say that there is nothing in the ideas of sense not innate to the mind, and this would include the form of direct thoughts.[16] What is of interest in the *Notes* for our purposes is the view that even the contents of direct sensory thoughts are produced by a mental faculty. In speaking of innate sensory ideas, I therefore intend to refer to these percepts rather than the universal concepts provided by reflection.

(b) *The question of consistency*

Having clarified the notions of innateness and sensory idea employed in the response to Regius, we must confront the objection that the response itself can be discounted. There are two ways in which such an objection could be supported. First, the critic could hold that the claim that sensory ideas are innate to mind is merely an incidental one found in a single text, and thus cannot be given much weight. This is easily countered, however, for the claim is anticipated in earlier writings. Perhaps the most striking instance is Descartes's remark to Mersenne, seven years prior to publication of the *Notes*, that all ideas are innate because the sensory organs "do not bring anything that is such as the idea which arises in us" (*se reveille en nous*) on the occasion of motions in these organs (AT iii. 414). There are other, more subtle, forms of anticipation that I shall mention later.

For the present, however, I want to consider a second and more serious argument that the view of the *Notes* cannot be accepted as Descartes's own because it is inconsistent with principles entrenched in his system. For instance, the claim that sensory ideas are innate seems to contradict the

---

[15] Descartes claimed in this letter that reflection can involve the employment of intellectual memory, and was reported by Burman to have remarked that intellectual memory is distinct from bodily memory because the former involves universal concepts (AT v. 149).

[16] Van de Pitte claims that the argument of the *Notes* supports only the conclusion that universal concepts, all of which structure experience, are innate. I take this interpretation to restrict Descartes's position too severely. Van de Pitte's interpretation will be considered further in I (d) (2) below.

suggestion in this same text that they are adventitious rather than innate. Alluding to a distinction drawn in Meditation III (at AT vii. 37–8), Descartes told Regius that innate ideas "proceed neither from external objects, nor from a voluntary determination of my will, but solely from a faculty of thinking in me; so that I call ideas which are the forms of these thoughts 'innate' to distinguish them from others which are adventitious or factitious" (AT viii-2. 358). The implication in both works is that sensory ideas proceed from external objects and thus are adventitious. Given the threefold distinction of ideas, it seems that Descartes is committed to denying that sensory ideas are innate.

There is a way around this difficulty. When Descartes claimed in the *Notes* that sensory ideas are innate, he meant merely that they are produced by a faculty of mind. This allows for the view that such ideas are adventitious in the sense that they arise from a mental faculty only when the mind is stimulated by certain bodily motions. When he stated that certain ideas are innate rather than adventitious or factitious, on the other hand, he meant to deny that such ideas arise either immediately upon particular sensory stimulation or by means of a voluntary combination of elements supplied by sense experience.

Descartes therefore suggested two different senses of 'innateness'. Ideas are innate in a *narrow* sense when they derive from an intellectual faculty of mind rather than from sensory or volitional mental faculties. These do not include sensory ideas that arise directly upon the stimulation of the mind by external objects. Ideas are innate in a *broad* sense, on the other hand, when they are produced by any sort of mental faculty. Given the view of the *Notes* that even sensory ideas are produced by a mental faculty, it follows that such ideas are innate in this broader sense. It is true that Descartes did not explicitly invoke this distinction between narrow and broad senses of 'innateness'. Yet such a distinction serves quite naturally to render various parts of the response to Regius consistent. This provides sufficient support for the conclusion that the Descartes of the *Notes* would have endorsed such a distinction had it been presented to him.[17]

This does not remove all difficulties, though, since Descartes himself suggested in certain texts that sensory ideas derive from external objects rather than from the mind. In *Les Passions de l'âme*, for instance, he held that sensory states of soul are passions, because "it is often not our soul which makes them such as they are, and the soul always receives [*reçoit*] them from

---

[17] A similar reconciliation of Descartes's remarks has been offered by Adams, 75–8, and Clarke, 48–54. Such a distinction was previously suggested by French commentators such as E. Gilson, *Discours de la méthode: Texte et commentaire* (Paris 1925), 327–8; G. [Rodis-] Lewis, *Le Problème de l'inconscient et le cartésianisme* (Paris 1950), 84–7; and M. Gueroult, *Descartes selon l'ordre des raisons* (2 vols, Paris 1968), i. 101–3.

things that are represented by them" (AT xi. 342). The claim that sensations are received from external objects also plays an important role in the proof of the existence of bodies outlined in the *Meditations* and the *Principles*. Descartes argued in Meditation VI that the mind cannot have an active faculty that produces sensory ideas, and, further, that God would be a deceiver if the ideas "were transmitted [*emitterentur*] from a source other than external things" (AT vii. 80). He also claimed in *Principles* II. 1 that "whatever we sense undoubtedly comes [*advenit*] to us from something that is distinct from our mind" (AT viii-1. 40).[18] Surely Descartes cannot be taken at his word, then, when he tells Regius that all sensory ideas must be formed by mind.

Such a conclusion would be too hasty. There are various ways in which texts emphasizing the passivity of sensation can be reconciled to a literal reading of the remarks in the *Notes* pertaining to the sensory faculty of mind. In the *Passions*, for instance, sensations are contrasted with volitions, the latter of which are experienced "as proceeding directly from our soul and as seeming to depend on it alone" (AT xi. 342).[19] The suggestion here is that sensations come from external objects in the sense that they do not arise in the soul by means of volitional activity. This does not conflict with the claim that sensory ideas are produced by a mental faculty, for this claim does not entail that the operation of this faculty is volitional. Moreover, Descartes implied that sensory ideas do not depend on the mind alone when he told Regius that the triggering of the mental faculty by the appropriate corporeal motions is required for the formation of these ideas.

The critic may object that this solution overlooks the denial in Meditation VI that the mind can possess an active faculty that produces sensory ideas. But the nature of the faculty discussed in this text must be examined with care. In Meditation VI, Descartes began his consideration of the active faculty by referring to the discussion in Meditation III. There he had considered the commonsense view that sensory ideas must derive from external objects because "I know by experience that these ideas do not depend on my will, and hence do not depend simply on me" (AT vii. 38). The fact that sensations are involuntary, he noted, is insufficient to establish that they have an external source. In support of this, he suggested the possibility of an unknown faculty "which produces these ideas *without any assistance* from external things", similar to the faculty responsible for dreams (AT vii. 39, emphasis mine).[20] Given the allusion to this in Meditation VI, Descartes can

---

[18] For the view that sensory ideas come from external objects, see also *RO* II, v: AT vii. 135, 367.

[19] See also the 1644 letter to Mesland at AT iv. 113.

[20] Descartes's reference to dreaming is surely meant to bring to mind the dream argument of Meditation I. Wilson has argued convincingly in *Descartes* (London 1978), 17–31, that Descartes took this earlier argument to show that, since we do not think that dreams represent reality, and since there is nothing that distinguishes waking experience from dreaming, there is no reason to

be seen as concluding there only that *this sort* of faculty cannot exist in me. Whereas the active faculty of mind discussed in the *Meditations* does not depend on external events, however, the innate sensory faculty of the *Notes* is so constructed that its operations do depend on the presence of certain motions in the brain. The active mental faculty rejected in Meditation vi cannot be identified with the innate sensory faculty posited in the *Notes*.

But even if the faculties cannot be identified, it may still be that the argument against the one can be offered against the other. To assess this point we must consider the specific argument in Meditation vi. Descartes noted that there are only two faculties of mind: the passive faculty of intellect and the active faculty of will.[21] The faculty of sensation is held to be a mode of the intellectual faculty (AT vii. 79). The implication is that any other non-volitional faculty of mind must likewise be a mode of this intellectual faculty. He then argued that the active faculty that is the source of sensory ideas in me cannot be such a mode, for "clearly it presupposes no intellectual act on my part" (AT vii. 79). What Descartes appears to have had in mind is that, since the intellect is a passive faculty for the apprehension of ideas, a distinct active faculty not involved in such an apprehension cannot be a mode of it. Neither can this active faculty be a mode of the will, since it had been established in Meditation iii that sensory ideas arise in the mind involuntarily. If it is a mode of neither my intellect nor my will, it must be a mode of some other substance.

Nothing here serves to preclude the innate sensory faculty of the *Notes*. Descartes did not suggest in this work that this faculty is something over and above the faculty of sensation; rather, he employed it to explain the manner in which the mind apprehends sensory ideas. This faculty still is passive in the sense employed in the *Passions*, for it does not involve an act of will. The faculty also is a mode of intellect because it is involved in the apprehension of sensory ideas. The innate sensory faculty is naturally identified with the passive faculty of sensation and thus does not appear to be within the scope of the argument of Meditation vi.[22]

---

think that waking experience represents reality accurately. Likewise, the argument of Meditation iii may be construed as follows: Since dreams may derive from a mental faculty, and since the involuntariness of sensation does not serve to distinguish it from dreams, it may be that sensation derives from a similar sort of faculty. D. Garber notes this connection between the dream argument as construed by Wilson and the faculty argument of Meditation iii in 'Semel in vita', in Rorty, 114 n. 42.

[21] This view of mental faculties supports the account of error supplied in Meditation iv (e.g., in AT vii. 56–57), and is presupposed in other texts in which Descartes discusses the operations of mind (cf. *PP* i. 32: AT viii-1. 17; the 1641 letter to Regius at AT iii. 372; and *PA* i. 17: AT xi. 342).

[22] In taking the innate faculty of the *Notes* to be the faculty of sensation, I dispute Janet Broughton's description of it as a "meta-faculty" that "regulates the mind's faculty for having sense-ideas" ('Adequate causes and natural change in Descartes' philosophy', in *Human nature*

Descartes emphasized both in Meditation VI and in Part II of the *Principles* that, since God is not a deceiver, sensory ideas must arise from material objects. Here again, though, there are indications that he was not thinking of the same sort of derivation of ideas in these texts as he was in the *Notes*. When he offered proofs of the external world, for instance, he did not address the question of the manner in which motions in the brain give rise to sensory ideas; he was more concerned to show that sensory ideas are not produced by an act of will and that external objects play a role in the production of sensory ideas. As we have seen, the innatist position of the *Notes* is consistent both with the claim that sensations are not produced by the will and with the claim that external motions are required for the production of sensory ideas.

Moreover, Descartes's view in Meditation VI that bodies have an "active faculty" of "producing or bringing about" sensory ideas (*producendi vel efficiendi*: AT vii. 79) need not preclude the operation of the innate mental faculty of the *Notes*. One could hold that the active faculty in an external body produces motions in the brain, which, in turn, cause a faculty of mind to produce sensory ideas. In this sense, sensory ideas could still derive from the active faculty of an external body without arising directly from motions in the brain. It is interesting to note that in the *Principles* Descartes in fact dropped the reference to an active faculty in bodies, writing simply that particular corporeal motions "bring it about [*efficient*] that we have various sensations" (AT viii-1. 40). But motions may "bring about" sensations by triggering the operation of the innate sensory faculty of mind.[23] Remarks in Meditation VI and *Principles* II. 1 concerning the importance of bodies in sensation do not contravene the nativist account of sensation in the *Notes*.[24]

This is not to say that we can attribute to Descartes a wholly consistent view of sensory interaction. I cited above his claim in the Second Responses that sensory ideas inform the mind when it "attends to" images in the brain. Nor is this passage unique; he referred in several texts, early and late, to the

---

and natural knowledge, ed. A. Donagan and others (Dordrecht 1986), 119). If Broughton were correct, the innate sensory faculty would fall within the scope of the Meditation VI argument after all. I do not think, however, that her interpretation is warranted by the texts. There is no mention in the *Notes* of a separate regulative function of this faculty. Descartes spoke of the innate faculty simply as a faculty for forming sensory ideas that is designed to operate in a particular manner.

[23] The French translation of *PP* II. 1 speaks of *l'idée [qui] se forme en nous à l'occasion des corps de dehors* (AT ix-2. 64). This supports my claim that Descartes's proof of the external world need not conflict with the view of the *Notes* that bodily motions serve as occasions for the formation of sensory ideas by a faculty of mind.

[24] In 'Descartes on the origin of sensation', Wilson presents a similar reconciliation of the proof of the existence of the material world in Meditation VI and *PP* II. 1, on the one hand, and the remarks in the *Notes*, on the other. Though I developed the main lines of my position independently, Wilson's paper is responsible for several improvements in my discussion here.

fact that the mind turns toward such images in sense experience.[25] He spoke at times as if the mind senses by seeing images in the brain, thus violating the strictures of the *Notes*. What I have been concerned to argue, though, is that neither Descartes's proof of the existence of the material world nor his position that the mind is passive in sensation presupposes that the mind must perceive something in the brain in order to have sensory ideas. This view, therefore, is less central to his thought than it might at first appear. And this fact, in turn, allows us to take the position of the *Notes* seriously.[26]

(c) *The critique of scholastic transmission*

Thus far I have provided an explication of the conclusion of the *Notes* and have defended the position that this conclusion is consistent with doctrines vital for Descartes. I have yet to consider the argument for the conclusion. Descartes himself provided such an argument when he told Regius that rejection of the mental faculty leaves one with an untenable view of sensory processes. He claimed that, in order to affirm the alternative position that the mind receives ideas from the senses, one must accept a theory according to which "things send ideas to the mind through the sense organs". According to Descartes, the position that *simulacra* are transmitted to the mind by external objects is entailed by the claim that the mind merely receives ideas from bodies. Surely, he told Regius, we cannot believe that bodies literally transmit little images of themselves to the mind by way of the senses.

Descartes had attacked this transmission view of sensation earlier, in the *Dioptrics*, when he referred to "all those little images flitting through the air, called 'intentional species' [*espèces intentionnelles*], which so exercise the imagination of the philosophers" (AT vi. 85). The philosophers here, clearly the schoolmen of Descartes's day,[27] were said to offer such a view because

---

[25] Cf. *TH*: AT xi. 176–7; *Med.* vi: AT vii. 73, v. 162. As I shall note below, this sort of claim is also present in certain parts of the *Discourse*. It could be argued that in his more mature writings, at least, Descartes was speaking only metaphorically when he referred to the mind as attending to figures in the brain. But the fact that he used this sort of metaphor reveals that the transmission view continued to retain some sort of hold on him.

[26] The view of the *Notes* that bodily motions are occasions for the formation of sensory ideas by the mind was also taken seriously, and even accepted, by followers of Descartes such as Arnauld (see Arnauld and Nicole, *La Logique ou l'art de penser*, ed. P. Clair and F. Gerbal (Paris 1965), 46) and La Forge (see the passage from his work cited in note 8).

[27] Kepler had offered a transmission view of sensation. (For the context of this view, see G. Hatfield and W. Epstein, 'The sensory core and the medieval foundations of early modern perceptual theory', *Isis* 70 (1979), 363–84.) Yet the philosophers, or the proponents of the vulgar philosophy, were for Descartes the schoolmen (AT iii. 420; cf. AT i. 421, iv. 30). In the *Notes*, he defended himself against the view that he took ideas to be forms distinct from the faculty of thought by noting that "there is no one more opposed than I to the useless lumber of scholastic entities" (AT viii-2. 36).

"they saw how easily a picture can stimulate thought [*pensée*], and so it seemed to them, in the same way, thought must be stimulated by little pictures formed in our head, to conceive the objects that affect our senses" (AT vi. 112). Forgetting that he himself had spoken of such mental stimulation, Descartes offered a *reductio ad scholasticum* of the view that mind is totally receptive in sensation. The *Notes* offers the innate mental faculty in order to avoid an appeal to resembling images that fly to the mind.

Interpreters of the *Notes* often pass over this attack on the scholastic position. Given the importance of the attack both in the remarks to Regius and in the *Dioptrics*, however, it is worth considering whether this picture of the schoolmen bears any resemblance to their own view. To aid such a consideration, I turn to the account of sensation offered by Eustachius a Sancto Paulo (Eustache de Saint-Paul) in his *Summa philosophiae*, a work that Descartes told Mersenne he had been reading with some care.[28] Earlier in 1640 he mentioned to Mersenne the works of certain scholastic commentators that he had read some twenty years before;[29] it is far from clear, however, that Descartes had paid these works the attention that he paid the text of Eustachius. To be sure, he came across this text three years after publication of the critique of the scholastic account of sensation in the *Dioptrics*. None the less, he evidently took Eustachius to offer a view of sensation of the sort criticized in his earlier essay, for he suggested later in the *Notes* that the same objections hold. Thus it is fair to take Eustachius as representative of the schoolmen criticized by Descartes in this work.

Eustachius's view of sensation is on the whole in line with the teachings of Thomas Aquinas (though, as we shall discover, Eustachius did not follow Aquinas in all respects). He concurred with Aquinas, for instance, in taking sensation proper to involve both a material alteration of the sense organ by the perceived object and an intentional (*intentionalis*) modification involving the production of a sensible species that is a likeness (*similitudo*) of a quality of

---

[28] Eustachius (1573–1640) was a French Cistercian professor of philosophy and theology at the Sorbonne. Descartes wrote to Mersenne in 1740 that, having read his newly purchased copy of Eustachius's text, he found it to be "the best book that has ever been done on this material" (AT iii. 232). He even revealed a plan to publish an annotated version of this work alongside what became the *Principles* (ibid., 233, 259–60). The plan was dropped after the death of Eustachius in 1640, both because he could no longer give permission for use of his work, and because Descartes came to think that an explicit comparison of his view and that of the scholastics was no longer necessary (ibid., 260, 286, 470). The edition of Eustachius's work that Descartes studied, and that I will cite, is *Summa philosophiae quadripartita* (Cambridge 1640) [hereafter '*SP*', followed by book and page numbers]. All translations are my own.

[29] At AT iii. 185, Descartes mentioned the following Jesuit authors of popular commentaries on the works of Aristotle: Spanish Cardinal Franciscus Toletus (Francisco Toledo) (1532–96); the Portuguese Conimbricenses, who were the faculty at the University of Coïmbra; and the Mexican Antonius Rubius (1548–1615), a student of Toletus. Below I cite Toletus's commentary on *De anima*.

that object. This resemblance is explained by the inherence in the species of a form qualitatively similar to one inhering in the object perceived.[30]

On Descartes's reading of this sort of account, the species is a likeness of an object because it is an image sent from the object. Yet Eustachius himself explicitly rejected such a transmission view of sensation. He claimed that sensation "does not occur by means of a traversal [*transitionem*], in the way in which an arrow is dispatched [*emittitur*] towards a target by a marksman, but instead by means of a continual propagation in the way in which warmth reaches [*pervenit*] the warmed object by means of the fire".[31] The object is not understood to produce images that fly off towards the eye. Rather, the account offered is that the object has a form by means of which a medium is altered. Admittedly, Eustachius suggested that a form is somehow passed on to the sense organs by means of a "continual propagation",[32] and there may be difficulties in understanding how such a propagation occurs. But he clearly indicated that this process need not involve the presence of a material image sent from the object.[33] To take the propagated form to be such an image, moreover, is to confuse the qualitative change in the percipient, which occurs by means of a form, with the material processes by means of which such a change occurs. If there is an objection to Eustachius's account on this point, Descartes has yet to formulate it.

Descartes also noted, however, that the schoolmen were led to posit species because they saw "how easily a picture can stimulate our thought to conceive the objects depicted in it". He took his scholastic contemporaries to be claiming that, just as an external picture may stimulate thought, so may an

---

[30] Cf. Aquinas's position in *Summa theologiae* (London 1964–76) [hereafter *ST*], Pt I, qu. 78, art. 3–4; I. 84. 3; I. 85. I ad I. Eustachius called the sensible species *intentionales* in *SP* iii. 290. The species is further described as a *similitudo* in *SP* iii. 297. Both Aquinas and Eustachius emphasized that the sensible species is not the object of perception, but is only the means by which the qualities of objects are perceived.

[31] *SP* iii. 291.

[32] The need for such propagation is revealed by the claim of Eustachius that the sensory organ can receive a form only from something in immediate contact with it (see the text provided by Gilson, *Index scolastico-cartésien* (Paris 1913), sec. 417). Interestingly enough, Ockham denied the principle that there can be no action at a distance and thus rejected the need for propagation. A. Maier discusses this view further in 'Das Problem der "Species sensibiles in medio" und der neue Naturphilosophie des 14. Jahrhunderts', in *Ausgehendes Mittelalter* (3 vols, Rome 1964–77), ii. 419–51, at 433–44.

[33] Aquinas claimed that the impression of sense does not occur *"per modum defluxionis, ut Democritus posuit, sed per quandam operationem"* (*ST* I. 84. 6). He therefore with Eustachius rejected the notion that little material pictures are sent from the object. The term *'quandam operationem'* also signals a lack of commitment to a specific explanation of the manner in which a form is passed to a percipient, and Eustachius spoke in similarly vague terms. J.-L. Marion, in *Sur la théologie blanche de Descartes* (Paris 1981), 243 n. 12, suggests that the Cartesian caricature of scholastic theories of perception arose from a confusion of Aristotelian *eidos* with Democritean *eidola*. The point that the scholastics were not committed to the images of Democritus was made previously by Gilson in *Études sur le rôle de la pensée médiévale dans la formation du système cartésien* (Paris 1951), 21–2.

internal picture give rise immediately to mental sensation. But this characterization no more captures the scholastic position than Ryle's discussion of what he called "Descartes's myth" captures Descartes's own thought.[34] There are two obvious difficulties with Descartes's caricature of the schoolmen. First, Eustachius could not have accepted that little pictures in the brain are the objects of sensation. With other schoolmen, he emphasized that sensible species are not the objects of perception but rather theoretical entities employed in an account of perception.[35]

The second, more significant difficulty is that Eustachius would not have spoken of sensation as involving the *thought* of images at all. Descartes's concept of thought is most similar to the scholastic concept of an intellectual operation.[36] Schoolmen such as Eustachius held that intellectual operations do not involve a corporeal organ, whereas they took the sensory power to operate only through such an organ. The sensory power is thus involved only in modifications of the sense organs. This explains the view of Eustachius that the corporeal souls of brutes as well as the incorporeal souls of humans possess the power of sensation. Scholastic sensation does not involve the stimulation of thought as Descartes understood this notion. Eustachius did claim that there are intellectual operations on material supplied by sensation, but the account of these operations is not as simple as Descartes suggested. Using Augustinian language, this schoolman argued that, since the rational soul is of a higher order than the body, the latter cannot bring about an alteration in the former.[37] There must be an agent intellect that "abstracts" the intelligible species. By means of this production, the potential intellect is able to receive an intellectual aspect of objects, thereby allowing for knowledge.[38] This abstractive operation of the intellect takes one beyond the sensory processes common to humans and brutes to an activity that is found in the human soul alone.

In order to appreciate the extent to which Descartes's caricature distorts the actual view of the schoolmen, it is useful to consider scholastic discussions of the role of the human soul in sensation. Aquinas mentioned the view, which he attributed to Plato, that "the soul is somehow excited so as to

---

[34] G. Ryle, *The concept of mind* (London 1949), ch. 1. For a critique of Ryle's reading, see E. M. Curley, 'Dialogues with the dead', *Synthèse* 67 (1986), 33–49.

[35] See *SP* iii. 292. Cf. *ST* i. 85. 2. In this respect, perhaps, sensible species are similar to the images in the brain posited by Descartes (in those passages in which he rejected the view, implied by the transmission account, that the mind sees these images).

[36] Eustachius referred to operations proper to the soul (*operationes proprias animae*) in *SP* iii. 329. Aquinas spoke of the power (*potentia*) that has the soul as its subject, and to the acts (*actus*) of this power (*ST* i. 77).

[37] Eustachius employed Augustine's neoplatonic notion of different orders of reality in *SP* iii. 337. Cf. *ST* i. 84. 6.

[38] As with sensible species, both Aquinas and Eustachius emphasized that the intelligible species are not what is known directly by the intellect, but are the means by which knowledge of objects is attained. Cf. *ST* i. 85. 2, i. 87. 3; *SP* iii. 332.

form sensible species in itself".[39] He noted somewhat cautiously that Augustine "seems to touch on" the opinion of Plato, citing Augustine's claim that "the body does not feel, but the soul through the body, which it uses as a kind of messenger to form [*ad formandum*] in itself what is announced from without".[40] Aquinas countered this view not by indicating the ease with which a material object stimulates the human soul, but rather by objecting that sensation involves merely the reception of the sensible species in the sense organ, and thus that it pertains to the soul-body composite, not to the soul alone. He held that the principle that the body is of a lower order than the soul is irrelevant at the level of sensation, though he granted that it is important at the level of intellection.[41] Eustachius sided with Aquinas when he affirmed that the sensory power inheres in the physical sense organ rather than in the human soul.[42]

Even this preliminary examination of the scholastic context reveals that the initial Cartesian critique of scholastic theory has missed its mark. Schoolmen such as Eustachius are committed neither to flying images nor to the view that in sensation the mind is easily stimulated by pictures. Had Descartes relied only on difficulties with the crude transmission view in rejecting the scholastic account of sensation, such a rejection certainly would be without firm support.

(d) *Resemblance and mental activity*

Fortunately, Descartes had more to offer in response to the account of sensation offered by the schoolmen. Eustachius conformed to Aristotelian

---

[39] *ST* I. 84. 6.

[40] This passage, cited in *ST* I. 84. 6, is from Augustine's *De Genesi ad litteram*, XII. 24, in *Patrologiae cursus completus*, *Series latina*, ed. J. Migne (221 vols, Paris 1844–64) [hereafter PL], xxxiv. 475. Cf. *De musica*, VI. v. 9–10: PL xxxii. 1168–70. For more on the Augustinian view of sensation, see P. B. Kälin, *Die Erkenntnislehre des Hl. Augustinus* (Sarin 1920), 8–40; M. A. I. Gannon, 'The active theory of sensation in St Augustine', *New scholasticism* 30 (1956), 154–80; R. H. Nash, *The light of the mind* (Lexington, Ky. 1969), 39–59; R. A. Marcus, 'Augustine. Sense and imagination', in *Cambridge history of later Greek and early medieval philosophy*, ed. A. H. Armstrong (Cambridge 1967), 374–9.

[41] *ST* I. 75. 4. The positions of Augustine and Aquinas on sensation are contrasted by J. Hessen, *Augustins Metaphysik der Erkenntnis* (Leiden 1960), 251–4, 258–60. Toletus mentioned the view (which he attributed to Plotinus and Simplicius rather than Plato and Augustine) that sensation involves the activity of the soul. Following Aquinas, he countered with the Aristotelian position that sensation is a passive feature of the soul-body composite rather than an activity of the human soul itself (Franciscus Toletus, *In tres libros Aristotelis De anima commentarii* (Lyons 1591), 251–3).

[42] There was some dispute among schoolmen over the subject of the sensory power. The more traditional view accepted by Aquinas and Toletus was that the subject is the soul-body composite (*ST* I. 77. 8; Toletus, *De anima*, 251–3). On the other hand, Suarez at one point suggested the deviant position that the body itself (albeit a body informed by a soul) is the subject (*De anima*, III. iii. 3). Eustachius did not directly address this question, which I take to be an indication that he assumed the standard Thomistic line.

doctrine when he claimed that the sensible species involved in sense experience resemble bodily qualities. Descartes objected, however, that certain sensory ideas *cannot* be similar to such qualities. He stated in the *Principles*, for instance, that when we form the judgement that colours resemble qualities of objects, "we do not really know what it is we call a colour; nor can we understand any similarity between the colour which we suppose to be in objects, and that which we experience to be in sensation" (1. 70: AT viii-1. 34). This dispute over the intelligibility of the scholastic position that the form of colour actually does exist in the sense organs and in objects suggests that Descartes's account of sensation was built on more than ridicule of the crude transmission view. There appear to be deeper reasons for the position in the *Notes* that there cannot be "any similarity between" sensory ideas of colours and sounds and corporeal qualities, and thus that such ideas must be innate. I begin with a discussion of Descartes's deeper reasons for his rejection of scholastic doctrine, and then consider the grounds for his alternative position that the mind is active (in a non-volitional manner) in sensation.

1. *The rejection of resemblance.* Throughout his philosophical life, Descartes attempted to replace scholastic appeals to sensory and qualitative forms with an account of the bodily aspects of sensation solely in quantitative terms. Yet the grounds for this replacement shifted over time. In the early and unfinished *Regulae ad directionem ingenii*, Descartes had presented his alternative to the scholastic account as assumptions (*suppositiones*) that are "helpful" in avoiding "troubling consequences" (AT x. 412–15). He indicated elsewhere in this work that he offered a hypothetical view of sensation as part of a prolegomenon to an account of our knowledge of nature.[43] Undoubtedly influenced by the work of Mersenne, Descartes appealed to such a view in order to support the claim that material objects are capable of mathematical analysis.[44]

In a letter to Mersenne in 1630, however, Descartes announced that the "foundations of physics" lie in metaphysical truths "more evident than the

---

[43] Descartes's account of sensation is presented in *RI* XII, but he had indicated earlier in *RI* VIII that, prior to an investigation of the nature of particular objects, one must consider the nature of the knowing subject and the nature of the objects known (cf. AT x. 395–6, 398).

[44] In *La Vérité des sciences* (Paris 1625), Mersenne conceded to the sceptic that knowledge of essences is impossible, but claimed none the less that a mathematical science of appearances is possible. He held, in particular, that the science of optics provides an explanation of the connection of appearances. As J. Schuster notes in 'Descartes' *Mathesis universalis*, 1619–28', in *Descartes: Philosophy, mathematics and physics*, ed. S. Gaukroger (Brighton 1980), 41–96, it is likely that Descartes's employment of the theory of sensation in *RI* XII was inspired by the work of his friend, Mersenne. None the less, as Schuster also claims, Descartes was not satisfied with a piecemeal science of appearances since he wished to present a more systematic theory of nature than that provided by Mersenne. For more on the thought of Mersenne, see R. Lenoble, *Mersenne ou la naissance du mécanisme* (Paris 1942); P. Dear, *Mersenne and the learning of the schools* (Ithaca, NY 1988).

proofs of geometry" (AT i. 143–4). Whereas previously he had started from his account of sense experience, using that account to support his account of nature, he now suggested that any explanation of natural processes, including those processes involved in sensation, must be rooted in an evident metaphysical foundation.[45] He took this foundation to displace scholastic metaphysics, the latter of which is supported by tenets "easy to overturn" (AT iii. 231).[46]

Descartes held in his later writings that the weakness of the metaphysical thought of the schoolmen derives ultimately from the fact that such thought is grounded in the sensory prejudices of youth. In developing this contention, he indicated that from early on the mind is preoccupied with the body. This preoccupation involves the domination of the faculty of sensation, a faculty he took to arise from the union of mind and body.[47] This domination so clouds the mind that it is unable to distinguish what pertains to body from what pertains simply to the mind. A particular instance of this confusion is the belief that sensation itself reveals the true nature of material objects. In the *Principles*, Descartes wrote that

there are none of us who have not judged from the earliest years that all that we have sensed is something existing external to our mind and quite similar to our sensations, that is, the perceptions we had of them. Thus, on seeing, for example, a colour, we supposed we see a thing positioned outside us, and quite similar to the idea of the colour that we experienced within us then; and this was something that, because of our habit of judging thus, we seemed to see clearly and distinctly, so that we took it for something certain and indubitable. (1. 66: AT viii-1. 32)

According to Descartes, the habits of youth lead to hasty judgements concerning bodies. Only by freeing the mind from the shackles of the prejudice that bodies resemble our sensations can one apprehend the clear and distinct concepts that frame the true account of the material world. Descartes took the scholastics to be mired in the senses, and thus told a correspondent that their forms and qualities are of no more use in natural philosophy than is the childhood judgement that bodies resemble sensations (AT iii. 648).[48]

---

[45] One indication of this methodological shift from the *Regulae* is Descartes's remark to Mersenne in 1630 that he had written a treatise on the metaphysical foundations of physics in 1629 (AT i. 146; cf. the 1637 letter to Mersenne at AT i. 350). This manuscript may have been destroyed by Descartes and in any case was not found among the papers collected after his death (AT x. 5–12).

[46] See also AT vii. 596–7. My account of Descartes's shift is similar to that found in G. Hatfield, 'The senses and the fleshless eye', in Rorty, at 61–2.

[47] See note 10, both for texts in which Descartes stated that the faculty of sensation depends on mind-body union and for an indication of the different accounts that he provided of the nature of the human being constituted by this union.

[48] This Cartesian view of scholasticism is discussed further by Gilson, *Études*, 168–73.

For the schoolmen, there is no shame in the fact that an account of nature is rooted in sensory judgement. Natural philosophy for them must rely on an abstraction from the particulars of sense, since it is simply a consideration of the bodies of experience in so far as they share a common form or nature.[49] Therefore, postulation of qualities such as colour and taste, far from being unjustified, is required if one is to have an account that coheres with the world of common sense. It is precisely this commonsensical position, however, that Descartes wished to reject. That is one of the reasons why he noted at the start of the *Meditations* that "once in life, everything ought to be overturned completely and ought to be rebuilt from first foundations, if I want to establish something firm and lasting in the sciences" (AT vii. 17). This remark indicates that the Cartesian programme involves two steps. The first is to overturn the commonsense view of nature of the sort endorsed by the schoolmen. The second is to establish indubitable metaphysical foundations on which legitimate sciences can be built. These steps purportedly yield an alternative to scholastic explanation that is "firm and lasting".

Whereas the schoolmen held that intellectual knowledge quite properly derives from sensory knowledge, Descartes took knowledge of bodies that are sensed, and knowledge of the nature of sensation itself, to depend on insight into metaphysical foundations. He believed that such an insight reveals that "extension in length, breadth, and depth constitutes the nature of corporeal substance" (PP I. 53: AT viii-1. 25). This concept of matter, in turn, shows that

nothing whatever pertains to the account of body, except only that it is a thing with length, breadth, and depth, capable of various shapes and motions. . . . [C]olours, smells, tastes, and such are only certain sensations existing in my thought, and differing no less from bodies than pain differs from the shape and motion of the weapon striking pain; and finally, heaviness, hardness, the power of heating, attracting, purging, and all other qualities that we observe [*experimur*] in bodies, consist solely in motion or privation of motion, and the configuration and situation of parts. (RO vi: AT vii. 440)

The identification of matter with extension thus dictates an account of the physiology of sensation that adverts only to geometrical properties. The sight of different colours, for instance, is explained in terms of the mechanical effect of particles of light on the optic nerves and, by means of these nerves, on the flow of animal spirits, i.e. subtle bodily fluids, to the pineal gland.[50]

---

[49] The position that physics rests on an abstraction from sensory particulars was endorsed by Eustachius in *SP* i. 138–41, iii. 110–13, and iv. 1–4. See the discussion of the scholastic position in G. Hatfield, 'First philosophy and natural philosophy in Descartes', in *Philosophy, its history and historiography*, ed. A. J. Holland (Dordrecht 1985), at 149–51.

[50] For the details of Descartes's account of the physiology of sensation, see *Diop.* vi: AT vi. 130–34; *PA* I. 10–16: AT xi. 334–42.

Descartes did not claim, of course, that the precise details of this account arise directly from intellectual insight into the nature of matter. He stated repeatedly that determination of the particular configurations of bodies must rely on observation or experiment.[51] But he did take his concept of matter to delimit any intelligible account of sensory stimulation. This concept is the one that precludes scholastic appeals both to the intentional aspects of sensible species and to qualitative features of bodies.

Contrary to the intimations of Descartes's rhetoric, then, the fundamental difference between Cartesian and scholastic accounts of the bodily aspects of sensation does not consist in the fact that the latter requires flying images while the former eschews them. Rather, Descartes took an Aristotelian theory of perception to err in giving heed to the sensory prejudices of youth and thus in failing to adhere to a clear and distinct conception of corporeal substance. A portion of Descartes's rejection of the scholastic view of physical sensory stimulation in the *Notes* therefore derives from his concept of matter and from his corresponding account of material processes.

2. *The active sensory role of mind.* We have yet to discuss the claim to Regius that the mind plays an active role in sensation. Descartes referred Regius to the *Dioptrics* for a more complete account of his view of this sensory role of mind. There are ways in which this earlier work anticipates the view of the *Notes*; I have discussed some of these and will mention others presently. Yet it is the Responses to the Sixth Objections to the *Meditations*, first published four years after the *Dioptrics*, that provides the more precise account of this role. In this text, Descartes distinguished the following three grades of sensation. "The immediate effect on corporeal organs by external objects", the first, physiological grade of sensation, involves only the mechanical effect of the object on the sense organs and the brain. A second grade includes "all that immediately results in the mind owing to the fact that it is united to a corporeal organ so affected". Finally, there are "all those judgements which, occasioned by the motion of the corporeal organs, we have been accustoned to make from our earliest years". This third grade is "occasioned", because it involves the distinctively mental act of judging. Since these acts are often rapid and go unnoticed, the vulgar often identify them with the sensation itself. None the less, Descartes held that these judgements are more properly attributed to the intellect (or more precisely, to non-sensory mental faculties) than to the senses (AT vii. 437–8).[52]

---

[51] Descartes emphasized in the *Discourse*, for instance, that in framing explanations of "more particular things", the natural philosopher must employ "many special observations" (*expériences*: AT vi. 64). D. Garber, in 'Science and certainty in Descartes', in *Descartes: Critical and interpretive essays*, ed. M. Hooker (Baltimore 1978), 149 n. 1, cites some of the literature that emphasizes that Descartes allowed for experimental observation in natural philosophy.

[52] Descartes's distinction between the various grades of sensation had been anticipated by others, most notably by Augustine, who had claimed in *De Genesi* that there are three sorts of

Descartes suggested in this text that his discussion of the three grades of sensation merely reiterates the view of the *Dioptrics*. Indeed, the overlap between the discussions in the *Dioptrics* and in the Sixth Responses is significant. The *Dioptrics* states that of the six qualities perceived by sight, "light, colour, position, distance, size, and shape", the first two "alone properly belong to the sense of sight" (AT vi. 130). The discussion in this text of the other four qualities emphasized the role of judgement in the determination of these qualities.[53] This distinction between the two kinds of sensory qualities seems similar to the view in the Sixth Responses that sensations of light and colour belong to grade (2), whereas "size, distance, and shape" involve further judgement, and thus belong to grade (3). Moreover, in a passage from the *Dioptrics* considered below, Descartes held that sensation is a mental state "instituted by nature" (*institués de la nature*) to arise in the soul by means of the action of a bodily image (AT vi. 130). Such a claim foreshadows the view in the Sixth Responses that grade (2) "includes all that immediately results in the mind because it is united to a corporeal organ affected in this way" (AT vii. 436).

However, the accounts in the Sixth Responses and the *Dioptrics* differ in emphasis. As I have indicated, in the former work Descartes noted the distinction between the contribution of the senses in grade (2) and the contribution of the intellect in grade (3). The distinction is not incidental to this text. Descartes's critics had objected that the senses can correct errors in the other senses (AT vii. 418) and Descartes responded by emphasizing that the mature judgement of the intellect corrects such errors (AT vii. 439). In the *Dioptrics*, on the other hand, he was not as concerned to distinguish sensory and intellectual elements, and so wrote that bodily motions give rise both to sensations of light and colour and to knowledge of position by means of the institution of nature (AT vi. 130, 134–7). The remarks in the Sixth Responses revise and do not merely repeat the account of sensation offered in the *Dioptrics*.

Be that as it may, the distinction in the Sixth Responses between the first two grades of sensation complements Descartes's discussion in the *Notes*. Grade (1) serves to explain the view of the *Notes* that only certain corporeal motions approach the mind by being present in the brain. In both the Sixth Responses and the *Notes*, he adverted to the caricature of the schoolmen presented in the *Dioptrics*, on which they accept intentional forms that fly to

---

vision: bodily, spiritual, and intellectual (XII. 6–8: PL xxxiv. 458–9). There is an anticipation of Descartes's point that sensation proper (in Augustine's terms, spiritual vision) must be distinguished from sensory judgement. Toward the end of II (a), below, I emphasize another similarity between the accounts of sensation offered by Augustine and Descartes.

[53] For reference to the fact that judgement is involved in our determination of size and shape, see AT vi. 140. The famous reference to the determination of distance "as if by a natural geometry" is found at AT vi. 137–8.

mind. And in all of these writings, he indicated that there can be no qualitative or intentional aspects at the first grade of sensation. This position was clearly stated in the Sixth Responses when Descartes claimed that explanation of the "immediate affection of the corporeal organs by external objects . . . can be nothing other than the motion of the particles of the same organs, and the change of shape and position proceeding from this motion" (AT vii. 436–7). Such strictures on an account of bodily processes involved in sensation simply follow from Descartes's view of what is proper for an explanation of bodily processes in general.[54]

Grade (2) involves the production of sensory ideas in the mind. Descartes stated that this production is possible owing to "the fact that the mind is so intimately conjoined with the body, that it is affected by the movements which occur in it" (AT vii. 437). He emphasized that the sensory ideas produced are not capable of falsity, on the ground that error requires judgement.[55] In the *Notes*, there is a distinction drawn between these ideas and judgements such as "that this or that idea which we have now immediately before our mind refers to a certain thing situated outside us"; and only the former are taken to be innate (AT viii-2. 359). This is in accord with the view, presented in the letter to Mersenne cited earlier, that "all those [ideas] which involve no affirmation or negation are innate". The ideas of sense do not involve affirmation or negation, because they are distinct from the judgements made concerning them (AT iii. 414).[56] The ideas that arise directly from the intimate union of mind and body in this manner are thus the ones that Descartes held to be innate.

Certain commentators offer a different conception of the relation of the argument of the *Notes* to the distinction of the grades of sensation. They argue that innate ideas play no role in grades (1) and (2) of sensation, but enter only with the activity of intellect and will in grade (3).[57] This interpretation may seem to be supported by the fact that Descartes spoke of the judgements of grade (3) as being "occasioned" by motions in the brain, just as he spoke in the *Notes* of the content of sensory ideas as being produced on the occasion of these motions. This terminological link appears to indicate

---

[54] The details of this account of sensation, if not its grounds, derive from *RI* xii: AT x. 412–15. See also the accounts offered in *TH*, *Diop.*, and *PA* I. 10–16: AT xi. 145–99, vi. 115–28, xi. 334–42.

[55] See *RO* vi: AT vii. 438; *Med.* iii: AT vii. 35, 44.

[56] Descartes stated in the *Notes* that "over and above perception, which is a prerequisite of judgement, we need affirmation and negation to determine the form of the judgement" (AT viii-2. 363). He also claimed that sensations in themselves are incapable of falsity (or truth) in Meditation iii (AT vii. 37). He did hold, notoriously, that certain sensory ideas have a sort of material falsity; but I indicate in ii (a), below, that such falsity derives from the fact that these ideas are regularly linked to false judgements concerning external objects.

[57] Van de Pitte, 363–6; and McRae, 41–5.

that what this work takes to be occasioned are judgements concerning sensory ideas.[58]

The appearance in this case is deceptive. In his response to Regius, Descartes linked the fact that there is an occasional connection between bodily motions and sensory ideas to the fact that the latter are innate. He never argued, on the other hand, that judgements of the third grade of sensation must be innate since they arise on the occasion of sense experience. The occasioning here reveals only that these judgements add to those elements present in sensation. To see what Descartes had in mind, recall his claim in Meditation III that acts of will have forms beyond those that represent. The act of affirming that heat is in the fire, for instance, is constituted not only by ideas representing heat and fire but also by the form of affirmation (AT vii. 37).[59] Descartes did not say, however, that the additional forms involved in judgement are innate to mind. Indeed, I have already cited passages from the 1641 letter to Mersenne and the *Notes* in which he stated in no uncertain terms that judgement is an exception to the doctrine that everything in our sensory ideas is innate to mind. He therefore indicated that only the representational content of sensory ideas is innate. These considerations should suffice to indicate that the occasioning mentioned in the response to Regius is distinct from the occasioning of sensory judgement.

Descartes stated that the sensory effects of grade (2), though occasioned in the sense explicated above, are correlated with certain motions in the brain due to the intimate union of mind and body. I have emphasized that the scholastics took sensation to involve sensible species that present the qualities of bodies to the perceiver. On Descartes's understanding, this presentational likeness allows for awareness of different bodily qualities. Having rejected the doctrine that sensations in general resemble qualities of bodies, though, it is incumbent on Descartes to offer an alternative conception of the manner in which non-resembling sensations are linked to the world. This he had attempted to do prior to the Sixth Responses, in *Le Monde*, by pointing to the relation that words bear to thoughts. He wrote in the latter work:

Now if words, which signify nothing except by human institution, suffice to make us conceive of things to which they bear no resemblance, then why could nature not also have established a certain sign which would make us have the sensation of light, even if this sign has nothing in itself similar to the sensation? Is it not thus that nature has instituted laughter and tears to make us read joy and sadness in the face of men? (AT xi. 4)

---

[58] Although Van de Pitte does not employ the passage from the Sixth Responses in precisely this manner, he claims that Descartes took only the elements added at grade (3) of sensation to be innate. The account presented by McRae is linked more directly to my remarks since he holds that the innate faculty of the *Notes* simply is the faculty of judgement.

[59] For further discussion of this position, see Sellars, 259–65.

Bodily images that give rise to sensations thus are non-resembling signs rather than perfect images of external objects. Sensations are linked to the world by virtue of being linked to bodily signs of objects.[60]

In using this sign analogy, Descartes appears to have suggested that the mind is aware of those bodily motions that are responsible for sensation. The mind does have an awareness, after all, of the laughter and tears by means of which it reads joy and sadness. More generally, signs seem to serve as signs in virtue of the fact that they are read or comprehended. Yet at one point in the *Dioptrics* Descartes indicated that he did not wish to take the analogy this far when he ridiculed the position that one is aware of something in the brain, "as if there were yet other eyes within our brain with which we could perceive [*appercevoir*] it". In order to avoid this implausible position, he offered the alternative view that movements in the brain "are instituted by nature to make [the soul] to have such sensations" (AT vi. 130), even though he suggested such a position when he noted in this same text that we sense the size of an object by comparing our knowledge of the distance to "the size of the images they imprint on the back of the eye" (AT vi. 140).

There is another aspect of the sign analogy, however, which Descartes embraced more consistently. This analogy can be seen as implying that the mind is active in sensation. Just as the mind actively interprets written or spoken signs, so it responds actively to corporeal motions by forming sensations. Descartes indicated that mental activity is a consequence of the sign analogy when he stated in *Le Monde* that "it is our mind which represents to us the idea of light each time our eye is affected by the action which signifies it". The representative activity of mind is linked with the fact that bodily motions serve as signs. He continued this remark by claiming that, because physical processes merely signify sensory ideas, the latter are "formed in our mind on the occasion of our being touched by external bodies" (AT xi. 4–6).[61] This view, recorded in a relatively early work, is retained in the *Notes*, for in the latter the occasional connection between the presence of certain motions and the formation of sensory ideas, on the one hand, and the mind's possession of a productive faculty, on the other, are affirmed in the same sentence.

Descartes therefore employed the sign analogy to show that the mind is active in sensation, though he emphasized in one portion of the *Dioptrics*, at least, that this activity is not the result of a conscious mental apprehension of images in the brain. But given this caveat, there seems to be little sense to the view that the bodily motions that constitute such images are *signs*. If these

---

[60] On the sign analogy, see Yolton, ch. 1; Marion, 231–63.

[61] For other passages in which Descartes linked the displacement of scholastic resemblance to the view that motions in the brain are occasions for the production of sensation, see *TH*: AT xi. 143–4; *Diop.*: AT vi. 114.

motions are not grasped by the mind, how are they able to serve as signs for it? A response to this question turns on Descartes's claim in Meditation VI that the connection of motions and sensations is established so as to ensure that there are "other things in bodies, from which these various sensory perceptions come, variations corresponding to them [i.e. to the various sensory perceptions], though perhaps not similar to them" (AT vii. 81). By ordaining that certain sensations are produced when the appropriate motions are present, "God or nature"[62] can be said to establish a code. Motions in the brain are thus signs to the mind in the metaphorical sense of being part of a code instituted by God. This code links the motions, and the alterations in external objects which give rise to these motions, to the formation of sensory ideas by the mind.[63]

Descartes employed the language of signs most often in order to explain the production of sensations that he took to bear no resemblance to qualities of bodies. Thus there is the reference to the sensation of light in the passage from *Le Monde* cited above, and the allusion to the theory of signs in Meditation VI, where the claim is made that brain impulses "give the mind a signal for having a certain sensation, namely the sensation of pain in the foot" (AT vii. 88). In the *Principles*, moreover, he introduced his discussion of the sign analogy with the claim that it "is *especially* true of the confused [thoughts], which are called sensations or feelings" that the mind is stimulated to have them when bodily motions are present (IV. 197: AT viii-1. 320, my emphasis). This point is made in an alternative manner in the *Notes*, which says that sensory ideas such as those of pain and colour "must be *so much the more* innate" if "our mind is able, on the occasion of certain corporeal motions, to exhibit them to itself" (AT viii-2. 359, my emphasis). Because motions lack any resemblance to these ideas, the former must be merely the occasion for the production of the latter. Yet these motions are still signs in Descartes's metaphorical sense, since nature has correlated their presence with the activity of an innate mental faculty.

Descartes even encouraged the view that the sign analogy applies *only* to sensations that bear no resemblance to the qualities of bodies. Bodily signs lead to the formation of the second grade of sensory effects, but he claimed at one point in the Sixth Responses that the sensations so produced include "perceptions of pain, pleasure, thirst, hunger, colours, sound, taste, odours,

---

[62] The phrase '*Deus aut natura*' is used in *PP* I. 28: AT viii-1. 15 (cf. *Med.* VI: AT vii. 80). God is said to establish the connection between bodily motions and sensory states in *TH*: AT xi. 143; and *Med.* VI: AT vii. 87.

[63] I borrow the term 'code of nature' from Marion's interesting discussion of the sign analogy cited in note 60. Descartes had suggested the view that sensation is linked by nature to certain bodily configurations in the brain in *RI* XII: AT x. 413.

heat, cold, and the like" (AT vii. 437).[64] There is no mention of sensory ideas that bear some resemblance to the qualities of bodies. It is interesting to note on this score that he deviated from the sign analogy in the *Dioptrics* when he stated with respect to the formation of these ideas: "And if, in order to depart as little as is possible from opinions commonly received, we prefer to maintain that the objects we sense truly send images of themselves inside our brain, it is necessary that we remark that there are no images that must wholly resemble the objects that they represent." It suffices for the images to represent their objects only in an imperfect manner, just as engravings represent "forests, towns, men, and even battles and storms" by means of resemblance only in shape. Even this resemblance in shape is imperfect, given that, in accordance with the rules of perspective, engravings "often represent circles better by ovals than by other circles; and squares by rhombuses rather than by other squares" (AT vi. 112–13). By introducing the engraving analogy, Descartes appears to have endorsed the transmission view with respect to ideas such as those of various figures, with only the caveat that these ideas do not bear an exact resemblance to what is present in the brain.

As indicated earlier, Descartes sometimes did speak, even in the *Dioptrics*, as if the mind literally contemplates images in the brain. He seems at times to have been under the sway of the transmission view. But the remarks from the Sixth Responses and from the *Dioptrics* cited above do not necessarily indicate such an influence. Elsewhere in the Sixth Responses, for instance, he noted that grade (2) includes not only sensations of colour and light reflected from a stick, but also sensations of "the extension of the colour, the boundary, and the position" of this stick (AT vii. 437). Thus he held that this grade includes sensations that resemble somewhat the qualities of bodies as well as sensations that bear no such resemblance. Furthermore, when Descartes used the engraving analogy in the *Dioptrics*, he did so hypothetically and only "in order to depart as little as possible from accepted opinions". He may have intended to use the engraving analogy merely as a rhetorical device in order to show that, even on purported scholastic principles, the soul need not contemplate images that bear a precise resemblance to the bodies represented.[65] In any event, after criticizing the view that there are other eyes in the brain that perceive figures, he suggested that all sensory ideas are

---

[64] In this work Descartes referred back to the claim in Meditation VI that "confused modes of thinking" such as "sensations of hunger, thirst, pain, and so on" arise from the intermingling of mind and body (AT vii. 81).

[65] Descartes may also have introduced the two analogies in order to emphasize the difference between sensation of colours and sounds, on the one hand, and perception of modes of extension, on the other. On his view, the latter, unlike the former, are able to bear some resemblance to external objects and to figures in the brain that signify such objects.

instituted by nature to arise from corporeal motions (AT vi. 130). The sign analogy therefore pertains to all sensory ideas.[66]

Descartes told Regius, moreover, that an innate faculty produces ideas of figure and motion along with ideas of pains, colours, and sounds. To be sure, he also said that the latter ideas are more innate, and this may seem to suggest that the former ideas are derived to some extent from corporeal motions. But as in the *Dioptrics*, so here he may have wanted to use the principles of the transmission theorists against them. Even if something were transmitted to mind, he appears to have intended to say, we need not suppose that what is transmitted corresponds to what arises in the mind. In the *Dioptrics* Descartes went on to replace (albeit not rigorously) talk of the mind peering into the brain with the language of natural ordination that is coupled with the sign analogy. Likewise, in the *Notes* he held that sensory ideas are formed by a mental faculty on the occasion of bodily motions, rather than transmitted to the mind by means of these motions. I take Descartes's appeals to bodily signs, the ordination of nature, and the activity of the innate mental faculty to be interconnected ways of suggesting a more sophisticated view of sensation than the views he attributed to Regius and the schoolmen. The response to Regius is not an aberration but is the continuation of a line of thought present, though not fully developed, in the *Dioptrics* and in Descartes's other early discussions of sensation.

Hence Descartes had more to offer in response to the schoolmen than ridicule of the transmission view. He proposed a rejection of the scholastic position that bodily qualities resemble sensory ideas such as those of colour and sound, and thus offered a fundamental reorientation of our view of the material world. He also took this rejection to show that certain ideas cannot be received from bodies by way of the senses. The sign analogy provides another means of conceiving the relation between bodily motions and the non-resembling sensory ideas to which they give rise.[67] In the *Dioptrics*, and more consistently in the *Notes*, Descartes held that this analogy suggests a view of sensation that is more sophisticated than the view that he took to be

---

[66] Descartes also spoke elsewhere in a more general manner of motions as being "ordained by nature" to make the soul have passions (e.g., at AT xi. 369).

[67] Although Descartes offered his sign theory as an alternative to the scholastic account, this theory is in some ways reminiscent of the view of the schoolmen. Eustachius, among others, spoke of the mental word (*verbum mentis*) which serves as a sign (*signum*) of the natures of external objects (*SP* iii. 340–41; cf. *ST* I. 85. 2 ad 3). The sign metaphor was also linked by the schoolmen to the fact that the intellect is active in the production of concepts drawn from sensory experience. Yet it is important not to make too much of these similarities. For instance, Descartes spoke of the bodily motion rather than the mental product as the sign. Moreover, the sign analogy is employed in the *Notes* to explicate the production of the *particular* forms of sensory thought, whereas the scholastics often focused on the production of universal forms of thought (but see the discussion of Eustachius in II (a), below).

linked to the scholastic resemblance doctrine. Motions in the brain are not resemblances of objects viewed by mind but are merely the occasions for the formation of sensory ideas by a mental faculty. Once one has an account of sensation in terms of an ordination of nature that links motions and the mental formation of sensory ideas, there is no need for appeal to the mental contemplation of resembling images. This route to the innate mental faculty may be somewhat longer than Descartes indicated in the *Notes*. Yet it is the most complete argument that I have been able to draw from the Cartesian texts for the move from the claim to Regius that sensory ideas "have no similarity with corporeal motions" to the conclusion that the motions "give occasion" to the mind "to form them . . . by means of a faculty innate to it".

II. THE INADEQUACY OF THE ARGUMENT

Descartes thus offered the innate faculty of the *Notes* in order to counter both the resemblance doctrine and the position that the mind receives its ideas by viewing images in the brain. But while the new response has more behind it than a criticism of transmission, one could object that he still took the alternative to his account to require that the mind view bodily images, and thus continued to see his opponents as adhering to the crude transmission view. I would not want to dispute this objection; indeed, in the end I will insist on it. But in order to appreciate the force of the objection, we must consider two different objections to Descartes's account of sensation which are suggested by the positions of his contemporaries. The first, alluded to above but not developed, stems from the scholastic view that human sensation does not include an intellectual element. Descartes had the resources to respond to this view, though such a response in fact undermines the argument of the *Notes*. The other objection, offered by Regius himself, is that, even if sensations are mental in nature, they need not be produced by mind. I take both objections to press Descartes to focus less on difficulties concerning transmission and resemblance when arguing for the innate sensory faculty of mind.

(a) *Sensory ideas as mental*

Descartes insisted in the *Dioptrics* that "it is the soul that senses and not the body" (AT vi. 109). This claim evolved by the time of the *Notes* into the view that human sensation involves the production of the intellectual content of sensory thought by an innate mental faculty. From the scholastic perspective, one fundamental difficulty with this final view is that human sensation does not include any intellectual content, since it consists merely in the alteration of the corporeal sense organs. Given that human and animal sensation consists only in this sort of alteration, Descartes's addition of a second grade of sensation would seem unwarranted. The schoolmen could have objected at this point that he must justify the claim that human sensation, in distinction from the sensation of other brutes, includes intellectual content.

Descartes himself appears to have provided comfort to critics who would on these grounds reject the account of sensation in the *Notes*. Earlier I indicated that in certain texts he seems to have denied that sensory ideas such as those of colour and sound, which do not resemble modes of extended substance, have objective reality. One such passage is in Meditation III, where he claimed that sensory ideas of qualities such as "light and colours, sounds, odours, tastes, heat and cold" may be materially false in the sense that the ideas "represent what is not a thing as if a thing" (*non rem tanquam rem representant*) (AT vii. 43-4). This appears to indicate that these ideas represent nothing and thus have no objective reality. Such a suggestion seems to be reflected also in the claim in the *Principles* that the sensations of "taste, odour, sound, heat, cold, light, colour, and the like . . . represent nothing located outside thought" (I. 71: AT viii-I. 35).[68] Such a position would tend to undermine the view in the *Notes* that an innate faculty of mind is required to produce the content of sensory ideas such as those of colour and sound.

Yet Descartes did say in Meditation III that *all* ideas are "as if images of things". The indication there seems to be that even sensory ideas represent objects. Moreover, he held in Meditation VI that bodies formally contain what is contained objectively in sensory ideas, even though bodies may not be "entirely such as I comprehend them by sense" (AT vii. 80). The position that sensory ideas can represent bodies they do not resemble is anticipated in earlier discussions of sensation. Descartes had written in *Le Monde*, for instance, that the object of the sensory idea of sound is "the motion of the parts of the air", even though this idea does not provide a "true image" of its object (AT xi. 5). Likewise, he wrote in the *Dioptrics* that, while we do not sense images that perfectly resemble external bodies, nevertheless we have sensations "of just as many different qualities in . . . bodies as there are differences in movements caused by them in the brain" (AT vi. 114). The sensations do not resemble the properties of bodies, but nevertheless signify (or are "of") these properties. Admittedly, Descartes was more concerned in this work to hold that *bodily images* signify external objects. Yet the passage

---

[68] Wilson has argued that Descartes's remarks in Meditation III and *PP* I. 71 commit him to just this position (*Descartes*, 100–119). More recently, in her 'Descartes on the representationality of sensation', in *Central themes in early modern philosophy*, ed. J. Cover and M. Kulstad (Indianapolis 1990), 1–22, she provides an interpretation similar to the one I offer below.

just cited indicates that correlations between images and objects, on the one hand, and between images and sensations, on the other, allow sensory thought itself to direct the mind to these objects.

What, then, of Descartes's account of material falsity? This account is not inconsistent with the claim that sensory ideas represent objects. First, Descartes did not attempt in Meditation III so much to offer a theory of material falsity, as to counter the view of the schoolmen that we understand the nature of bodily qualities such as heat and cold that they hold to resemble the ideas of these qualities. Furthermore, when he stated that certain sensory ideas represent what is not a thing as if it were a thing, he may have meant no more than that we judge that the ideas represent some resembling quality that they in fact do not represent. His point in the end is that we cannot determine, merely by introspection, exactly what sensory ideas such as those of heat and cold do represent; this is why he concluded that such ideas are confused and obscure.[69] But none of this constitutes a denial of the claim that these sensory ideas represent bodily states perhaps unknown to us. By means of the natural correlation between the sensory ideas and the bodily states, these ideas are able to indicate the presence of (and in this sense to represent) the states even though they are unable to indicate their precise nature.[70] There is something in sensory ideas that directs the mind to bodies, and it is this feature of these ideas that the *Notes* takes to be produced by an innate mental faculty.

Remarks in the *Principles* also indicate that non-resembling sensory ideas represent the features of bodies. As we have seen, Descartes stated in this work that sensations of taste, odour, sound, and the like do not represent anything external to mind. Yet he could have intended to say simply that these sensations do not resemble certain qualities that exist external to mind. This interpretation is suggested by his claim earlier in this text that if a person "examines what it is which this sensation of colour or pain represents, as if existing in the coloured body or in the painful part, he will notice [*advertet*] that he is wholly ignorant of it" (I. 68: AT viii-I. 33). Consistent with the view in Meditation III, this passage indicates that non-resembling sensations actually represent something in bodies, although the sensations are

---

[69] For the claim that sensory ideas are confused and obscure, see *Med.* III: AT vii. 44; *RO* IV: AT vii. 234. Descartes also held that sensations are clear and distinct when considered merely as sensory states (cf. *PP* I. 68: AT viii-I. 33). These positions need not be inconsistent; Descartes could claim that, while sensations *qua* operations of mind are clear and distinct, the same sensations *qua* representations of features of bodies are confused and obscure since sensory ideas reveal these features in a confused and obscure manner.

[70] I believe, but cannot argue here, that it is possible to provide a similar interpretation of Descartes's admittedly confusing response to Arnauld's objections concerning material falsity. (Arnauld's remarks are at AT vii. 206–7; Descartes's response at 231–5.)

so confused that we remain ignorant of the nature of what in bodies is represented.

To this point I have been speaking as if Descartes referred only to sensations that do not resemble modes of bodies, such as those of colour and sound, as confused and obscure. But there are several passages in which he referred to sensations that do bear some resemblance to modes of bodies in similar terms. In Meditation VI, for instance, he noted that sensations of particular geometrical properties of bodies such as "that the sun is of such a size and shape", as well as those of "light, sound, pain, and the like", are "very doubtful and uncertain" (AT vii. 80). The view that even sensory ideas of modes of extension do not accurately indicate the nature of what is in particular bodies is suggested by the remark in the *Principles* that all perceptions of the senses—including, presumably, perceptions of these modes—"do not teach us, except occasionally and by accident, what exists in [external bodies] themselves" (II. 3: AT viii-1. 41–2). All sensory ideas, then, fail to indicate reliably the precise nature of the particular bodies they represent and for this reason are confused and obscure. Descartes did believe that "we know [*agnoscimus*] more evidently what it is for shape to be [in bodies] than what it is for colour to be [in bodies]" (I. 69: AT viii-1. 34); he allowed that sensory ideas of shape, as opposed to those of colour, at least generically resemble something that can exist in bodies. Yet he also claimed that neither sort of sensory idea reveals which particular features certain bodies actually possess. To be sure, in the *Notes* (as well as in *Le Monde* and the *Dioptrics*) he emphasized more that sensations do not resemble images in the brain than that they do not resemble external bodies. None the less, I take him to have provided a position consistent with that found in the *Meditations* and the *Principles* when he argued in his response to Regius that sensory ideas of figures and motions, as well as sensory ideas of colours and sounds, fail to resemble (and, by implication, that they are confused representations of) the bodily states to which they are linked.

While these remarks may serve to reveal the consistency of Descartes's position, they do not provide an argument against the scholastic objection that human sensation includes no intellectual content, confused or otherwise. I take Descartes to have suggested an argument when he claimed in the Sixth Responses that the particular intellectual operations at grade (3) employ the sensory ideas provided at grade (2). The materials for some of our judgements concerning external objects are supplied by the sensory ideas that represent these objects. Since these sensations are used in this way by the intellect, there is as much reason to attribute them to the mind as the intellectual operations themselves.

At one point Descartes defended his view of sensation by arguing in just this manner. In his contentious remarks on the *Meditations*, the Jesuit Bourdin had objected that, since brute animals and humans alike have sensory thought, only the ability to engage in reflexive consideration of thought can be a property unique to the incorporeal human mind.[71] Descartes responded:

The initial thought, by which we notice [*advertimus*] something, differs no more from the second thought by which we notice that we noticed before, than [the second] differs from a third by which we notice that we have noticed that we have noticed. Nor is any reason able to be asserted, if the first [thought] is conceded to a corporeal thing, why the second is not also. Accordingly, it must be stressed that our author errs . . . perniciously. . . . For in removing the true and most intelligible difference which is between corporeal and incorporeal things, namely that [the latter] think but not [the former], and in place of it substituting what in no way can be seen to be essential, namely that [the latter] consider [*considèrent*] that they think but [the former] do not consider, he does all that in itself is necessary to impede lest the real distinction of the human mind from the body be understood. (AT vii. 559–60)

Sensory experience of bodies, it is suggested here, does not differ in kind from intellectual reflection on such experience. To hold with Bourdin and other scholastics that merely corporeal beings have sensory thought is thus to admit the possibility that such beings can engage in higher intellectual operations as well. In order to block this dangerous consequence, Descartes held that sensory thought pertains to the mind rather than to bodily organs. This is not to say that he denied that animals have sensation in any sense. He wrote to More, after all, that he did not wish to deny "sensation" to animals "in so far as it depends on a bodily organ" (AT v. 278). That is, Descartes did not deny that animals have physical processes that are similar to those that accompany human sensation. What he opposed is the position that creatures without intellect have the sort of sensory thought that humans possess.[72] For this reason, I believe, he found it necessary to postulate grade (2) of human sensation.

Descartes sometimes indicated another sort of argument for the postulation of grade (2) of sensation that is linked in an interesting way to the view of his scholastic contemporaries. I have in mind his suggestion that sensory content plays a role in the intellectual activity of abstraction. In a passage cited previously, for instance, he told Arnauld that the intellect is able to reflect on

[71] This sort of view is not unique to Bourdin, but was in fact quite popular in the seventeenth century. Gassendi, for instance, argued along these lines. For further discussion of the reflection argument, see E. and F. S. Michael, 'Two early modern concepts of mind', *Journal of the history of philosophy* 27 (1989), 29–48.

[72] Marjorie Grene has charged that there is "a fundamental incoherence in the Cartesian teaching about emotion", and in particular that Descartes offered conflicting answers to the question of whether animals have passions akin to those present in humans (M. Grene, *Descartes* (Brighton 1985), ch. 2). This inconsistency can be eliminated, however, once it is recognized that Descartes spoke of passions in two ways: either as bodily processes or as the mental upshot of these processes. He consistently emphasized that animals devoid of reason have passions in the first sense but not in the second (cf. AT vi. 46).

particular sensations and to connect them conceptually with other sensations (AT v. 192). This accords with the account of abstraction in the *Principles*, where it is held that "universals arise solely from the fact that one and the same idea is used for thinking of all individual items which resemble each other" (I. 59: AT viii-I. 27). We have access to sensory thoughts of particulars present at grade (2) and by means of this access form universals. The human intellect therefore makes some use of such sensory thought and for this reason human sensation must involve some sort of intellectual content.

Aquinas himself would have rejected this line of argument since he denied the view that the intellect can know particulars directly. According to Aquinas, only forms that represent the universal features of objects can be present in the intellect, since to be so present the form must be abstracted from individuating material conditions. He did grant that the intellect can know particulars indirectly by "turning to phantasms" (*convertendo se ad phantasmata*), but he remained adamant that there are no intelligible forms of particulars.[73] Later schoolmen, however, were not satisfied with this position. In his commentary on Aristotle's *De anima*, for instance, the Jesuit Toletus objected that Aquinas's notion of an intellectual *conversio ad phantasma* is itself unintelligible; citing Scotus, he claimed that it is better to say that the intellect turns to intelligible species that represent particulars.[74] And indeed, most seventeenth-century schoolmen, Eustachius included, preferred the Scotist view of the intelligibility of particulars to Thomistic orthodoxy.[75] Even more explicitly than Toletus, Eustachius affirmed that the intellect can receive the intelligible forms of particulars, as opposed to universal forms.[76] He emphasized that reflection on the forms of the intellectual conception of particulars is in fact a necessary condition of the abstraction of universals.[77] This account of abstraction is reminiscent of that found in the *Principles*; surprisingly enough, on this point Eustachius is not so far from Descartes. It is true that Eustachius himself did not wish to deviate from the position that human sensation proper involves only the reception of species in the sense organ. Yet since he held that intelligible

---

[73] *ST* I. 86. I. Aquinas took phantasms to be sensible species that are stored in one of the internal senses. Eustachius followed him on this point (see *SP* iii. 316–18).

[74] Toletus, *De anima*, 468–9.

[75] See the documentation of the Scotist influence on seventeenth-century scholastic thought in G. [Rodis-] Lewis), *L'Individualité selon Descartes* (Paris 1950), ch. I. There is in particular a discussion on pp. 28–30 of the Scotist nature of Eustachius's view.

[76] *SP* iii. 332. In this passage, Eustachius took *res spirituales, sive universales sive particulares* to be *per se intelligibiles*, and claimed "*singularia sensibilia proprio ac peculiari conceptu a nobis intelligi*".

[77] In *SP* iii. 335, Eustachius held that "singulars are known prior to universals, for the intellect is not able to attain to a cognition of universals unless it has first abstracted from singulars; wherefore it is necessary that the singular is first, itself made new as a universal".

forms of particulars are supplied prior to reflection by means of sensation, he appears to be committed to the view that sensory processes include an element that one cannot attribute to animals devoid of intellect. The way is cleared for Descartes's conclusion that human sensation involves a second grade not present in the case of brutes.

If he had admitted that sensation supplies content for intellection, Eustachius would thereby have been committed to the view of the *Notes* that human sensation involves the activity of mind. As indicated previously, schoolmen such as Eustachius inherited from Augustine the neoplatonic tenet that body, being of a lower order than mind, could not act on it. Eustachius himself inferred that the material elements of sensation could not be the efficient cause of an alteration of intellect, owing to this difference of orders. Such elements instead merely dispose the agent intellect to create a certain sort of intelligible species.[78] If the form of a particular is to play a role in the operations of intellect, however, it can no more be the product of physical processes alone than can intelligible universal forms. And since Eustachius claimed that reflection on the forms of the intellectual conception of particulars is a prerequisite for the act of abstraction, the production of these forms must precede this act. The sort of production that Eustachius is forced to posit appears strikingly similar to that present in Descartes's grade (2) of sensation.

With respect to this similarity, it is interesting that, when speaking of the activity of the intellect, Eustachius used the phrase '*vim efformandi*'. The gerund here has the same root as the gerundive '*efformandas*', the term employed in the *Notes* to describe the operation of the innate sensory faculty.[79] I am not claiming that Eustachius anticipated the account of sensation found in the response to Regius, or that Descartes actually derived this account from Eustachius's text. There is too much evidence against the former claim and not enough for the latter. My point is conceptual rather than historical: Eustachius could have been led to accept the sort of sensory activity that Descartes proposed or, alternatively, Descartes could have brought Eustachius to this view by exploiting certain elements present in the text of the schoolman.

In fact, there is a gap between the way in which Descartes could have criticized schoolmen such as Eustachius and the way in which he did criticize them, and this gap is quite significant. We have constructed a Cartesian response to the schoolmen that emphasizes the need for an intellectual

---

[78] In *SP* iii. 338, Eustachius claimed that "a phantasm is not the efficient cause of the production of intelligible species, because a corporeal thing is not able to be the efficient cause of the production of a spiritual thing, but only has itself a disposition for their production".

[79] See Eustachius, *SP* iii. 337, and the portion of the *Notes* quoted toward the start of this paper.

element of human sensation. Yet neither the *Dioptrics* nor the *Notes* acknowledges the existence of this issue. On the contrary, Descartes assumed in the former work that the schoolmen accept such an element when he ridiculed them for holding that the mind is easily stimulated by pictures. Had he considered their position with more care, he would have seen that this caricature could not be accurate. If the schoolmen did admit that there is a stage of sensation at which the intellect is presented with a particular, they could not have held that it is stimulated with ease. Rather, they would have been compelled to hold, owing to their acceptance of Augustinian strictures on interaction, that it is the soul itself which produces the form of the intellectual conception of the particular. Such activity would be required regardless of the stance on the resemblance of intellectual forms to bodily qualities. Certainly, Descartes's conception of grade (1) of sensation involves an important shift away both from the scholastic appeal to the intentional features of sensible species and from the scholastic view that these species resemble the qualities of objects. But in the dispute over the presence of an innate sensory faculty of mind, it is the intellectual content of human sensation and not resemblance or transmission that is the central issue between Descartes and the schoolmen.

A more direct consideration of the position of Augustine serves to reinforce this point. Here is someone who shared with later followers of Aristotle the tenet that sensations resemble bodily qualities.[80] Yet Augustine also concluded in a passage cited above that in sensation the soul uses the body "as a kind of messenger to form in itself what is announced without". There is no compelling evidence that Descartes was aware of this text. Nevertheless, the passage itself anticipates the conclusion of the *Notes* that bodily motions "give occasion" to the mind "to form [sensory ideas], at this time rather than another, by means of a faculty innate to it". Descartes often found no difficulty acknowledging the claim of correspondents that certain of his views were anticipated in the writings of Augustine.[81] Given the implication of the *Notes* that the rejection of the resemblance doctrine is a necessary element of any argument for the conclusion that the mind is active in sensation,

---

[80] Augustine claimed in *De Genesi* that in sensation there is a mental image that bears a likeness to the physical object represented (XII. 22: PL xxxiv. 462). See the discussion of this position in B. Bubacz, *St Augustine's theory of knowledge* (New York 1981), 22, 103–7. For the Aristotelian scholastic, the resemblance of the sensible species to the qualities of bodies was established by the fact that the species contains a form similar to the one present in the object. Augustine differed from schoolmen such as Aquinas and Eustachius, however, in taking an immaterial image, rather than the qualities of bodies, to be the object of sensation.

[81] Arnauld often reminded Descartes of his debt to Augustine (see AT vii. 197–8, 205, 217; Descartes responded in *RO* IV: AT vii. 219). Descartes happily acknowledged the debt in a letter to Mesland of 1644 (AT 113), but in a 1640 letter to Colvius he had been more concerned to show how he differed from Augustine (AT iii. 247). For further discussion of this relationship, see Stephen Menn's contribution to the present volume.

however, he could not in similar comfort have acknowledged that Augustine had derived such a conclusion without rejecting this doctrine.

(b) *Sensory ideas as formed by mind*

We have seen that the schoolmen are committed to the position that any intellectual content of sensation must be produced by the soul itself. But the assumption that such content must be innate in Descartes's sense actually was questioned by Regius. As I have argued, Descartes linked the need for a productive mental faculty to the rejection of the scholastic doctrine of resemblance. In a response to Descartes's attack on his pamphlet, Regius argued in effect that the presence of the faculty does not follow from this rejection. He wrote:

> It is not an objection that light, colours, odours, and all sensible qualities are conceived by us in a confused manner and not under the concept of motion. For it does not follow from this that the ideas of such qualities are innate in us: but that the motions themselves, in which the nature of such qualities consists, are provoked by the objects, and are created by insensible particles of material objects, and thus are able to be perceived and conceived by us, by reason of their smallness, not distinctly but rather in a confused manner.[82]

Regius had stated in thesis 19 of his pamphlet that "all sensation is the perception of some corporeal motion" (AT viii-2. 346), and in the passage above he noted that it does not follow from the fact that these sensations do not resemble the motions that they are innate. The argument presented explicitly is that this is so because the possibility of perception depends on the presence of motions sent from external objects. Descartes did not deny this sort of dependence; indeed, he indicated that motions are needed to trigger the operation of an innate mental faculty. But Regius may be read more sympathetically as claiming that the motions themselves rather than a faculty of mind give rise to the confused perceptions.

Descartes stated that he had never read anything in the writings of Regius, save what he copied from others, "which in my view did not contain some error" (AT viii-2. 365). And though Descartes did not have an opportunity to comment on Regius's response, since it was published after his death, had he read it no doubt he would have claimed to find errors in it. In the *Notes* Descartes indicated that Regius's position that mind may be a mode of body fails to distinguish the distinct attributes of thought and extension (AT viii-2. 350–51, 356). I think it likely that he would have seen this sort of error as

---

[82] Regius, *Philosophia naturalis*, 1. 5 (my translation). This work, a retitled edition of *Fundamenta physices*, was first published in 1654. The Latin text of this passage is reproduced in *Lettres à Regius*, 206–9.

infecting Regius's view of the nature of sensory qualities. Relevant here is Regius's claim above that qualities such as light, colours, and odours *consist in motion*, which appears to suggest that these qualities simply are motions in the brain. It would have been in character for Descartes to urge that the qualities perceived are ideas in the mind and thus are distinct from the motions in the brain that give rise to them. Given this view, it simply does not follow from the fact that the motions arise from external objects that the sensory ideas in the mind are not innate. Had Regius attended more carefully to the distinction of mind and body, one can almost hear Descartes say, he would not have offered such a muddled objection to the account of sensation in the *Notes*.

Yet in his response Regius did suggest a distinction between motions in the brain and the perceptions or conceptions of these motions. Moreover, he claimed elsewhere that revelation establishes that the perceiving mind is a substance distinct from body.[83] He thus could have agreed with Descartes, against the schoolmen,[84] that there is a distinction to be drawn between sensory qualities as perceptions of mind and as bodily elements. When Regius said that these qualities consist in motion, he could have intended to affirm that the sensation of red is a confused sensation of small motions in the brain.[85] Perhaps his remarks, then, are not so muddled after all.

---

[83] See AT viii-2. 343. Regius, who received his medical training in Padua, undoubtedly was influenced here by the view of the Paduan Pomponazzi, who claimed in his 1516 *De immortalitate animae* that we can know the doctrine of the immortality of the soul only by faith, not by reason. For a discussion of the influence of Pomponazzi's work on early modern thought, see Michael, 'Two early modern concepts of mind', 32–9. While critics such as Voetius doubted the sincerity of Regius's appeal to revelation, I think that there is no evidence that he was disingenuous. See Rodis-Lewis, *Lettres à Regius*, 15–16; Dibon, 285–7. In 'The myth of Renaissance atheism and the French tradition of free thought', *Journal of the history of philosophy* 6 (1968), 233–43, P. O. Kristeller defends Pomponazzi against a similar charge of insincerity.

[84] And also against Gassendi, who argued that there is a distinction between the sensitive soul, which apprehends external objects by means of sensory images, and the intellectual soul, which is able to engage in intellectual reflection without the use of sensation. See the discussion of Gassendi's position in Michael, 'Corporeal ideas', 40–44; and 'Two early modern concepts of mind', 41–8. In other respects, however, Regius's critique of Descartes's doctrine of innate ideas resembles that offered earlier by Gassendi. On the relation between the views of Gassendi and Regius, see Rodis-Lewis, *Lettres à Regius*, 14–17; Dibon, 286–7.

[85] Regius's view that we perceive motions in the brain, though not distinctly, seems to resemble somewhat the account of sensation offered by Leibniz in his *Nouveaux essais sur l'entendement humain*. Responding to Locke's suggestion that God arbitrarily annexes certain sensations to bodily motions, Leibniz stated there that sensations have features that "express" the various bodily motions with which they are linked. He took the sensations to be confused because the mind runs together and thus cannot distinguish these various features (see the passages in Leibniz, *Sämtliche Schriften und Briefe* (Akademie edition, in progress), VI. vi. 131–3, 403–4; this pagination is repeated in the Bennett and Remnant translation). It is interesting to note, however, that Leibniz claimed in this work that strictly speaking these sensations are produced by the mind, rather than by the bodily motions they express (ibid., 71–4). Leibniz was somewhat closer to the view of the *Notes* on this particular point than to the

One could argue, in further defence of Regius, that the *Notes* unfairly suggests that he accepts the same sort of misguided view of sensation that Descartes attributed to the schoolmen. Regius followed Descartes, after all, in endorsing a mechanical account of the bodily processes involved in sensation.[86] In thesis 19 of his pamphlet, accordingly, he rejected the tenet that we sense intentional forms transmitted to mind (AT viii-2. 346). None the less, the claim in Regius's response above that we perceive small motions does recall the position, implied by the old transmission account, that the mind senses by peering into the brain. Descartes seems to have been correct, in the end, when he suggested that Regius accepts the very position that is (incorrectly) taken in the *Dioptrics* and the Sixth Responses as well as the *Notes* to be the weak link in the scholastic account of sensation. The view of sensation in the *Notes* is perhaps superior to that offered by Regius in so far as the former avoids the seemingly implausible claim that the mind senses motions in the brain.

These difficulties with Regius's response may go some way towards vindicating the remarks in the *Notes*. There is, however, another aspect of this response that Descartes cannot easily dismiss. Regius implied that Descartes commits a fallacy when he attempts to derive the innateness of ideas of sensory qualities from the fact that these ideas do not resemble bodily motions. This objection is important for our purposes, and even more so in light of the position offered by Locke. In his *Essay* Locke claimed in rather cavalier fashion, and without mention of Descartes, that it "would be impertinent to suppose, the *Ideas* of Colours innate in a Creature, to whom God hath given Sight" (*Essay*, I. ii. 1). Little more is said in this work of the nature of the impertinence, though a similar point is developed in Locke's critique of the position of Malebranche that God rather than body is the cause of sensation.[87] In Book III of *La Recherche de la vérité*, Malebranche had supported his view that bodies do not cause sensations in part by attacking a

position of Regius, though I have argued elsewhere that Descartes did not intend in the *Notes* to deny that bodily motions play some causal role in the production of sensory ideas (T. M. Schmaltz, 'Sensation, occasionalism, and Descartes' causal principles', in *Minds, ideas, and objects*, ed. P. D. Cummins and G. Zoeller (Atascadero, Cal. 1992), 37–56). For a fuller discussion of the Leibnizian account of sensation, see M. D. Wilson, 'Confused ideas', in *Essays on the philosophy of Leibniz*, ed. M. Kulstad, *Rice University studies* 63 (1977), 123–37.

[86] For discussion of the Cartesian roots of Regius's mechanical physiology, see P. Mouy, *Le Développement de la physique cartésienne 1646–1712* (Paris 1934), 85–91; P. Sloan, 'Descartes, the sceptics, and the rejection of vitalism in seventeenth-century physiology', *Studies in the history and philosophy of science* 8 (1977), 22–8.

[87] Locke completed *An examination of P. Malebranche's opinion of seeing all things in God* by 1695, but it was not published until after his death. He also composed a response to the view of Malebranche's English disciple, John Norris, published posthumously with the title, *Remarks upon some of Mr Norris's books, wherein he asserts P. Malebranche's opinion of our seeing all things in God*. For a helpful discussion of the relation of Locke's view to that of Malebranche and Norris, see C. J. McCracken, *Malebranche and British philosophy* (Oxford 1983), ch. 4.

caricature of the scholastic theory of sensation of the sort suggested by Descartes in passages already considered in section I (c) above.[88] Locke pointed out that the scholastic view could be rendered more sophisticated, but held that in the end the more sophisticated version is untenable. He also emphasized, however, that even given this untenability, "the perception we have of bodies at a distance from ours, may be accounted for, as far as we are capable of understanding it, by the motion of particles of matter coming from them and striking on our organs".[89] The schoolmen had a misguided view of sensory processes, he argued, but the position that sensations are produced by alterations in the sense organs is none the worse for that. Indeed, Locke claimed that God would not have contrived such a complex structure of the sense organs were this structure unable to produce sensations. He thus concluded that it would be insulting to God to take these motions to be inefficacious.[90] Though only the thesis that God causes sensations is at issue here, these considerations serve to explain Locke's dismissal in the *Essay* of the position that sensory ideas are innate. He was motivated by the position that bodily motions produce sensory ideas, whether or not the motions resemble these ideas. I take a similar position to have inspired Regius's response to Descartes.

One could object that there is no explanation here of how motions could by themselves produce sensations. Locke did recognize this difficulty and admitted that he could not explain "how ideas are incited in me by motion"; in the end, he was forced to appeal to the fact that God "annexes" sensory states to certain bodily affections.[91] Of course, Locke held that we do not know enough about the nature of sensation to determine how this annexation is accomplished. With Regius, he emphasized that we cannot even know apart from revelation whether matter can think.[92] This scepticism may well

---

[88] Nicolas Malebranche, *De la Recherche de la vérité*, III. ii. 2.

[89] Locke, *Examination*, sec. 9.

[90] *Examination*, secs 9–10; *Remarks*, secs 3, 13–14.

[91] *Essay*, IV. iii. 6, 28; *Examination*, secs 10, 15–16. The nature of Locke's appeal to divine annexation is, of course, a matter of scholarly dispute. In 'Mechanism, superaddition, and the proof of God's existence in Locke's *Essay*', *Philosophical review* 90 (1981), 210–51, M. R. Ayers argues that this appeal serves merely the epistemological function of indicating our ignorance of the precise nature of the necessary mechanical connections between sensation and motion that Locke assumed to be present in nature. For a different reading of Locke's appeal, see M. D. Wilson, 'Superadded properties: the limits of mechanism in Locke', *American philosophical quarterly* 16 (1979), 143–50; ead., 'Superadded properties: A reply to M. R. Ayers', *Philosophical review* 91 (1982), 247–52; E. McCann, 'Lockean mechanism', in Holland, 209–31. Wilson and McCann provide reason to think that Locke appealed to divine annexation because he doubted that there are any such necessary mechanical connections, and thus to think that this appeal has some ontological bite to it.

[92] Regius declared in the second thesis of his broadsheet that "so far as the nature of things is concerned, the mind is able to be either a substance or a mode of a certain corporeal substance" (AT viii-2. 342). Locke's assertion that matter may think, for all we know, is found in *Essay*, IV. iii. 6.

be a useful antidote to Descartes's dogmatic assertions regarding mind and matter. Yet there is still a respect in which Descartes's discussion of sensation is superior to that of Locke. Without any explanation of how God annexes sensations to motions, Locke's appeal to God seems to be little more than the invocation of a *deus ex machina*. Descartes also appealed to sensory connections established by God or nature when he employed the sign analogy, but he gave some indication of how this connection is established when he adverted in the *Notes* to the operation of an innate mental faculty. The sensory faculty could be seen as at least partially filling an explanatory gap in the Lockean account of sensation.

The problem with the argument of the *Notes*, though, is that it does not draw attention to this gap. In this work and elsewhere, Descartes was preoccupied with the question of whether the mind sees images that are sent from objects and that do not resemble sensory ideas; he did not consider the more general question of whether the bodily motions that constitute these images could alone produce sensory ideas in the mind.[93] Once one sees that the schoolmen did not adopt the transmission view attacked in the *Dioptrics*, the Sixth Responses, and the *Notes*, and also sees that differences over the innate sensory faculty of mind do not stem from the rejection of the resemblance doctrine, the more general question gains in importance. What is required is an argument for the claim that it must be a mental faculty rather than bodily motions that produces sensory ideas. There may be compelling reasons for the postulation of the innate mental faculty drawn from Descartes's system,[94] but they were not offered in the response to Regius. Descartes's argument for the innate sensory faculty of mind therefore does not prove to be satisfactory.

This is not to say that the *Notes* is without worth. Remarks in this work are

---

[93] Yolton claims that Descartes employed the sign analogy because he "was confronted with the difficulty of how causation could work across categories, between body and mind, from physiology to psychology" (Yolton, 22). Broughton argues along similar lines that the argument in the *Notes* arises from the fact that Descartes cannot take sensory states of mind to be caused by bodily motions which differ in nature from these states (Broughton, 115–19). (Such a position has been suggested most recently by N. Jolley in *The light of the soul* (Oxford 1990), 40–42.) By setting the *Notes* in historical context, I hope to have shown that neither the sign theory nor the view presented to Regius was motivated by difficulties concerning the causal interaction of entities with different natures. Moreover, as I argue in 'Descartes's causal principles', there is no reason to think that Descartes himself was bothered, or need have been bothered, by the sort of difficulties emphasized by Yolton and Broughton.

[94] It may be thought, for instance, that elements of Descartes's system preclude the claim that bodies have causal powers to produce sensations. For different ways of defending this claim, see G. Hatfield, 'Force (God) in Descartes's physics', *Studies in the history and philosophy of science* 10 (1979), 113–40; D. Garber, 'Understanding interaction', *Southern journal of philosophy* 21 (1983), Suppl. 15–32; Schmaltz, 'Descartes and Malebranche'. I have not been concerned with this difficulty, focusing as I have on the argument of the *Notes*. I would want to argue, however, that Descartes should have been more concerned with this sort of difficulty in that work.

related in an interesting way to the sign analogy, and they suggest an account of sensory processes that avoids recourse to a mental contemplation of images in the brain. But the argument in this text does not go far enough. In the *Dioptrics* Descartes noted that, once the resemblance doctrine is rejected, the problem is simply to know how images in the brain "can enable the soul to sense all the qualities to which they correspond [*rapport*]—not how they can resemble these objects" (AT vi. 113–14). Had Descartes not focused so much on issues concerning resemblance and transmission in his writings on sensation, he might have been able to garner a more powerful defence of the account in the *Notes* of how bodily images can enable the soul to have sensory ideas.[95]

Department of Philosophy
Duke University

[95] I am grateful to Karl Ameriks for invaluable discussion of earlier drafts of this essay, and to Fred Freddoso, Dan Garber, Christia Mercer, and Margaret Wilson for improvements in the final version which were made possible by their remarks. Thanks also to M. A. Stewart for very helpful editorial assistance in the preparation of the manuscript.

3

OCCASIONALISM AND THE MIND-BODY PROBLEM

STEVEN NADLER

One of the more popular myths in the traditional account of the development of metaphysics in the seventeenth century regards the genesis and historico-philosophical significance of the doctrine of occasionalism, or the theory that God alone is a true causal agent, in whose operations *qua causa* are included all the phenomena of nature. According to the story usually told, some early modern thinkers, committed to Descartes's philosophy, and to mind-body dualism in particular, were unable to explain how two substances so radically different in essence could interact. Since unextended thought and matter as pure extension have absolutely nothing in common (either essentially or in regard to the kinds of properties of which each is capable), and thus no means by which they might be able to "engage" one another, it becomes inexplicable, and even inconceivable, how a body can be the cause of mental events (thoughts, sensations) and how a mind can cause motions in the body with which it is united. When confronted with such a problem, the story runs, Cartesians asserted that no such interaction really takes place and retreated to a *deus ex machina*. What appears to be true causal interaction is really God's constant activity in producing thoughts on the occasion of certain bodily motions (especially in the brain) and motions in the body on the occasion of certain volitions in the mind, all in accordance with general laws established beforehand. On this reading, occasionalism is first and foremost an *ad hoc* response to the mind-body problem as it is faced by Cartesian dualism.[1]

© Steven Nadler 1997

[1] This, of course, is the standard textbook account. See F. C. Copleston, *A history of philosophy* (9 vols, London 1946–75), iv. 176ff.; G. Boas, *Dominant themes of modern philosophy* (New York 1957), 103. This reading, however, is also found in recent scholarly work. See R. A. Watson, *The downfall of Cartesianism, 1673–1712* (The Hague 1966), 2, 98; D. Radner, *Malebranche* (Assen 1978), 10–12; A. G. A. Balz, *Cartesian studies* (New York 1951), 213; L. J. Beck, *The metaphysics of Descartes* (Oxford 1965), 269; W. von Leyden, *Seventeenth-century metaphysics* (London 1968), 216; S. V. Keeling, *Descartes*, 2nd edn (Oxford 1968), 224.

There are, however, several very good reasons for questioning this commonly accepted view.

1. It is clear that those seventeenth-century thinkers who did have recourse to a thoroughgoing occasionalism did so not only in order to account for apparent mind-body interaction, but to account for apparent causal relations among bodies as well.[2] Nicolas Malebranche, for example, in both *The search after truth* and *Dialogues on metaphysics*, argues that it is no more conceivable how one body can move another than how a body can be a true cause of thoughts in the soul or how volitions in the soul can move the body.[3] Thus it can be argued that the problem, for Malebranche, is as equally one of the physics of force as of the metaphysics of dualism. And Géraud de

Leibniz bears much responsibility for the popularity of the standard reading. He clearly believed that Cartesian occasionalists resorted to "continuous miracles" by God only after they had recognized that the soul in its "diversity" from the body "can have no influence whatsoever" upon it. See 'First truths', in *Philosophical papers and letters*, trans. and ed. L. E. Loemker, 2nd edn (Dordrecht 1969), 269; letter to Arnauld, 9 Oct. 1687, ibid., 340; 'Considerations on vital principles and plastic natures, by the author of the system of pre-established harmony', ibid., 587.

Lately, however, a more accurate picture of the arguments and motivations behind occasionalism is beginning to emerge in the critical literature. T. M. Lennon, for example, argues that the traditional reading is "utterly without historical foundation"; see his 'Philosophical commentary', in Nicolas Malebranche, *The search after truth*, trans. T. M. Lennon and P. J. Olscamp (Columbus, Oh. 1980), 810ff. See also C. J. McCracken, *Malebranche and British philosophy* (Oxford 1983), 89ff.; L. Loeb, *From Descartes to Hume* (Ithaca 1981), 210–22. These scholars, however, who do question the standard account do so, for the most part, by insisting that the occasionalist solution to the mind-body problem is really just an extension of a more general analysis of causal relations. My argument, on the other hand, denies that the specific mind-body problem as we have come to know it was even recognized by the relevant thinkers; it was not even recognized as a special case of some more general causal problem (although, as will become clear below, I do agree that occasionalism *is* being offered to resolve *some* problems about mind-body interaction which stem from a more general account of causation).

[2] Occasionalism comes in a number of different varieties and with several different scopes. See J.-F. Battail, *L'Avocat philosophe Géraud de Cordemoy* (The Hague 1973), 141–6. By "thoroughgoing" occasionalism, I here understand the occasionalist doctrine as applying to *all* apparent interactions among natural phenomena—between and within minds, between bodies, and between minds and bodies. Some important thinkers, on the other hand, were only partial occasionalists. Antoine Arnauld, for example, restricted it to sensations "caused" in the mind by the body; see his *Des Vraies et des fausses idées* (1683), in *Oeuvres de Messire Antoine Arnauld* (43 vols, Paris 1775), xxxviii. 349. And I believe Louis de la Forge *not* to be an occasionalist in regard to mind-body interaction: see his *Traité de l'esprit de l'homme* (1666) (Paris 1974), 224–46, although, as I discuss below in note 7, La Forge's position is not entirely clear. See N. K. Smith, *Studies in the Cartesian philosophy* (London 1902), 87 n. 2.

[3] See Malebranche, *The search after truth*, VI. ii. 3, and Elucidation XV; *Dialogues on metaphysics*, VII. All subsequent translations from the *Search* are from the Lennon-Olscamp edition, referred to as 'LO' followed by page numbers. References to the original *De la Recherche de la vérité* (1674) are to the 1712 edition as re-created in *Oeuvres complètes de Malebranche*, dir. A. Robinet (20 vols, Paris 1960–75), i–iii, ed. G. Rodis-Lewis. Henceforth, the *Oeuvres* are referred to as 'OC' followed by volume and page numbers. Translations from the *Dialogues* are by W. Doney (New York 1980), referred to as 'D'; the original, *Entretiens sur la métaphysique*, is in OC xii.

Cordemoy insists that

If there is any meaning in saying that the soul moves the body, it is in the same sense that it can be said that a body moves another body. For as one body is said to move another when on account of their impact it happens that that which moved the former now moves the latter, so a soul can be said to move a body when on account of its desire it happens that that which was already moving this body now moves it in the direction in which this soul wants it to move. And it should be noted that it is a convenient way of speaking ordinarily to say that a soul moves a body and that one body moves another.[4]

As Thomas M. Lennon has argued, the priority here is on a general analysis of causation. "Occasionalism was argued on grounds far transcending the mind-body problem. The view that only God can be a real cause of mind-body interaction was only a consequence of a metaphysics adopted by the Cartesians in their general account of change."[5] The relevant analysis of causation had ramifications in both contexts: the purely physical realm of bodies in motion (and at rest) and the psychophysical realm of mind-body interaction.

2. Some Cartesians call upon occasionalism *only* in order to answer questions about interaction between bodies. Louis de la Forge, one of the more important expositors and followers of Descartes in the mid-seventeenth century, insists that "the will can well be the efficient cause of all the things we notice to depend on it in this alliance [between mind and body]",[6] although he does reduce mind-body interaction to a "mutual correspondence and concourse and reciprocal dependence" in the states of the two substances. It is only when he comes to the question of how one body moves another body that he employs the constant and necessarily efficacious activity of God.[7]

3. The three most important thoroughgoing occasionalists of the seventeenth century did not even believe that there was any special mind-body problem that needed resolving. Malebranche, Cordemoy, and Arnold

[4] Géraud de Cordemoy, *Le Discernement du corps et de l'âme* (1666) (in a later edition, *Six discours sur la distinction et l'union du corps et de l'âme*), Discourse VI, in *Oeuvres philosophiques* (Paris 1968), 152.

[5] Lennon, 'Commentary', 810. This point is also argued by Loeb, 217–20. See also W. Doney, 'Malebranche', in *The encyclopedia of philosophy*, ed. P. Edwards (8 vols, New York 1967), v. 142–3.

[6] *Traité de l'esprit de l'homme*, 227. See also 245: "It ought not to be said, nevertheless, that God does everything, and that the body and the mind do not truly act [*n'agissent pas véritablement*] upon one another."

[7] There is, however, some disagreement on whether La Forge is an occasionalist in the mind-body realm. In agreement with my reading that he is not, see F. Bouillier, *Histoire de la philosophie cartésienne*, 3rd edn (Paris 1868), i. 513; Smith, 87; H. Gouhier, *La Vocation de Malebranche* (Paris 1926), 89. For the contrasting view, see McCracken, 95; Watson, 72; Lennon, 811; and, if I understand him correctly, Balz, 94–9. I develop my argument at greater length in 'The occasionalism of Louis de la Forge', in *Causation in early modern philosophy*, ed. S. Nadler (University Park, Pa. 1993).

Geulincx all denied that the mind and the body causally interact in any real sense (and likewise for bodies among themselves). But they did so not for any reasons which we should recognize as deriving from a scepticism or concern about how two substances differing essentially can interact. In fact, whatever reasons they do present for denying mind-body interaction (and, consequently, for calling upon God to effect the necessary changes) either derive immediately from identical reasons at work against body-body interaction; or, if they are reasons specific to mind-body relations, do not derive from problems or inconsistencies perceived to be inherent in Cartesian ontological dualism.

In arguing against the standard textbook reading, I limit the scope of this paper to considerations falling under (3): the mind-body problem played no role at all in motivating the occasionalisms of Malebranche, Cordemoy, and Geulincx. I do not directly address (1), as it has been well argued for in the recent literature.[8] Moreover, (3) is a much stronger claim, since the reading represented by (1) still leaves open the possibility that occasionalism *is* being offered as a solution to the mind-body problem. (1) simply argues that, while occasionalism may indeed have been intended to resolve the mind-body problem, it was also meant to take care of an equally pressing body-body problem; and the two (distinct) problems have their source in a more general theory of causation (that is, given the general Cartesian account of change mentioned by Lennon, one specific problematic arises for mind-body interaction—namely, the mind-body problem itself—and another, different problematic arises regarding bodies among themselves). I, on the other hand, argue that, while Malebranche and others do offer occasionalism to account for the apparent causal relations between mind and body, there is *no* sense in which their occasionalism was a solution to a perceived specific mind-body problem (as it was and is usually understood) regarding interaction, a problem allegedly due to their commitment to dualism.

The scope of this paper is also limited in that it is confined to this negative thesis, without examining what positive motivations lay behind occasionalist doctrines—for example, what other perceived problems in Descartes's metaphysics or physics might have led to Malebranche's views on causation; or what theological premises regarding God's relationship to the creation play a role therein.

I. THE MIND-BODY PROBLEM

The mind-body problem, particularly as it is understood by those who have given us the traditional view of the development of occasionalism, is the

---

[8] See Lennon, McCracken, et al. (above, note 1).

question of how two such essentially different substances can causally influence the properties of one another. This problem is first raised for Descartes by Gassendi in the fifth set of Objections to the *Meditations* (1641). After querying Descartes on the possibility of union or "intermingling" between something "incorporeal, unextended and indivisible" and the extended divisible body, Gassendi takes up the issue of mind-body causation: "Since you admit that you feel pain, how, may I ask, do you think you are capable of having this sensation if you are incorporeal and unextended? . . . The general difficulty still remains of how the corporeal can communicate with the incorporeal and of what relationship may be established between the two."[9]

Princess Elisabeth gives a more acute statement of the problem in her letter to Descartes of 6 May 1643, where she asks Descartes

how the soul of man can determine the bodily spirits to perform voluntary actions, since it is only a thinking substance. For it seems that every determination of motion comes about by means of impulse upon the thing moved, such that it is pushed by that which moves it, or yet by the qualification and figure of the surface of the latter. Contact [*l'attouchement*] is required for the first two conditions, and extension for the third. But you completely exclude extension from the notion which you have of the soul; and contact seems to me to be incompatible with the nature of an immaterial thing.[10]

Thus presented in its classical aspect, the mind-body problem is essentially a *conceptual* problem, not a factual one. There obviously is the kind of mental state/physical state correspondence which we recognize as sensation and voluntary movements of the body—I do feel heat when my body approaches the fire, and my arm moves up when I will to raise it. The question is, can these facts coherently be described as cases of real causal activity between unextended thinking and thoughtless extension? Or, in other words, assuming a commitment to mind-body dualism, is it conceivable that two substances which differ essentially act upon one another?[11] Elisabeth, for one, seems to have trouble making sense of the claim, given the unextended, immaterial nature of the soul.[12]

---

[9] *Oeuvres de Descartes*, ed. C. Adam and P. Tannery (11 vols, Paris 1974–83), vii. 344–5 (henceforth 'AT' followed by volume and page numbers). Translation from *The philosophical writings of Descartes*, trans. J. Cottingham and others (3 vols, Cambridge 1985–91), ii. 239 (henceforth 'CSM' followed by volume and page numbers).

[10] AT iii. 661.

[11] A fuller statement of the mind-body problem would have to make reference to certain causal principles, particularly ones which require some kind of "likeness" (essential or otherwise) between cause and effect, as well as some metaphysical premises about substance, mode, etc. See D. Radner, 'Is there a problem of Cartesian interaction?', *Journal of the history of philosophy* 23 (1985), 35–49.

[12] I am not claiming here that Descartes is subject to a problem of mind-body interaction. Radner (1985) does argue this. For the opposing view, see R. C. Richardson, 'The "scandal" of Cartesian interactionism', *Mind* 91 (1982), 20–37; Loeb, 134–49.

It should be noted that this particular conceptual problem about interaction is quite distinct from any conceptual problems which may arise regarding interaction between entities of the same ontological kind. Thus, body-body interaction might be problematic (given, for example, a conception of motion as a non-transferable mode of a body), but not for the same "dualistic" reasons that presumably render mind-body interaction problematic. Moreover, the mind-body problem is certainly *not* a subspecies of some more general conceptual problem regarding interaction between finite substances. While such a more general problem *would* entail conceptual difficulties regarding mind-body interaction (as well as similar difficulties for body-body interaction), they are not the conceptual difficulties which are identified here as the mind-body problem. This particular account of the problem and its distinguishing features is important for my argument below.

II. MALEBRANCHE AND THE INEFFICACY
OF NATURAL CAUSES

It is significant for my thesis if Malebranche, perhaps the most important and well known of the occasionalists, did not present his occasionalism as a response to the mind-body problem, either in whole or in part. In fact, close examination of the relevant texts reveals that none of the arguments Malebranche offers for denying real mind-body interaction, hence for affirming God as sole cause in this arena, exhibits a concern for the special problem noted in section I, although other conceptual problems which lead to this denial play an important role in his doctrine.[13]

Malebranche's picture of causation can be summarized as follows. God has established general laws regarding the relations between bodies, the relations of mental events to other mental events (e.g. beliefs to volitions) and the relations between minds and bodies. Such laws specify, for example, that when one body strikes another, the second body moves in a given direction with a given speed; or when certain motions occur in the brain, corresponding sensory thoughts appear in the mind. But, strictly speaking, the one body

---

[13] Thus I am arguing against Watson when he claims that "Malebranche met the problem about [mind-body] causal interaction by denying that there is interaction between mind and matter. This seems to be an *immediate* result of his adherence to the ontological dualism and the causal likeness principle. It is because of the complete difference or unlikeness between mind and matter that Malebranche insists they cannot interact" (*Downfall*, 98, my emphasis). I also argue against Radner, when she insists that Malebranche's occasionalism *is* a response to general problems in Descartes's interactionism, and to the mind-body problem in particular. She provides evidence for the more general claim but does not argue for the particular one: see 'Is there a problem of Cartesian interaction?', 44–9. See also Loeb, 217ff., where he suggests (but nothing more) that Malebranche's occasionalism is not a response at all to a mind-body problem.

does not cause the motion of the other body, and the brain motions do not cause the sensation. Rather, bodily impact serves as an occasion upon which God exerts power and moves the second body accordingly; and the brain motions present a similar occasion for God to produce the required sensations ('accordingly' and 'required' here refer to the fact that these causal operations follow the general laws that God has established).

One finds in Malebranche four separate arguments for the denial of mind-body interaction. Each argument by itself is believed by Malebranche to establish the following claims: mind cannot act on body, body cannot act on mind, body cannot act on body, and God is the true and only causal agent.

1. The first argument that Malebranche offers is based on the causal principle that in order for one thing, A (of whatever ontological type), to count as the cause of another thing, B, there must be a "necessary connection" between the existence of A and the existence of B (where 'A' and 'B' can stand for substances or states of substances). "A true cause as I understand it is one such that the mind perceives a necessary connection [*liaison nécessaire*] between it and its effects."[14] But we can find no such connection between any human mental event and a corresponding physical event; for example, between any volition to move my arm and my arm actually moving.

Since the idea we have of all bodies makes us aware that they cannot move themselves, it must be concluded that it is minds which move them. But when we examine our idea of all finite minds, we do not see any necessary connection between their will and the motion of any body whatsoever. On the contrary, we see that there is none and that there can be none. We must therefore also conclude . . . that there is absolutely no mind created that can move a body as a true or principal cause.[15]

When we consider God, however, as an infinitely perfect being, we see that there *is* such a necessary connection between God's will and the motion of bodies, since it is logically impossible that an omnipotent being should will to move a body and it does not move.[16]

One might be tempted to insist that the "no necessary connection" claim made in reference to the finite human mind and a body is just one way of putting the mind-body problem: how can we conceive a necessary connection between such disparate things, i.e. between an entity which is unextended and indivisible, and hence incapable of local contact, and another entity which is extended and mobile? But this would be to miss the main thrust of the argument. The emphasis here is on the *finiteness* of the mind, not its "mentalness" or immateriality. Since it is finite and hence not omnipotent,

---

[14] *Search*, VI. ii. 3 (LO 450, OC ii. 316).

[15] *Search*, VI. ii. 3 (LO 448, OC ii. 313).

[16] "It is a contradiction that He should will and that what He wills should not happen" (ibid.).

the human mind's success in willing an effect x will be contingent upon factors other than its merely having willed x. This is not an empirical claim, but a conceptual one. It is part of what it means to be a finite mind both that its understanding falls short of omniscience, and that it is less than omnipotent. And what can omnipotence mean, Malebranche is insisting, other than that there is a necessary connection between will and effect? Thus, when Malebranche says in this context that "there seems to be some contradiction" in saying that humans are the true causes of movements in their bodies, the contradiction follows from his strict definition of 'cause' (as involving necessary connection), together with the fact that a human will is finite. It is not a contradiction within dualism *per se*.

My claim that finiteness and not mentalness is the problem is supported by the conclusion of the argument, namely, that there must be an *infinite mind* (God) which is responsible for the motion of the body. Malebranche obviously here sees no conceptual problem in the claim that something mind-like, hence something essentially different from body, can move body.

Finally, this same argument can be, and *is*, used to demonstrate the causal inefficacy of bodies among themselves and of the body upon the mind.[17] In other words, Malebranche is arguing generally against the reality of causal relations between any finite substances—material or immaterial. Mind-body interaction is problematic, and thus depends on the agency of an infinite will, *not* because of any ontological differences between mind and body, but because it is a species of finite causation, which *is* inconceivable given Malebranche's strict definition of 'cause'.

2. Malebranche's second argument is likewise based on a conceptual problem—namely, the "inconceivability" that any "natural cause", any finite mind or material body, should have "a force, a power [*puissance*], an efficacy to produce anything".[18] My idea of body (that is, the clear idea of pure extension), for example, represents it as having only one property: the entirely passive faculty of "receiving various figures and various move-ments".[19] It certainly does not represent body as having any active power. In fact, I perceive such a power as *in*compatible with the notion of pure extension, since it cannot be reduced to or explained in terms of "relations of shape, divisibility, and distance". Thus, bodies cannot act on minds or on other bodies.

Second, whatever knowledge I have of my soul (and, for Malebranche, such knowledge is minimal and not based on any clear idea) does not involve the perception of any power, whether to move the body or even to produce its

---

[17] *Search*, VI. ii. 3 (LO 450, OC ii. 316), v. i (LO 338–9, OC ii. 129); *Dialogues*, VII. 12 (D 161, OC xii. 163–4).
[18] *Search*, Eluc. xv (LO 658, OC iii. 204).
[19] *Dialogues*, VII. 1–2 (D 145–9, OC xii. 148–51).

own ideas. All I perceive through inner consciousness is an actual volition to move my arm upwards, and all I notice in my body is that my arm is subsequently raised. But I perceive, either by inner consciousness or by reason, *no* power on the part of the soul by means of which it might effect this motion.[20] It is in this sense that "those who maintain that creatures have force and power in themselves advance what they do not clearly perceive".[21] Indeed, according to Malebranche, I perceive a general incompatibility between the idea of a created finite being and such a power or productive faculty.[22] Only in my idea of the will of an infinite being do I clearly and distinctly recognize any element of power whatsoever.

Once again, as in argument (1), real interaction between mind and body is ruled out (and divine governance required) because the notion of such productive interaction between two created and finite substances is conceptually incoherent, and not because of any perceived mind-body problem. Mind cannot act on body, body cannot act on mind—but for the *same* reasons that the mind cannot cause mental events (ideas) and the body cannot cause physical events (motion in another body). The more general problem about power, in fact, short-circuits even raising the specific mind-body question, since for Malebranche it does not even make sense to ask whether created unextended mind can exert effectively its inherent power on extended body (and vice versa). That is, the question of the coherence of mind-body interaction in a dualistic system cannot even be raised if we are dealing from the start with two entities which have no causal efficacy at all.

3. The third argument is based not on any conceptual problem, but on a contingent fact. Even if we had the *power* to move our bodies, we clearly lack the knowledge required to do so.

For how could we move our arms? To move them, it is necessary to have animal spirits, to send them through certain nerves toward certain muscles in order to inflate and contract them, for it is thus that the arm attached to them is moved. . . . And we see that·men who do not know that they have spirits, nerves, and muscles move their arms, and even move them with more skill and ease than those who know anatomy best. Therefore, men will to move their arms, and only God is able and knows how to move them. If a man cannot turn a tower upside down, at least he knows what must be done to do so, but there is no man who knows what must be done to move one of his fingers by means of animal spirits. How, then, could men move their arms?[23]

Malebranche is thus setting an epistemic condition on the notion of "cause": in order to count as the cause of effect *E*, a thing must know how (*savoir*) to

---

[20] *Search*, Eluc. xv (LO 670–71, OC iii. 227–8).

[21] Eluc. xv (LO 658, OC iii. 204).

[22] *Search*, vi. ii. 3 (LO 450–51, OC ii. 316–18); Eluc. xv (LO 658, OC iii. 204). As I note, this applies even to the soul's inability to produce its own ideas; see *Search*, iii. ii. 3 (LO 222ff., OC i. 422ff.); Eluc. xv (LO 671, OC iii. 229).

[23] *Search*, vi. ii. 3 (LO 449–50, OC ii. 315).

bring about *E*. He then appeals to the evident fact that this condition is not satisfied by our minds in order to show that we do not, in fact, cause those body motions which we consider voluntary. This same condition, however, rules out not only the mind's causal efficacy upon the body, but also the mind's ability to produce its own ideas.[24] It also rules out any causal efficacy one might want to attribute to bodies (since, as non-thinking beings, they necessarily cannot satisfy the relevant epistemic condition).[25]

In other words, God is needed as cause here because no finite being, mental or otherwise, happens to have the knowledge necessary to act causally. It should be clear that the considerations specific to the mind-body problem do not play a role in this argument, since (a) the reasons at work here, as in the last two arguments, are effective in ruling out causation even within the same ontological category; and (b), as we saw, the specific mind-body considerations are of a conceptual nature, while this particular argument appeals to a matter of fact.[26]

4. Malebranche's most powerful argument against real interaction, and the one which he appears to believe to carry the most weight, appeals to God's role as creator and sustainer (i.e. re-creator) of the universe. To his mind, the argument shows that it is an "absolute contradiction" that minds should move bodies, but it does so by showing that it is a contradiction that *anything* besides God alone should move a body.[27]

---

[24] See *Search*, III. ii. 3 (LO 223, OC i. 424–5); Eluc. xv (LO 669, OC iii. 226).

[25] This is the kind of argument used by Geulincx to rule out real interaction: see his *Metaphysica vera* (1691), Pt I, Quinta scientia.

[26] That this is an argument "from fact" is underscored by the line immediately following the quoted passage and leading into another argument: "But not only are men not the true causes of the movements they produce in their bodies, there even seems to be some contradiction (in saying) that they could be" (LO 450, OC ii. 316). It should be noted that, later, Malebranche does seem to present the same argument as a conceptual problem: "How is it conceivable that the soul should move the body?". In order to do so, the number of the soul's volitions would have to be as great as the almost infinite number of collisions or impacts that would occur in the particles composing the relevant bodily spirits. "But this is inconceivable, unless we allow in the soul an infinite number of volitions for the least movement of the body, because in order to move it, an infinite number of communications of motion must take place." But since the soul is finite, particular, and limited, it is necessarily not capable of an infinite number of volitions, nor of knowing exactly "the size and agitation of an infinite number of particles that collide with each other when the spirits are in the muscles" (Eluc. xv: LO 671, OC iii. 228). Still, it should be clear that, even with this presentation of the argument, the kind of conceptual problem at work is not the one associated with the mind-body problem; and it would seem that (a) is still true with regard to this reformulation.

[27] The argument does not appear in the *Search* at all, but only in the *Dialogues* (VII. 13). It is found in a very similar form in La Forge, *Traité*, ch. 16, pp. 239–40; and in embryonic form in Descartes himself—see *Principles of philosophy*, II. 39, and *Le Monde* (AT xi. 44–6, CSM i. 96–7). For a discussion of this argument and an analysis of its non-occasionalist form in Descartes, see D. Garber, 'How God causes motion: Descartes, divine sustenance, and occasionalism', *Journal of philosophy* 84 (1987), 567–80. My claim about the scope and strength of the argument is based on the fact that Malebranche himself introduces it by granting the epistemic condition ("Let us

God's activity is required not only to create the world, but to sustain it as well. To insist otherwise is to mistake the kind of dependence creatures have upon God. And from God's point of view, there is no essential difference between the divine activity as creator and the divine activity as sustainer. "If the world subsists, it is because God continues to will that the world exist. On the part of God, the conservation of the creatures is simply their continued creation."[28] Now when God conserves/re-creates a body, it must be re-created in some particular place and in some relation of distance to other bodies. If God conserves it in the same (relative) place from moment to moment, it remains at rest; if it is conserved successively in different places, it is in motion. But this means that God is and can be the *only* cause of motion. As Malebranche puts it later, the motion of a body is only its being transported by a divine act (or, more accurately, by a series of divine acts). "The moving force of a body is, then, simply the efficacy of the volition of God who conserves it successively in different places. . . . Hence, bodies cannot move one another, and their encounter or impact is only an occasional cause of the distribution of their motions."[29] And what applies to bodies as apparent causes of motion applies also to minds. As Theodore, Malebranche's spokesman in the *Dialogues*, says to Aristes in his typically hyperbolic manner:

Here you are in the world without any power, as incapable of motion as a rock, dumb as a log, as it were. Your soul can be united to your body as closely as you please . . . yet what advantage will you derive from this imaginary union? What will you do to move merely the end of your finger, to utter merely a one-syllable word? If, alas, God does not come to your aid, you will only make efforts in vain. . . . It is only the Creator of bodies who can be their mover. This principle is sufficient to stop—why do I say 'stop'?—to annihilate all your alleged faculties.[30]

Malebranche indicates explicitly that the point of his argument here is to prove that finite mind cannot act on body, by showing, first, that only God is a motive force, and hence that *no* created being can move a body.[31] In a sense, the ultimate conclusion is a trivial one: first he shows that nothing but God can move bodies, and then concludes that *a fortiori* minds cannot move bodies. Mind-body interaction is here problematic because of more general principles regarding the nature and source of motion, not because of dualism.

suppose that you know quite well what no one knows . . . let us suppose that you are acquainted with the anatomy and the action of your mechanism" [D 163, OC xii. 165]), and *could* even grant the "inherent power" condition, since such a power should necessarily and always be superseded by God's infinite, all-encompassing, and constantly exerted power.

28 *Dialogues*, VII. 7 (D 153, OC xii. 157).
29 *Dialogues*, VII. 11 (D 159, OC xii. 161–2).
30 *Dialogues*, VII. 13 (D 162–3, OC xii. 165).
31 *Dialogues*, VII. 4 (D 151, OC xii. 154); VII. 10 (D 157, OC xii. 160).

In fact, the occasionalism in this case is grounded directly in the essence of God and God's relation to creation, and hence precedes, and serves as a premise in, the argument for the claim that minds do not act on bodies (nor bodies on minds). As in argument (2), the specific question about interaction that supposedly creates the mind-body problem is forestalled and cannot even be coherently raised.

We have examined, then, the four explicit arguments Malebranche offers in support of his occasionalism. In none of them do we encounter a worry or a concern about how two substances as unlike as mind and body can interact. In fact, they all presuppose that at least one mind interacts with bodies: namely, God.

If Malebranche's occasionalism is a response to a perceived explanatory failure in Cartesian ontological dualism, there is no evidence for this view in the arguments themselves. What about elsewhere in the texts? Is there *any* evidence that Malebranche was concerned with the specific mind-body problem? There are two passages which appear to point towards the traditional reading and to imply that Malebranche's occasionalism is, indeed, an attempt to shore up Cartesian dualism.

Early on in the *Search*, Malebranche, in his discussion of sensation, argues that the natural cause of a sensation in the mind need not itself contain the sensation.

For just as light need not be in my hand for me to see light when I strike my eyes, so heat need not be in the fire for me to feel it when I bring my hands near it, nor does any sensible quality I perceive have to be in the object. It is enough that they cause some disturbance in the fibers of my flesh so that my soul to which it is joined may be modified by some sensation. There is no relation, it is true, between instances of motion and sensations. But neither is there any relation between the mind and body, and since nature or the will of the Creator allies these two substances (however opposed in their nature they may be [*toutes opposées quelles sont par leur nature*]), it should not be surprising if their modifications are reciprocal.[32]

Malebranche seems to be saying here that since it is inconceivable how two substances differing essentially (*par leur nature*) can interact, it must be God who effects the causal relationship.

A similar, although more forceful and explicit (and, for my thesis, problematic) passage is found in Book V, 'The Passions':

For I cannot understand how certain people imagine that there is an absolutely necessary relation between the movements of the spirits and blood and the emotions of the soul. A few tiny particles of bile are rather violently stirred up in the brain— therefore, the soul must be excited by some passion, and the passion must be anger

---

[32] *Search*, I. xii. 5 (LO 59–60, OC i. 141–2). The first and second editions have '*toutes inalliables*' instead of '*toutes opposées*'.

rather than love. What relation can be conceived between the idea of an enemy's faults, or a passion of contempt or hatred, on the one hand, and the corporeal movement of the blood's parts striking against certain parts of the brain on the other? How can they convince themselves that the one depends on the other, and that the union or connection [*alliance*] of two things so remote and incompatible [*inalliable*] as mind and matter could be caused and maintained in any way other than by the continuous and all-powerful will of the Author of nature?

He then goes on to suggest that the belief that bodies really communicate motion to each other, although mistaken, has "a certain plausibility", given their essential likeness.

For in the final analysis, this prejudice or error has a certain basis: bodies seem to be essentially related to bodies. But the mind and the body are two kinds of being so contrary to one another that those who believe that the soul's emotions necessarily follow the movement of the spirits and blood believe something without the faintest plausibility. Certainly, only our own inner experience of the union of these two beings and an ignorance of God's continuous operations on His creatures could make us imagine a cause of this union other than the always efficacious will of God.[33]

Could one hope for a more explicit statement of the mind-body problem and the necessary recourse to occasionalism?

My answer to this question is Yes, and that in fact what these two passages present is not really a concern with the mind-body problem, nor a subsequent call upon God to effect interaction *per se*. Note, first of all, that each argument, and the immediate context of each argument, concerns only the apparent activity of the body upon the mind in causing sensations (in the first case) and passions (in the second case). One response I might make, then, would be that the specific question of mind-body interaction is here moot, since we know from our clear idea of extension that bodies are inactive by nature and lack any power to cause any effect—whether that effect be in the mind or in another body. But this particular response is unsatisfying, especially since Malebranche has not yet, at this point in the text, demonstrated the causal inefficacy of body.

A more relevant and important response, however, one which is truer both to the immediate passages themselves and to their place in the *Search*, is available. What Malebranche is concerned with in the two passages is *not* interaction between two essentially different substances, if 'interaction' is taken to mean simply the causal production of effects on one another—in this case, body upon mind. I suggest that at this point this is not yet the problem for Malebranche. That is, the question here is not the *general* one of interaction, but rather a question concerning how and why the *particular* causal relations we see do obtain. Why is it that, given certain determinate

---

[33] *Search*, v. i (LO 338–9, OC ii. 129).

motions in the brain, this and only this particular mental event occurs? Why is it that, once "a few tiny particles of bile are rather violently stirred up in the brain", the soul is "excited by some passion, and the passion must be anger rather than love"? We fail to see any necessary connection between these specific motions and that specific thought. But the question of relation here, then, is the *semantic* one between certain bodily motions and the corresponding idea or passion (for example, as he notes, between "the corporeal movement of the blood's parts striking against certain parts of the brain" and "the idea of an enemy's faults, or a passion of contempt or hatred")—why is a set of motions translated into mental event *A* rather than mental event *B*? Such a relation appears somewhat comprehensible, he is saying, when we are dealing with bodies alone. We think we can see clearly the relation that obtains between a particular kind of motion at impact in one body and the consequent motion of the affected body, and why it is that the effect in the second body is that particular motion and not another. But why should one kind of brain motion be attended by the passion, say, of hatred, rather than the passion of love? This is what we cannot clearly comprehend. But this question of "translation" from physical event to mental event must be distinguished from the metaphysical question of interaction that motivates the mind-body problem. God is called upon in these two passages to explain the semantic connection (*alliance*) or correspondence between particular event *A* in the body and particular event *B* in the mind, not the causal relation *per se* between mind and body.[34] And once the "prejudice or error" is dispelled, God is also needed to explain why one particular kind of motion in body *A* is followed by just this motion in body *B* and no other.[35]

More generally, I might further add that, if the mind-body problem was truly a problem which Malebranche sought to overcome with his occasional-ism, it seems rather odd that there are only two short passages which even

[34] Descartes explicitly makes a similar point in the opening passages of *Le Monde*. Even though there is a radical difference between the objects or events which cause (*produissent*) sensations in us and the sensations themselves (e.g. the motions of a feather and the tickle), none the less nature could have established that such and such motions were productive of such and such sensations in the mind (AT xi. 3–6, CSM i. 81–2).

[35] For those who are still unsatisfied by this response, I might add the following. Malebranche is insisting in the second half of the second passage that the obstacle to our conceiving the plausibility of the relation between mind and body is that these are beings "so contrary to one another". The French term used here is *'si opposées'*. In Elucidation xv, he denies that the will is the true cause of the arm's movement, of the mind's ideas, and of other things accompanying its volitions, "for I see no relation whatever between such different things" (LO 669, OC iii. 226). Note that here the phrase *'si differents'* is used not only with regard to mind and body, but also with regard to mind and *idea*! This suggests (but, I admit, only suggests) that the kind of difference or opposition involved in the first instance (*si opposées*) is not the ontological one between unextended mind and extended body. Can it be the kind of difference that necessarily exists between any two distinct individual things, whether of the same ontological type or not?

seem to discuss the kinds of problems which might arise when trying to explain the relationship between two substances of radically different natures—passages, indeed, which are very general, sketchy, and incomplete (since they refer only to the action of body upon mind), and which do not even occur in the three main contexts in the *Search* and the *Dialogues* in which Malebranche is concerned to argue explicitly for his occasionalist theory of causation. If the mind-body problem *is* the problem calling for such a theologically-weighted theory, why not argue so?

III. CORDEMOY: THE WILL AND THE BODY

If Malebranche is the most famous, and perhaps the most important, of the thoroughgoing occasionalists, Cordemoy can at least lay a credible claim to being the first.[36] Moreover, there is no question that Malebranche was significantly influenced by Cordemoy's *Le Discernement du corps et de l'âme*, published eight years before the first edition of the *Search* appeared.[37] By looking at Cordemoy's treatise, then, we can see whether the mind-body problem had a role to play in the early stages of the development of seventeenth-century occasionalism. The answer, as I show, is that at least in Cordemoy's influential work it did not. There is no indication that Cordemoy, who in many respects was a Cartesian, found any serious conceptual difficulties in the claim that the mind acts on the body. His argumentation for occasionalism is quite interesting, since he does find such difficulties in the claim that bodies can act on other bodies (and on minds). This inefficacy on the part of bodies requires, then, the activity of some mind as the cause of the motion of bodies. But Cordemoy's arguments that the mind which performs this role is not the human mind are based on certain contingent facts about the human being which are accessible to everyday observation—that is, we can see that it is just not our minds which move our bodies.

---

[36] Due notice should be taken of Johannes Clauberg (1622–65), the German Cartesian—see his *Conjunctio corporis et animae*, chs 13–16. For a discussion of his influence in the development of occasionalism, see W. Weier, 'Der Okkasionalismus des Johannes Clauberg und sein Verhaltnis zu Descartes, Geulincx, Malebranche', *Studia Cartesiana* 2 (1981), 43–62; and A. G. A. Balz, 'Clauberg and the development of occasionalism', 2 pts, *Philosophical review* 42 (1933), 553–72; 43 (1934), 48–64. Moreover, La Forge's *Traité* was published in 1666, the same year as Cordemoy's *Le Discernement du corps et de l'âme*. There is reason to believe that Cordemoy and La Forge discussed many of the relevant issues. See P. Clair, 'Louis de la Forge et les origines de l'occasionalisme', *Recherches sur le XVIIème siècle* (1976), 63–72, for a discussion of the historical significance of La Forge in the development of the doctrine.

[37] Malebranche cites the sixth Discourse of the *Discernement*, 'De la distinction de l'âme et du corps', at *Search*, I. x. 1 (LO 49, OC i. 123).

Cordemoy's argument that bodies cannot act on other bodies, and that in order to find the "true cause" of the motion of bodies one must "seek outside bodies themselves", follows "the method of the Geometers" and proceeds a priori from certain definitions and axioms. The first axiom states that nothing has "from itself" (*de soy*, i.e. essentially) that which it might lose while remaining what it is. Thus, since any body can lose its movement while not ceasing to be a body, no body is the source of its own movement. Nor, then, is any body the first cause of the motion of bodies, since such a first cause would have to have motion from itself. Thus it must be a mind which is the "first mover" of bodies, since there are only two sorts of substances—mind and body (third axiom). And this mental first cause must also be that which continues to move bodies, since (by Cordemoy's fifth axiom) an action can be continued only by the agent which initiated it. Thus, given the nature of bodies (i.e. what belongs to them essentially and what does not) and of causation, it is necessarily the case that bodies have no motive force in themselves, no efficacy to move themselves or to be the true cause of motion in another body.[38] Note that, while real body-body interaction is here ruled out on conceptual grounds, Cordemoy apparently has no problem with the claim that mind acts on body. In fact, his strict dualism (in his third axiom he states that "we can conceive only two kinds of substances, namely Mind . . . and Body") *requires*, in the context of the above argument, that mind-body interaction be not only conceivable, but also actual and ubiquitous.

The question remains, however, as to the identity of the mind(s) which is the source of motion in bodies. And here the character of Cordemoy's argumentation changes. While he states at first that the problem here is similar to that regarding body-body interaction, in that the human mind "cannot" be the cause of the movements of the body with which it is united, his arguments never establish *this* claim. Rather, Cordemoy proves only that our mind *is not* the cause of our bodily motions. As he notes, our own "weakness" (*foiblesse*) demonstrates to us the inefficacy of our mind upon our body.[39]

All of Cordemoy's evidence for this conclusion is taken from what he sees as the general independence of the body from the will and the will's general lack of control over the body. First, there are the involuntary movements of the body which both precede that body's being animated by a soul and cease before the soul has abandoned the body in death. These movements (e.g. the circulation of the blood, the beating of the heart) clearly do not obey our will,

---

[38] Discourse IV, pp. 135–9. In a subsidiary remark he claims that since the movement of body *B* is a state (*état, façon d'être*) of that body, *B* (when colliding with body *C*) cannot be the cause of *C*'s subsequent movement, since "the state of one body cannot ever be passed on to another" (p. 138; see also Discourse V, p. 150).

[39] Discourse IV, p. 143.

since by simply willing them to stop or change we can do nothing to affect them. Second, old age, exhaustion, and other conditions make it clear that, even with those movements which we would consider "voluntary", the body is not sufficiently subordinated to our will. "It is in vain that an old man desires to walk more quickly, or that a drunkard wills to walk a straight line; and anyone whose hand is frozen desires uselessly to move his fingers." Sleep overcomes us in spite of ourselves, and we often shiver no matter how hard we will to cease. In other words, we simply do not have the control over our bodies that we ought to (and would) have were our will the true cause of the body's motions. Thus, "if there remains any legitimacy to the claim that the soul moves the body, it is in the same sense that it can be said that a body moves another body".[40]

The mind, then, which is responsible for all motions in all bodies—animate and inanimate—is the sovereign mind (*Esprit souverain*) of God. Mind-body "interaction" is simply the constant activity of God's necessarily efficacious will whereby there is maintained a reciprocal correspondence between mental states and physical states. On the occasion of a volition in the human mind, the human body is moved by God accordingly. On the occasion of certain motions in the body, specific thoughts are caused in the mind, all in conformity with the laws God has established.

Nowhere in the arguments Cordemoy offers for this occasionalist account of interaction—indeed, nowhere in the *Discernement* at all—is there a trace of concern for the specific mind-body problem. In fact, Cordemoy several times insists that "the action of minds upon bodies *should not be thought more inconceivable* than that of bodies upon [bodies]", and he attributes the popular belief in such a greater inconceivability to a failure to consider the matter "exactly" and carefully.[41] To be sure, in both cases interaction is only apparent and not real. But for Cordemoy there is no *conceptual* difficulty peculiar to the mind-body case. As I have shown, the arguments that he presents against interaction all show only that mind and body do not, in fact, interact (i.e. the mind does not cause motions in the body; although he establishes his point in the other direction by showing that body is necessarily incapable of acting on anything), and are based on the contingent circumstances of the union of the two substances in a human being. None

---

[40] Discourse IV, pp. 140–42. Cordemoy does use one very brief argument which does not appeal to "facts" in this way and which does (to his mind) establish the conceptual "cannot" claim: If we could move our bodies, then the total quantity of motion in nature could be increased indefinitely, and the order of nature established by God would be upset (*troublé*).

[41] Discourse V p. 151, emphasis added: "A considerer la chose exactement, il me semble qu'on ne doit plus trouver l'action des esprits sur les corps plus inconceivable, que celle des corps sur les [corps]." See also 149: "Sans doute il n'est pas plus mal-aisé de concevoir l'action des esprits sur les corps, ou celle des corps sur les esprits, que de concevoir l'action des corps sur les corps."

rely on any special inconceivability stemming from the essential unlikeness of mind and body.[42] More generally, there does not appear to be any evidence for the view that Cordemoy was attracted to occasionalism as a solution to the mind-body problem, or that he even recognized the existence of such a problem. Like Malebranche, he found mind-body interaction as problematic (or, alternatively, as "conceivable") as body-body interaction. But the root of this problematic was not any inconsistencies generated by Cartesian dualism *per se*.

IV. GEULINCX: KNOWLEDGE AND CAUSATION

While Geulincx is usually cited as a central figure in seventeenth-century occasionalism, there is no evidence that his views on causation play any significant role in the development of the doctrine. In fact, his most important philosophical work and the one in which he presents his arguments for occasionalism, *Metaphysica vera*, does not appear in print until 1691, years after the theories of Cordemoy and Malebranche have been published (and twenty-two years after Geulincx's death). None the less, historians of philosophy do (and ought to) look at Geulincx for an understanding of occasionalism. And it seems proper, for this reason, to examine whether we find in his account any evidence for the claim that occasionalism was offered to solve the mind-body problem, hence any evidence to justify the traditional story.

Like Malebranche and Cordemoy, Geulincx is unconditionally committed to Cartesian dualism: "I do not recognize, nor is there, a third kind of being besides extension and thought."[43] Geulincx is also a thoroughgoing occasionalist—mind cannot act on body; body cannot act on mind; and body cannot

---

[42] McCracken, in his study of Malebranche, claims that "Cordemoy also argued that since mind (a thinking, unextended substance) and body (an extended, unthinking substance) have no common attribute, neither can be supposed to produce effects in the other; this too must be done by God" (*Malebranche*, 95). But in the pages from Cordemoy that McCracken cites, I cannot find any such argument. McCracken may have in mind a passage where Cordemoy claims that "a thing only acts on another thing in so far as the former can bring some change to the latter according to its nature [*suivant sa nature*]. Consequently, if a body acts on a mind, it cannot be by causing in the mind any change of motion, figure, or parts; for this mind has none of these things. No more can it be that if this mind acts on a body, it is by causing any change of thought therein, for this body has no thought to begin with" (p. 149). But Cordemoy's conclusion from this is *not* that there is a reason why minds and bodies cannot interact, a special reason which is different from the reason why bodies cannot interact. Rather, his point is that what mind-body "interaction" comes to is that thoughts (and not motions) occur in the mind when there are motions in the body, and motions (and not thoughts) occur in the body when there are thoughts in the mind. In other words, the "effect" in the mind from bodily motions will *not* be more motions, but rather the kind of effect that accords with the nature of the thing affected—i.e. they will be "mental", thoughts.

[43] *Metaphysica vera* (1691), Pt I, Sexta scientia, in *Opera philosophica*, ed. J. P. N. Land (The Hague 1892), ii. 151.

act on body. God, or an infinite will and understanding, alone is responsible for the changes and affections of things. But none of Geulincx's arguments for this conclusion evince any concern for the peculiarly dualistic conundrum which the mind-body problem represents. Mind-body interaction is ruled out, but for precisely the same reasons that body-body interaction is ruled out, and *not* because there is something particularly incomprehensible about how two radically different kinds of substance could interact.

Geulincx's arguments all rely on an "evident principle" that was seen above operating in one of Malebranche's arguments—namely, the principle of causation which stipulates that, in order for one thing to cause (*efficere*) another, it must *know how* to bring about the effect. As Geulincx insists, "it is impossible for someone to bring something about if they do not know how it is to be brought about. . . . What someone does not know how to do . . . they cannot do [*impossibile est, ut is faciat, qui nescit quomodo fiat . . . quod nescis quomodo fiat, id non facis*]".[44] This epistemic constraint upon causation both necessarily precludes bodies producing effects in minds (as well as on other bodies) and shows that as a matter of fact minds do not produce effects in bodies.

Bodies cannot act on minds (or on other bodies) because they necessarily fail to fulfil the epistemic condition. As non-thinking, inanimate beings, they *a fortiori* cannot have any knowledge required to bring about any effect whatsoever. "Fire, the sun, stones, all of these are only brute existents [*brutos*], devoid of any sense or knowledge [*sine sensu, sine cognitione*]."[45] Hence, if a sensation of warmth occurs in my soul when I am near a fire, the cause of this sensation cannot be the fire itself. It can only be a being who *knows* how and hence who is able to bring about such an effect. (The causal principle also rules out *my* being the cause of the sensation, since it is obvious that I, too, do not have the relevant knowledge of how to generate sensations and passions in the mind, no matter how much I may have learned about human psychology and physiology.)[46]

Minds cannot act on bodies and cannot be the true causes of any physical effects (more specifically, a mind cannot act on the body with which it is united and cannot be the cause of its movements), for the same reasons. When I will to move my tongue, my tongue moves. But I am completely in the dark as to how such movement is initiated in the body by the mind, ignorant of the physiological mechanisms at work and how they hook up with the volition.

---

[44] *Metaphysica vera*, Pt I, Quinta scientia, p. 150. In other words, mind-body relations are an instance of what medieval philosophers called 'equivocal causation'.

[45] Ibid.

[46] "Et qui mihi dico, me calorem non facere, me lumen et motum in praeceps non efficere, quia nescio quomodo fiant, cur non similiter igni, soli, lapidi idem illud improperem, cum persuadem habeam ea nescire quomodo effectus fiant, et omni cognitione distitui?" (ibid.)

Certainly, my body is moved according to my will in various ways: my tongue moves here and there in my mouth as soon as I want to talk; my arms stretch out, my feet move forward, as soon as I want to walk or swim. But it is not I who cause this movement, since I do not know how it is accomplished. With what impudence will I dare say that I did something which I do not know how to do? I do not know how, nor by means of which nerves and by which channels, this motion is to be communicated from the brain to my extremities.[47]

It is God who brings about such movements in the body—not *ad hoc* and arbitrarily, but on the occasion of the requisite event in the mind in accordance with some general law.

As further evidence that mind-body dualism is not the problem here, consider that Geulincx, like Malebranche and Cordemoy, is explicit in claiming that it *is* a mind which is the true cause of motion in bodies (and sensations in my soul)—"a being who knows [*sciens*], who desires [*volens*], that is to say, a thinking being [*cogitans*]".[48] The conclusion that occasionalists reach itself belies the traditional reading of the doctrine.

V. CONCLUSION

The conclusion to be drawn from my argument is not that no one in the seventeenth century offered occasionalism as a solution to the mind-body problem. Arnauld, for example, believed in real body-body interaction, but did not think that the body could cause *mental* states: "the motion of a body cannot have any other real effect than to move another body . . . it cannot cause any effect in a spiritual soul".[49] The source of his scepticism appears to be a concern about how the body could causally engage the mind, since the mind is unextended and thus incapable of coming into local contact with the body. He argues further that, since the soul obviously is not the cause of its own sensations on the occasion of the requisite bodily motions, their source must be God. But Arnauld, as this demonstrates, was an occasionalist only in a very limited sense—he was not committed to occasionalism as a full-bodied account of the nature of causal relations generally, as were Malebranche, Cordemoy, Geulincx, and others. It is these latter thinkers whom we ought to

---

[47] *Ethica*, Pt I, in *Opera philosophica*, iii. 32.

[48] *Metaphysica vera*, Pt I, Sexta scientia, p. 151. For a fuller discussion of Geulincx's occasionalism, see A. de Lattre, *L'Occasionalisme d'Arnold Geulincx* (Paris 1967).

[49] *Examen d'un écrit qui a pour titre: Traité de l'essence du corps et de l'union de l'âme avec le corps, contre la philosophie de M. Descartes* (1680), in *Oeuvres*, xxxviii. 146. Cf. note 2 above. For further discussion of Arnauld's occasionalism, see S. Nadler, 'Dualism and occasionalism: Arnauld and the development of Cartesian metaphysics', *Revue internationale de philosophie* 48 (1994), 421–40.

regard when examining the philosophical motivations for that account. As I have shown, the mind-body problem was not one of them.[50]

Department of Philosophy
University of Wisconsin at Madison

[50] Work on this paper benefited greatly from discussions with fellow participants in the National Endowment for the Humanities/Council for Philosophical Studies Summer Institute in Early Modern Philosophy (1988). I am also grateful to the NEH for the award of a Summer Stipend in 1988, and to Daniel Garber, Donald Rutherford, Richard A. Watson, and M. A. Stewart for their helpful comments. A portion of this paper was read at a colloquium in the Department of Philosophy at the University of Wisconsin at Madison. I thank the participants in that discussion for their comments and questions.

4

F. M. VAN HELMONT:
HIS PHILOSOPHICAL CONNECTIONS
AND THE RECEPTION OF HIS
LATER CABBALISTIC PHILOSOPHY

STUART BROWN

Franciscus Mercurius van Helmont was born at Vilvoorde in Brabant in 1614. His father was the famous medic and "chemist", Jean-Baptiste van Helmont. When the father died in 1644, Francis Mercury signed over his inheritance and spent most of the rest of his life in Holland, Germany, or England. In a number of respects he deserves his reputation as the prototypical "scholar gypsy",[1] and it is perhaps not very meaningful to raise the question of which country he really belonged to. He spent many years in Germany, spoke German fluently, and was there when he died in 1699. But the Netherlands were his base, in so far as he had one; Dutch was his native language, and more of his books were published in Amsterdam than anywhere else, except perhaps in London. In his own person he epitomized the role of the Netherlands as the crossroads of north European culture in the seventeenth century. By 1677 he was already a link between Christian cabbalists in Germany and others in England. And, partly through his own travels and partly through his being in the Netherlands, he was a mutual acquaintance of two very different philosophers who themselves never met—Leibniz and Locke.

The younger van Helmont was not known in his own time primarily as a philosopher but as a "chemist" and a physician. Though he had declined to take on the running of the family estate, he identified himself as his father's son in the world of learning. He was first widely known as the editor of various of his father's writings;[2] but by 1670 he had established a reputation

---

© Stuart Brown 1997

[1] M. H. Nicolson, 'The real scholar gipsy', *Yale review* 18 (1929), 347–63.
[2] *Ortus medicinae . . . edente authoris filio F. M. van Helmont* (Amsterdam 1648).

for himself as both a physician and an alchemist in his own right. His early visits to England were welcomed by Fellows of the Royal Society such as Robert Boyle, who wrote a paper on one of van Helmont's medical preparations.

Van Helmont was personal physician to Lady Conway for much of the 1670s, and this phase of his life is relatively well documented in the *Conway letters*.[3] Though he was by no means always successful in curing his patients, he enjoyed a reputation as a doctor in Germany and Holland as well as in England. The demand for his attentions made him the object of envious attack, as evidenced by the scurrilous satire on him entitled *London's plague from Holland*.[4] Cures attributed to him were still being published after his death in 1698.[5] His main medical book—his *Observations concerning man and his diseases*—was first published in Dutch and then in Latin in 1692. An English translation appeared during his final visit to England in 1693–4 under the short title *The spirit of diseases*.

Francis Mercury, like his father, had the reputation of being an adept. But his interest in alchemy and experimentation generally seems to have declined in the last twenty years of his life. His *An hundred and fifty three chymical aphorisms* is a rather spiritualized account of alchemy in which the author stresses that this science is "the gift of God".[6] It was first published in Latin at Amsterdam in 1688. An English translation was published, with *imprimatur*, in 1688, followed by a second translation in 1690 by one of his English admirers.[7]

This paper does not dwell on the younger van Helmont's career as a physician or alchemist. Nor does it deal, except marginally, with his Quaker connections, the aspect of his life that has been most thoroughly explored by

---

[3] *Conway letters: The correspondence of Anne, Viscountess Conway, Henry More, and their friends, 1642–1684*, ed. M. H. Nicolson (1930); rev. edn, ed. S. Hutton (Oxford 1992).

[4] A copy of this curiosity is to be found in the British Library.

[5] A work entitled *Thesaurus novus experientiae medicae aureus*, including cures by van Helmont, Boyle, and others, was published at Basel in 1704. In the same year, the same publisher also issued *Medicina experimentalis Helmontiana, or The newly discovered and most approved remedies of the excellent and highly enlightened Francis Mercury van Helmont, philosopher and adept*.

[6] This work is commonly credited to J. B. van Helmont. But that possibility seems excluded by the fact that it contains a letter purporting to be from the author, dated Vienna, 2 Sept. 1687. It may have been based on writings by his father; but it seems likely that the younger van Helmont was the author. He sent Leibniz a complimentary copy of the Latin edition.

[7] The full title, as in the 1690 English edition, is *An hundred and fifty three chymical aphorisms, To which, whatever relates to the SCIENCE OF CHEMISTRY may fitly be referred. Done by the labour and study of a country hermite, and printed in Latin at Amsterdam, Anon. 1688*. The 1690 translation was made by one N. N., who may be presumed to be the same N. N. as the author of *A letter to a gentleman touching the treatise entitled Two hundred queries*, a sympathetic presentation of F. M. van Helmont's ideas which had been published in the previous year. N. N.'s reason for producing a second translation is that the one by C. Packe in 1688 was too literal and many had complained they could not understand it. The 1690 edition also republished the Latin.

scholars already.[8] Instead it focuses on the reception of his cabbalistic philosophy and on his connections with philosophers, and with Henry More, Leibniz, and Locke in particular. These connections have not been neglected entirely,[9] except those with Locke.[10] In discussing them I give particular attention to a debate in which all participated, concerning the creation of matter. I hope to bring out how the issues involved are related to those about the mind-body relation as conceived in the seventeenth century. At least in their concern with this problem, the cabbalistic philosophers like van Helmont were addressing the same problems as the Modern philosophers, as Leibniz (and perhaps Locke too) rightly recognized.

As well as concentrating on van Helmont as a philosopher, I deal with a period of his life that has so far been neglected. During this period he was busy about the publication of his own writings and those of like-minded persons. The period began around 1677 and continued unabated for the rest of his life, though he depended increasingly in his old age on the assistance of others. Leibniz was one of those who helped him, and it is possible that this experience helped to confirm the stronger influence of cabbalism in Leibniz's later philosophy.[11]

To begin with, I give a brief account of two central doctrines of van Helmont's philosophy. He published a number of titles in Latin and in German and, in the 1690s, also in Dutch. But the language in which his work is best represented is English. So in the second part of the paper I discuss some of these English publications and try to explain the fact that he was so well represented in a language in which he was by no means fluent. I give some account of his English connections and, in particular, of his relation to Locke and of their common styles of philosophy. Finally, I consider his connection with Leibniz and argue that van Helmont's cabbalistic philosophy had much in common with Leibniz's monadology.

---

[8] Manuscript materials by Dr F. S. Darrow on this topic are to be found in the Friends' Library, London, and at Case Western Reserve University. See also W. I. Hull, *Benjamin Furly and Quakerism in Rotterdam* (Swarthmore, Pa. 1941); A. P. Coudert, 'A Quaker-Kabbalist controversy: George Fox's reaction to Francis Mercury van Helmont', *Journal of the Warburg and Courtauld Institutes* 39 (1976), 171–89.

[9] A. Becco, 'Leibniz et François-Mercure van Helmont: Bagatelles pour des monades', *Studia Leibnitiana*, Sonderheft 7 (1978), 119–41; S. Brown, 'Leibniz and More's cabbalistic circle', in *Henry More (1614–1687)*, *Tercentenary studies*, ed. S. Hutton (Dordrecht 1990), 77–95; Coudert, 'Quaker-Kabbalist controversy'.

[10] E. S. de Beer, in *The correspondence of John Locke* (8 vols, Oxford 1975–89), vols ii–vi, has made available some important documentary evidence not previously taken into account by students of van Helmont. The letters from Furly to Locke are of particular relevance. The *Correspondence* provides evidence, hitherto overlooked by van Helmont's would-be biographers, of his 1693–4 visit to England as well as his previously unremarked friendship with Locke.

[11] Since this paper was written, A. P. Coudert's *Leibniz and the Kabbalah* (Dordrecht 1995) has appeared. Coudert deals with the relationship between van Helmont and Leibniz in some detail, arguing that the development of Leibniz's philosophy in the 1690s was influenced by van Helmont's cabbalistic ideas.

I. TWO CENTRAL DOCTRINES OF VAN HELMONT'S CABBALISTIC PHILOSOPHY

The origins of van Helmont's interest in the Cabbala and in Hebrew studies go back to his childhood (and the influence of his father), and it was probably stimulated further by visits he made to Amsterdam in the 1640s. It is reflected in his first book on the truly natural Hebrew alphabet,[12] which he was working on while imprisoned by the Inquisition in Rome in 1661–2. This interest received a particular boost from his friendship with Christian Knorr von Rosenroth (1636–89). Van Helmont collaborated with him on a number of projects and helped him to bring together the major Latin collection of cabbalistic treatises of the period, *Kabbala denudata*, which appeared in two stages in 1677 and 1684.[13] This collection included, at van Helmont's instigation, a Latin translation of a work attributed to "the eagle of the cabbalists", Rabbi Isaac Luria,[14] whose theme—the revolution of souls through many lives—came to be regarded as van Helmont's chief doctrine. This aspect of the Lurianic Cabbala attracted Christians who were repelled by Calvinistic doctrines of predestination and who repudiated the idea of eternal damnation irrespective of moral desert. Van Helmont thought that proclaiming such an arbitrary and vindictive God would only serve as an obstacle to belief in any God.[15] This is the context to which the doctrine of the revolution of human souls belongs. The idea that we each have twelve lives should not be seen as an isolated conjecture, but as part of a theodicy, an explanation of how there can be evil in a world created by a wholly good God. Van Helmont linked the doctrine of the revolution of souls with that of a kind of progress of the soul and with the eventual salvation of every soul. He was already familiar with the doctrine of transmigration from a Pythagorean context; and it seems clear that one of the chief reasons why he was attracted to the Lurianic Cabbala was that it provided a way of interpreting the Bible as authorizing such a doctrine. Indeed, following a number of Christian neoplatonists of the previous two centuries, van Helmont sought to sanctify Pythagoras and Plato by suggesting that they "conversed with the learned

---

[12] *Alphabeti vere naturalis hebraici brevissima delineatio* (Sulzbach 1667). Knorr von Rosenroth's translation was published as *Kurtzer Entwurff des eigentlichen Naturalphabets der heiligen Sprache* (Sulzbach 1667). A Dutch translation was published in Amsterdam in 1697.

[13] *Kabbala denudata, seu doctrina hebraeorum transcendentalis et metaphysica atque theologica, opus antiquissimae philosophiae barbaricae variis speciminibus referentissimum*, ed. Christian Knorr von Rosenroth (2 vols in 3, Sulzbach 1677; Frankfurt 1684).

[14] This translation, under the title 'De revolutionibus animarum' was included in the 1684 volume of *Kabbala denudata*. The treatise was actually written by Hayyim Vital.

[15] D. P. Walker, *The decline of hell* (London 1964), 144.

among the Jews, and read the Scripture of the Old Testament, out of which they did learn, or receive the best things, which they professed".[16]

One central question in van Helmont's philosophical thinking is, as has already been noted, how to reconcile the existence of evil in the world with belief in an absolutely perfect Creator. For a cabbalistic or Platonic philosopher, this question is closely related to another: how can the existence of crass matter be reconciled with belief in everything originating from a God who is pure spirit?

The solution to the first problem lay in some form of "optimism" in which God becomes a perfect utilitarian, producing the maximum amount of good possible and allowing no more evil than is necessary. In this spirit van Helmont asked, making a characteristic use of the rhetorical question: "Is it not the Nature and end of God's vindictive justice, and indeed of all punishment, to aim at the good of those that are punished? Is not the Nature of all punishment Medicinal?"[17] No soul is ultimately lost. Evil, according to this optimistic solution to the problem, is necessary but ultimately transitory.

There is an analogous solution to the problem of the origin of matter, in which the counterpart to optimism is some form of idealism. Crass matter, being antithetical to God's nature, cannot result from that nature. Van Helmont—like other cabbalistic and Platonic philosophers—thought there was an inescapable logic about that statement. A philosophy that affirms the reality of matter must deny the existence of a spirit Creator. Thus, according to van Helmont, the "Pagan Philosophy" of Aristotle so uplifts matter as to become a form of "Atheism".[18] Following the argument the other way, the cabbalists were quickly led to a denial of matter. As Henry More put it in a summary of their position, they held that "Whatever there really is, is a spirit".[19]

More took it that the cabbalists were committed to denying a creation in the orthodox sense, i.e. a creation *ex nihilo*. The world comes about, according to cabbalistic and Platonic philosophers such as van Helmont, through a process of emanation from the divine nature. He suggested an analogy, as also did Leibniz, with the way our thoughts emanate from our minds.[20] Van Helmont, like Anne Conway but unlike Leibniz, was happy to

[16] F. M. van Helmont, *Two hundred queries moderately propounded concerning the doctrine of the revolution of humane souls, and its conformity to the truths of Christianity* (London 1684), 153. A Latin edition was included in *Opuscula philosophica* (Amsterdam 1690).

[17] Ibid., qu. 141.

[18] Van Helmont, *A cabbalistical dialogue in answer to the opinion of a learned doctor in philosophy and theology that the world was made of nothing* (London 1682), 11. (Originally published in Latin in *Kabbala denudata*, I.)

[19] Henry More, 'Fundamenta philosophiae', in *Kabbala denudata*, I. ii. 293–307, at 293.

[20] In his *Discourse on metaphysics* (1686), sec. 14, for instance, Leibniz remarked that God continually produces substances "by a kind of emanation, as we do our thoughts".

say that God creates "by intrinsical necessity", that the underlying spiritual
nature of the world results from God's nature.[21] But this aspect of cabbalistic
philosophy raised in the minds of the orthodox all the worries about God's
freedom and about pantheism that were notoriously associated in the late
seventeenth century with Spinozism. Such worries were amongst those that
turned More from being an enthusiast for the Cabbala to being a severe
critic.[22]

More wrote a piece for the 1677 volume of *Kabbala denudata* entitled
'Fundamenta philosophiae', in which he first summarized in sixteen axioms
what he took to be the cabbalistic theory of the origin and ultimate nature of
the world and then subjected it to a critique. Knorr von Rosenroth included
it, but also included a reply from van Helmont (307ff.) which is in the eirenic
and undogmatic question-and-answer style that he was later to develop
further. It is a dialogue between someone called "compiler" and a "cabbalist"
who presumably speaks for van Helmont himself. It was the first of van
Helmont's works to be published in English, appearing in translation in 1682
under the title *A cabbalistical dialogue in answer to the opinion of a learned
doctor in philosophy and theology that the world was made of nothing.*

The first of More's cabbalistic axioms was the principle "*ex nihilo nihil
posse creari*"—"Nothing can be created out of nothing". Van Helmont puts a
proto-Kantian construction on the principle, claiming that the word '*ex*' is
confined in its application to material causes and effects. In general, however,
he is willing to make use of similar abstract principles. The impossibility of
God's directly producing matter is defended on the basis of the principle that
"an efficient cause . . . cannot produce anything altogether unlike unto
itself" (*Cabbalistical dialogue*, 10). Van Helmont's solution is put forward as a
hypothesis: "Academically, and for Experiment sake; nor", he adds, "do I
require assent to them from any whatever" (17). His hypothesis is that spirits
emanate from God immediately, but that these spirits undergo a process of
degeneration. These "single . . . Spiritual . . . beings" or "Monades"
coalesce or congeal together at some stage during their degeneration, thus
forming matter (4). That is how the material world comes into being.
Material things are coalitions of monads in a fallen state from which they will
in time be freed. The history of the material world is thus only one stage in
the history of the universe, which is ultimately a history of immaterial beings.

Both the "optimism" and the immaterialism of cabbalistic philosophy were
in tune with some trends in the late seventeenth and early eighteenth
centuries, and provide links with the mainstream of philosophical thinking in
the period. The Christian cabbalists were also concerned with finding a
Biblical warrant for such ideas. Not surprisingly, Platonists such as More and

---

[21] *Cabbalistical dialogue*, 6.
[22] Coudert, 'Quaker-Kabbalist controversy'.

Conway could be drawn into taking an interest in the more esoteric aspects of the Cabbala. It seems that van Helmont brought Lady Conway to regard the project of the *Kabbala denudata* as of the highest importance. Her letters in the mid-1670s are full of her interest in the project and of her concern lest Knorr von Rosenroth ruin his health through overwork and so put its completion in jeopardy. Yet her book shows that she was not only a patron but an able philosopher in her own right.[23] The full title of that book, which she produced in note form, is *The principles of the most ancient and modern philosophy concerning God, Christ, and the creatures, viz. of spirit and matter in general: Whereby may be resolved all those problems or difficulties, which neither by the school nor modern philosophy, by the Cartesian, Hobbesian or Spinosan, could be discussed.* Conway's notes were eventually edited by van Helmont, translated into Latin and published in Amsterdam in 1690. This book was then retranslated into English and published in London in 1692. It was no doubt indebted to discussions with van Helmont, and the extant versions undoubtedly bear some traces of his editorial additions.[24] But the conception of the project and of its connection with the agenda of "Modern" philosophy is one which she owed, if to anyone in particular, to her earlier mentor in philosophical matters, Henry More.

By the time Anne Conway died in 1679, her previously close relationship with More was strained. More blamed van Helmont for drawing her away from the Anglican Church and into the Society of Friends. By this stage the two men, who had previously gained much from each other's company, had ceased to have any association. Van Helmont had, as we shall see, begun to write and publish his own cabbalistic philosophy. After Lady Conway's death, he lost his base in England and returned to wait on the Palatine Princess Elisabeth at Herford, who was then terminally ill.[25] Although his main period of residence in England was by this time over, he had by no means finished with the English. Indeed, although his own English was poor, van Helmont's cabbalistic philosophy is better represented by publications in the English language than any other. I shall now try to explain this anomaly.

[23] Van Helmont published Conway's *Principia philosophiae*, together with a work entitled *Philosophia vulgaris refutata* and his own *CC Problemata de revolutione animarum humanarum*, in *Opuscula philosophica* (1690). The English translation was made by one J. C., who had sought van Helmont out in Holland to see what books he could have permission to translate. This J. C. is almost certainly J. Clark, MD, who translated another of the *Helmontiana*, called *Seder olam, or The order of the ages*, "upon the Leave and Recommendation of F. M. Baron of Helmont".

[24] The task of sorting out the extent of van Helmont's editorial additions has not yet been attempted in earnest. But clearly the references to the 1684 *Kabbala denudata* cannot have been made by Conway herself. There is a new, briefly annotated, translation of Conway's work by A. P. Coudert and P. Corse (Cambridge 1996).

[25] Earlier in life van Helmont had been a courtier, and his connection with the Palatine Princesses and with Prince Rupert was of long standing. His visit to England in 1672 was initially on a mission on behalf of their mother, Princess Elisabeth of Bohemia, for whom he sought to obtain a pension from her nephew, Charles II.

II. THE PUBLICATION OF VAN HELMONT'S
CABBALISTIC PHILOSOPHY, 1677–99

In the period after 1680, van Helmont went out of his way to publish in English. From his own account, it seems that he judged that English readers would prove to be particularly receptive to his ideas. In coming to this conclusion, he was clearly encouraged by his stay at Ragley Hall in the 1670s. But More and Anne Conway were not the only people he found sympathetic to his way of thinking. One Samuel Richardson had written a book denying the eternity of hell—a book which van Helmont later reissued in Dutch translation.[26] There had been books attacking and defending reincarnation in the 1660s.[27] Van Helmont's ideas may have been controversial, but they were not strange in the English world of letters, and there seems to have been some vogue for them. Indeed, they seem to have been quite widely accepted in English Quaker circles, at least until the Friends began to be more preoccupied with orthodoxy. And it was his English Quaker connections who first encouraged him to publish in England and gave him the necessary assistance.[28] It is likely that the Quaker George Keith and even Conway herself helped to produce the Latin text of *A cabbalistical dialogue*. Keith certainly helped to produce *Two hundred queries*, a work that also dates from van Helmont's association with the Conway home at Ragley Hall but which was not published until 1684.[29] The Latin text of this work was, according to van Helmont, "translated into the English tongue beyond the seas, by a lover and searcher after hidden truth", and he seems to have brought the English manuscript with him to London in the early 1680s. It is not known who this

[26] Samuel Richardson, *A discourse on the torments of hell, the foundations and pillars thereof discover'd and remov'd* (1660).

[27] Henry More was willing to entertain the transmigration of souls as a probable hypothesis, as was his friend Joseph Glanvill in his *Lux orientalis* (1662). There were also books written in opposition to it, such as Samuel Parker's *An account of the nature and extent of the divine dominion and goodness, especially as they refer to the Origenian hypothesis concerning the pre-existence of souls* (1666).

[28] Amongst Friends from whom van Helmont received hospitality were Benjamin Furly in Rotterdam and James Claypoole in London (Hull, 117). Quakers who set down van Helmont's deliverances in writing included George Keith in the case of *Two hundred queries*. Quaker translators included Benjamin Furly in the case of Paulus Buchius's *The divine being and its attributes, philosophically demonstrated from the Holy Scriptures, and original nature of things. According to the principles of F. M. B. of Helmont* (1693), and Caspar Kolhans in the case of van Helmont's *Paradoxal discourses* (1685). Quaker publishers included Benjamin Clark in the case of *A cabbalistical dialogue*. Thomas Hawkins and Sarah Hawkins published *The divine being* and three other *Helmontiana* in the early 1690s.

[29] Van Helmont seems to have communicated his meaning in a mixture of languages and Keith put it down in writing, probably in Latin. In van Helmont's eyes the result involved contributions from Keith himself, perhaps for the sake of order or clarity. Keith later admitted having put van Helmont's thoughts in writing but denied being in any sense the author.

"searcher after hidden truth" was—though it may have been Benjamin Furly, the English Quaker who had made his home in Rotterdam.

Van Helmont's English Quaker connections included some printers, and a number of his London publications, including his first, were from the presses of known Quakers. He seems not to have found it so easy to publish books in Amsterdam. Van Limborch wrote to Locke in 1685 that van Helmont had returned from four years in England and was eagerly looking for someone to print the Latin manuscript of *Two hundred queries*.[30] But it was not until 1690 that the Latin version of this work finally appeared in the trilogy *Opuscula philosophica*. It was appropriate that it should have been published together with his edition of Conway's *Principia philosophiae*, since she was the "Person of Quality" at whose desire he and Keith had produced *Two hundred queries* in the first place.

As these cases illustrate, it is not always easy to decide how far, if at all, van Helmont can be said to be the author of a work that bears his name. There are also various anonymous or pseudonymous works with whose publication he was closely associated. Since he acted *in loco auctoris* in relation to certain works of which he was not the author, printers sometimes used his name as if he were. And in the case of certain other works of which he was actually the author, he adopted a pseudonym or did not give any name. In such confusing circumstances there is no consensus about the precise list of genuine van Helmont writings. There is a use, therefore, for the wider term *'Helmontiana'* to refer to writings van Helmont sought to publish or whose publication he encouraged, as well as those of which he was in some sense or to some extent the author.

Typical of the *Helmontiana* is a translation from the Latin published in London in 1684 and entitled *A dissertation concerning the pre-existency of souls*. The title page advertises the work as originally written "several years since, by the learned C. P. and now made English by D. F. D. P. upon the recommendation of F. M. H. their friend". "D. F." is possibly Dr Daniel Foote, a former Anglican clergyman who had been ejected from his living. Foote either wrote down or translated van Helmont's unpublished 'Observations', in which many of the anecdotes about him are related.[31]

Van Helmont seems to have had no difficulty in persuading people to co-operate in his publishing projects, either as scribes, ghost-writers, or translators. Furly never entirely forgave him for spiriting away Caspar Kolhans, who assisted van Helmont with some of his Dutch writings in the early 1690s. But in some cases he did not even have to ask for help. "J. B.",

---

[30] De Beer, no. 836.

[31] British Library, Sloane MSS 530. The manuscript dates from *c.* 1682. Foote's later involvement with Locke's "Dry Club" is noted below.

the scribe/ghost-writer for *Paradoxal discourses*,[32] was one of two would-be disciples who had sought van Helmont in Holland in 1684 and took the trouble to locate him in England.[33]

Paradoxal discourses is not van Helmont's best philosophical work. Locke could not make it out;[34] and even Leibniz was willing to dismiss it as largely unintelligible.[35] Given the curious circumstances of its production, perhaps not too much weight should be put on it, though it may throw some light on van Helmont's method of philosophizing about which J. B. and his friend had interrogated him. The method he adopted was, as J. B. put it, "an ancient Philosophical way of discussing, propounding all his Matters in Queries" ('Preface to the courteous reader'). J. B. and his companion had quizzed van Helmont about his methodology and reported the philosopher's replies. Van Helmont invited them to imagine that the true philosophy had been contained in a crystal ball called 'Know yourself' but that this had spitefully been broken in pieces, resulting in the fragmentary observations we make of Nature. All things in Nature "belong to and agree with one another", according to van Helmont. Most of those who called themselves philosophers were "without experience" and merely bickered about words. The true philosopher was like a judge who sought to piece together the truth from those who had experience of what they were talking about and who therefore were witnesses to at least part of the truth. It was because he believed that those who looked to him for the truth already possessed it, at least in part, that van Helmont made a practice of answering questions with questions. The style was deliberately undogmatic, hypothetical, "peaceable", and conversational.

Although he was often assisted in the preparation of his manuscripts, van Helmont did write some of them himself. He wrote a short exposition of the first chapter of Genesis in German (published in English translation with *A cabbalistical dialogue*), and it may be that some of his Dutch manuscripts were

[32] *Paradoxal discourses . . . concerning the macrocosm and microcosm or the greater and lesser world, and their union. Set down in writing by J. B.* (1685). There were Dutch and German editions (Amsterdam 1690, Hamburg 1691).

[33] One, who would have written it up in Latin, was said to have succumbed to the English weather and for this reason there was no Latin edition. The other visitor from the Continent, known only as J. B., made a point of following van Helmont's natural mode of discussing philosophical matters in the German text he prepared. "A Hollander" translated this German text into English and it was published in 1685.

[34] Furly wrote to Locke in 1692 that van Helmont's book "is fitter to be read by one that understands his philosophy beforehand" and that this was the reason for Locke's difficulties (De Beer, no. 1480). Were Locke to read a Dutch account of van Helmont's philosophy (*Aan merdingen van Fr: mer: van Helmont*, 1692), he could then read the earlier work "with more fruit".

[35] In his *New essays on human understanding*, Leibniz has his own spokesman express some agreement with van Helmont ("our friend"), but concedes that he was "otherwise full of meaningless paradoxes" (Leibniz, *Sämtliche Schriften und Briefe*, Akademie edition, VI. vi. 72).

straightforwardly dictated. But it seems that he had something of a reputation for relying on others in producing his books, more than someone should who claimed to be their author. Late on in life, he was encouraged to attempt a fuller cabbalistic account of the early chapters of Genesis. When the Latin edition of this work first appeared, Furly had sent a copy to Locke, noting that whoever drafted the Latin text used "High Dutch" (i.e. German) when slipping into the vernacular.[36] Van Helmont was likely to be caught out, Furly feared, in falsely pretending to be the author of a work that had actually been written by a German. His guess as to the real author was Knorr von Rosenroth, "with whose Plumes", as Furly put it, "the good old man decks himself".[37] In one respect this guess was far out, since Knorr had died eight years previously. But Furly was right in supposing that a German had been involved in drafting the work. That person was none other than Leibniz.[38]

Van Helmont's publishing activity in the period 1677–99 was impressive. In the English language in particular he had no fewer than nine pieces of his own published, and instigated the translation, if not the London publication, of six or seven books by others.[39] He also published frequently in German. But his London publication list is only rivalled by what he published in Holland. Most of his Latin and Dutch publications were printed in Amsterdam and most of what he wrote appeared in either Latin or Dutch,

---

[36] [F. M. van Helmont and G. W. Leibniz], *Quaedam praemeditatae et consideratae cogitationes super quatuor priora capita libri primi Moysis* (Amsterdam 1697). This work was published in Dutch as well as German in 1698. It was translated into English as *Some premeditate and considerate thoughts on the first four chapters of the first book of Moses called Genesis* (1701).

[37] De Beer, no. 2287.   [38] Becco, 'Leibniz et van Helmont'.

[39] In addition to the principal titles already cited, there were, of van Helmont's own writings, the following: 'A rabbinical and paraphrastical exposition of Genesis 1' (bound in with *A cabbalistical dialogue*, 1682); 'Appendix on the education of children' (bound with *Two hundred queries*, 1684); *An hundred and fifty three chymical aphorisms* (1688, discussed above); *The spirit of diseases; or Diseases from the spirit: laid open in some observations concerning man and his diseases* (1694); 'A few questions by way of exposition on each chapter of the Revelation of St John' (appended to *Seder olam*, 1694); 'An appendix of several questions with their answers concerning the hypothesis of the revolution of humane souls' (added to Buchius's *The divine being*, 1694). (It was van Helmont's custom, when he published works by others, to add a work of his own.) The posthumous translation of the collaborative work with Leibniz is likely to have been the initiative of one of van Helmont's English admirers.

Works written by others, but with whose translation and English publication van Helmont was in various ways associated, include the following, most of which have already been referred to: *A dissertation concerning the pre-existence of souls* by C. P. (1684); *Collectanea chymica* by J. B. van Helmont (1684); *The principles of the most modern and ancient philosophy* by Anne Conway (1691); *The vulgar philosophy refuted* by J. Gironnet (this title is referred to by William Clarke in a letter to Locke (De Beer, no. 1765); the Latin version was included by van Helmont in his *Opuscula philosophica* of 1690 and it is reasonable to expect he would have wanted to see it translated into English, but I have been unable to find a copy); *The talking deaf-man* by J. C. Amman (1692); *Seder olam* (anon., 1694); *The divine being* by Paulus Buchius (1694).

and sometimes both. Prior to 1690 he does not seem to have published in Dutch, but in the 1690s he seems to have published in Dutch rather than Latin. (He even had plans for a Greek-Dutch *en face* edition of the New Testament.) But, because what he published in Holland was in one or other of two languages and what he published in London was always in English, his work in the period after 1677 was much better represented in English than any other single language. This puts in perspective the extent to which van Helmont saw England as a specially fertile soil for his cabbalistic philosophy.

III. VAN HELMONT AND JOHN LOCKE

Locke would have long known the name of J. B. van Helmont, and may have met the son first in the 1670s, when Francis seems to have been involved with Boyle and others interested in iatrochemistry. But they were certainly acquainted by the late 1680s, when both were in Rotterdam and part of Benjamin Furly's circle and involved in his Lantern Club. They became good friends, and van Helmont spent much of the winter of 1693–4 as Locke's guest at the home of the Mashams at Oates. Locke seems to have retained a great affection for van Helmont and pressed Furly for news of him after van Helmont had left England for good in 1694.

Locke's library eventually contained seven *Helmontiana*, including the English editions of *A cabbalistical dialogue*, *Two hundred queries*, *Paradoxal discourses*, and the systematization of van Helmont's views called *The divine being and its attributes*. Van Helmont was apparently generous with presentation copies and it is reasonable to believe that some of the *Helmontiana* in Locke's library were presented to him by van Helmont himself, including his copy of *The divine being*, which was published in 1693 during van Helmont's last visit to England. Two of the Latin *Helmontiana* in Locke's collection may also be in this category—van Helmont's own *Observationes circa hominem eiusque morbos*, and the work entitled *Seder olam* that is generally, but mistakenly, attributed to him.[40] He would have been able to bring copies of the Latin editions of these works with him to Oates in October 1693. But the English editions were not published until 1694, probably after van Helmont had returned to London.

The letters from Furly to Locke assume that their reader will share their writer's good-humoured detachment about van Helmont's belief in reincarnation. And Locke seems generally to have been further removed from van Helmont's religious philosophy than Leibniz was. Leibniz, as we shall see in the next section, took an interest in cabbalistic theories of emanation

---

[40] Leibniz conjectured that this was the work of one of van Helmont's medical friends.

and, though not without qualification,[41] can be said to have held some such theory himself. Locke, by contrast, defended the creation *ex nihilo*, a doctrine frequently criticized in van Helmont's writings but particularly in *A cabbalistical dialogue*. Locke's treatment of the creation *ex nihilo* in the *Essay*, though it evidently reflects discussions with others, does not seem to be a direct response to van Helmont. He does mention an objection to the creation *ex nihilo* with which van Helmont would have agreed. Locke expresses this objection in his own way by saying we cannot conceive how God could have created matter. But whereas van Helmont argued in what might be called a rationalistic manner that what was inconceivable was therefore impossible, Locke's very characteristic response was to deny this inference. The fact that we cannot conceive how something is possible does not mean it is impossible, he thought. Indeed, according to Locke, the mystery of the creation is confirmed many times over in the mystery of how a thought can result in the movement of matter. For the effect of thought on matter, though unintelligible to us, was, according to Locke, "matter of fact, which cannot be denied" (*Essay concerning human understanding*, IV. x. 19).

Locke thought of the problem of the creation of matter as a special case of the problem about the relation of mind and body. "Make it intelligible," he wrote about the mind-body relation, "and then the next step will be to understand Creation" (ibid.). Locke took it for granted that it was beyond our capacity to give an intelligible account of creation. But, unlike the mind-body relation, creation is not properly regarded as "matter of fact which cannot be denied". On the contrary, in the case of creation, it needs to be shown that belief in it is even coherent. Cabbalistic accounts like van Helmont's can be regarded as attempts at producing an account of creation that is at least coherent. In this respect they play the same role and have the same kind of relevance as theodicies.

An attempt was made, interestingly enough, to draw Locke into the controversy that led eventually to the condemnation of van Helmont's cabbalistic ideas by the English Quakers. Matters came to a head on his last visit to England in 1693–4. When van Helmont was staying with Locke and the Mashams at Oates, they were visited by one of his Quaker disciples, William Clarke, and his doctrine of the revolution of human souls seems to have been a topic of discussion. Clarke wrote a book entitled *Eight queries*, in which he had defended van Helmont's view, and he seems to have believed that he and his book could depend on some support from Locke on the strength of their acquaintance at Oates. Clarke had been attacked in a book

---

[41] Leibniz rejected the pantheistic and deterministic tendencies of neoplatonic theories of emanation in favour of a free creation. But this did not deter him from using the word 'emanate' to characterize his own position, e.g. in *Discourse on metaphysics*, secs 14, 32.

published in 1694, entitled *An answer to some queries propos'd by W. C., or, A refutation of Helmont's pernicious error (that every man is often born, and hath twelve ages of tryal allow'd him in the world by God)*. Clarke was extremely upset by this book, and sent a copy of it, as well as his own, to Locke, pleading with him to write him a few lines, even anonymously, that could be used in his defence.[42] Locke's response is not known. What is known is that Clarke and van Helmont were not thereafter vindicated in the eyes of the English Quakers. By 1696 van Helmont was styling himself a "seeker" in a non-sectarian sense.

In his last years van Helmont returned to Brabant to settle his affairs. He found a female relation, one Madame Mermode, who became his devoted disciple. He named her in his will and she quickly made a good marriage. After he died in 1699, Mme Mermode turned to Leibniz for an epitaph for her famous relative. But despite Leibniz's injunctions, she appears to have done little if anything with van Helmont's unpublished remains. In the meantime, Locke had pressed Furly for all the details he could give of van Helmont since he had last seen him.[43] Furly suggested that van Helmont had been taken in by Mme Mermode, and that her motives in professing herself a "proselite" had been "cunning" rather than sincere. It is sad that he may have been right about this. He was more surely right too in judging the tone with which Locke would have been happy for him to conclude his account of the van Helmont story: "This is all that I can inform you concerning him since leaving England, save to say this Lady has a son in whom the Baron is supposed to be revolved already, it being very like him."

The Locke Correspondence throws some additional light on van Helmont's later life. But it raises more problems than it solves. What, in particular, was the basis for the friendship between Locke and van Helmont? Both were physicians with an interest in chemistry. Locke, though he may have had reservations (as Boyle had) about some of van Helmont's prescriptions, probably respected his work in these fields. But the special bond between them seems to have been forged by their common friendship with Benjamin Furly and their membership of his Lantern Club. Such clubs provided enclaves for free speculative discussion of religious matters. They were natural places of resort for those who enjoyed such discussions, but who could not generally engage in them because of the then widespread intolerance of anything that smacked of religious heterodoxy. Locke's fondness for such clubs is shown by the fact that he founded a similar club— the Dry Club—in London on his return. Van Helmont's disciple Daniel Foote was a member and, though there is no evidence of the cabbalist's involvement with the Dry Club, he would surely have been a welcome

---

[42] De Beer, no. 1765.   [43] Ibid., no. 2629.

visitor.[44] In such circles van Helmont could have floated his hypothesis of the revolution of human souls through twelve lives. Locke, for his part, could have aired his thoughts about whether God may have endowed matter with the power of thought. It is a reasonable conjecture (from Locke's manuscripts) that one topic they did discuss together was the question whether the punishments of hell were for the good of the sinner and therefore not strictly everlasting. A fragment in the Locke manuscripts appears to relate to the treatment of this question in *Seder olam*.[45]

This interpretation of the evidence that is available about the relationship between Locke and van Helmont offers a rather different perspective on Locke's *Essay* from the prevailing post-Enlightenment one in which the work appears as a forerunner to more positivistic and "critical" styles of philosophy. But, while Locke clearly was concerned "to examine our own Abilities, and see, what Objects our Understandings were, or were not fitted to deal with" ('Epistle to the reader'), his purpose seems to have been to encourage modesty and toleration in speculative matters. It does not seem to have been to provide a critique on the basis of which speculative systems might be dismissed. This is not the place to divert to the interpretation of Locke's *Essay*. It is sufficient to note that Locke cannot have been merely a bemused spectator of the discussions that were held in the various clubs with which he was associated. For, in the case of his Dry Club, the rules he constructed included one requiring all those present to give their opinion on the matter under discussion.[46]

Leibniz, like Locke, seems to have valued philosophical discussions with van Helmont.[47] Locke was, none the less, too different in his opinions to have been subject to any doctrinal influence from van Helmont. Leibniz, by contrast, was sympathetic to some of van Helmont's cabbalistic ideas and, it is argued in the next section, may have been influenced by them in adopting the radical ontology of his later philosophy.

IV. VAN HELMONT AND LEIBNIZ

In the 1690s, van Helmont took up an old friendship with the Palatine Princess Sophie, by then the Electress of Hanover. Various *Helmontiana* were

---

[44] Some indication of the bond between Furly, Locke, and van Helmont is to be found in Furly's remark: "Could we have your and the Barons good company, it would be very acceptable to us, and could we find, or frame such a society, as we have sometimes spoken of, and you now and again mention, we should have all the content we could wish for" (ibid., no. 1702).

[45] Bodleian Library, MS Locke c. 27, fo. 248.

[46] De Beer, iv. 571.

[47] Leibniz wrote in Nov. 1680: "je luy a parlé assez familierement il y a environ 8 ans, et il a parléz avec ingenûment" (*Sämtliche Schriften*, I. iii. 442).

sent to her, including the Dutch edition of Paulus Buchius's *Divine being* (*Het Gotlyk weezen*), a Dutch translation of Richardson's work denying eternal damnation (*Verhandeling van de helle*), and the Latin edition of *Seder olam*. Van Helmont was, in various ways, responsible for these publications, but was not in any sense their author. The Electress referred them to Leibniz for his comments.[48]

In 1696 van Helmont came to Hanover on a visit lasting several months. He conducted seminars each morning for Sophie's benefit, with Leibniz in attendance. Leibniz himself had first met van Helmont in 1672 and they quickly struck up a close rapport at that time. He had previously been much impressed by van Helmont's conversation. But though van Helmont's writings—like the writings of the cabbalists—contained many "fine thoughts" (*belles pensées*), they lacked "solid proofs" (*preuves assurées*).[49] Leibniz himself was concerned to argue for his ideas in terms he hoped his contemporaries would feel bound to accept. He belonged, as van Helmont did not, in the mainstream of late seventeenth-century philosophy. Van Helmont could only hope to win over those who, for one reason or another, were already inclined in his direction. Leibniz was so inclined and, while such influences should not be exaggerated, van Helmont seems to have made some impact on Leibniz's intellectual development at an important stage. I shall try to explain how this came about.

Leibniz's interest in the Cabbala seems to have been awakened or (more probably) reawakened[50] around the time of his two-month stay at Sulzbach in 1688 with van Helmont's cabbalistic associate, Knorr von Rosenroth. Leibniz was never himself a cabbalist, regarding the affinity of cabbalistic ideas with those of the Platonists as due to the influence of the latter on the former rather than the other way around.[51] But his seeing the cabbalistic philosophy as a form of Platonism explains what it was that attracted him to it, other than curiosity. When van Helmont visited Hanover, he found Leibniz willing to become involved in two of his publishing ventures. In 1697, at van Helmont's request, Leibniz saw to the publication of another edition of the van Helmont

---

[48] *Sämtliche Schriften*, I. xi. 18ff.

[49] This contrast is drawn in a number of ways by Leibniz, sometimes between "sublime thoughts" and "adequate proofs" (I. x. 58) and at other times between "fine ideas" and "solid foundations" (I. xi. 20). Leibniz also employed this distinction in relation to the Cabbala, to some part of which he believed a good sense could be given.

[50] There are many indirect sources through which German philosophy was influenced by the Cabbala, e.g. in the writings of Reuchlin and Boehme; and Leibniz was himself influenced by the "occult" tradition in German philosophy, as is evidenced by his curious 'Aurora' (*Die philosophischen Schriften von Gottfried Wilhelm von Leibniz*, ed. C. I. Gerhardt (7 vols, 1875–90; repr. Hildesheim 1960–61), vii. 54–6). Another source of influence on Leibniz was through his interest in an Adamic language and the art of Raymond Lull.

[51] For instance, see *Praemeditatae et consideratae cogitationes*, 2 (through Philo).

and von Rosenroth German translation of Boethius' *Consolation of philosophy*.[52] Then there was also his considerable involvement in the *Thoughts on the first four chapters of Genesis* already referred to. His own notes on those chapters appear to have been stimulated by his involvement in the van Helmont project and to show an influence on him of the cabbalistic theory of creation.[53]

The cabbalistic theory, as expounded by van Helmont and Conway, is an explanation for the existence of monads as degenerating spiritual particles that somehow give rise to matter. Leibniz appears to have taken over something like this theory. In these notes he denies the scriptural basis for a creation *ex nihilo*, and indeed rejects it as commonly understood. But it can, he goes on to say, be given a "good sense", meaning that there is no material, coexisting eternally with God, out of which the world was made. He concludes that it is right to say, with the author of the Epistle to the Hebrews (11: 3), that the visible is made from the invisible. This line of argument appears to have encouraged him in the thought that matter is a well-founded phenomenon that somehow results from the non-extended monads.

Confirmation of this interpretation is to be found in some 'Animadversions' Leibniz wrote a few years later on J. G. Wachter's *De recondita hebraeorum philosophia*. Wachter had sought to establish that Spinoza himself was a cabbalistic philosopher, and this suggestion seems to have revived Leibniz's interest in Spinoza. The cabbalists and Spinoza agree, Leibniz notes, that there is no way in which God could have created corporeal mass as the foundation of the world. Leibniz's observation is this:

There is some truth in these words but I think the matter has not been understood adequately. Matter does really exist. But it is not a substance, since it is an aggregate or resultant of substances.[54]

Leibniz seems here to be agreeing with the cabbalistic and Spinozistic argument that the world cannot be fundamentally material. What he here (and elsewhere) rejects is the suggestion (of the cabbalists) that matter does not exist at all, or (of Spinoza) that there could not have been a creator of the material world. His is the middle position adopted by van Helmont and Conway, that the fundamental realities of the universe—what all three call 'monads'—are spirits or spirit-like entities that emanate from God, and that the material world is somehow constituted by them or results from them. The material world is, in Leibniz's later phraseology, nothing more than a phenomenon,

---

[52] In sending a copy to the Electress Sophie, Leibniz remarked in a covering letter that "Mr Helmont has a particular liking for this book, because he thinks he can detect traces in it of Pythagorean thoughts" (*Die Werke von Leibniz*, ed. O. Klopp (11 vols, Hanover 1864–84), viii. 29).

[53] 'Notae in capita quatuor priora Geneseos secundum principia theologiae cuiusdam singularis, Gen. 1, 1 Creavit', in Leibniz, *Textes inédits*, ed. G. Grua (Paris 1948), 98.

[54] Leibniz, *Réfutation inédit de Spinoza*, ed. A. Foucher de Careil (Paris 1854), 26.

albeit a well-founded one, as a rainbow is. It results from monads in the way that secondary qualities are consequences of primary ones.

The details of Leibniz's account depend on a Modern and reductionist conception of the relation between the primary entities in the universe and the rest. Van Helmont too uses the notion of an appearance, but his image is of spirit appearing in the guise of matter:

> *Matter*, as such, is not a *Spirit*; but only that very Substance it self, which appeareth under the form of *Matter*, *viz.*, in its blindness and darkness, *to wit*, in that its *dull* rest, and privation of its former happiness, that was in sometimes past a Spirit, and yet *is fundamentally* and *radically* such, and will sometime hereafter be such again, as it is said.[55]

There are a number of differences in this account from that given by Leibniz. But both adopted what may be called a "privation theory" of matter. Again there is a parallel, from a neoplatonic view, with the problem of evil. Leibniz may have owed to Augustine the thought that evil is a privation. But its extension to matter was an obvious enough one within the neoplatonic and cabbalist traditions. The passive properties of matter are represented by Leibniz as inherent in created things as such. In the work known as the *Monadology*, Leibniz wrote that the created or derivative monads are produced from God (the original Monad) by "continual fulgurations of the divinity from moment to moment" (sec. 47). But they are "limited by the receptivity of the creature, whose essence is to be limited". Without such "receptivity" the creatures would be as God, "perfect", and therefore "pure activity", having "distinct perceptions" (see secs 49, 60). Having a body, i.e. being material, is linked by Leibniz with being "passive", having "confused perceptions", and being "imperfect". Being material is thus a privation of perfection.

All created monads must, according to this theory, have some matter attached to them. And so, from the point of view of a perfect Creator who is *actus purus*, the existence of *materia prima* can be explained as arising from the inherent limitations of created things rather than from any imperfection in the Creator. "God", Leibniz insists, "cannot deprive a substance of *materia prima*, for He would in that way make it pure activity [*actus purus*], which He alone is" (Gerhardt, ii. 324).

Leibniz had not previously tended to argue for his metaphysical atoms in this way. In the 'New system' of 1695, for instance, he adopts an autobiographical mode of presentation and invites his reader to follow him to his metaphysical atoms via a critique of the "Modern" (particularly, Cartesian) theory of matter. This other way of arguing is the one he continued to think appropriate for the readers of the *Journal des savants*. Yet there need be no inconsistency in his willingness to argue in both ways. And indeed nothing is

---

[55] *Cabbalistical dialogue*, 8, citing Rom. 8: 19–23; Eph. 1: 10; 1 Cor. 15: 28, etc.

more characteristic of Leibniz's mode of philosophizing than his willingness to deploy quite different styles of argument for the same conclusion. At the same time, there seems to have been some shift of emphasis in Leibniz's later writings, in favour of the more radically speculative type of argument.

What then was the influence of van Helmont? At least he was a tributary to a stream of neoplatonic and cabbalist influences on Leibniz's philosophy that became more marked in the last twenty years or so of his life. These influences are evidenced by his use of words like 'emanation' and, later, 'monad'. But I think Leibniz did more than adopt the term 'monad' as an alternate for the more familiar word 'substance'. He already believed that his fundamental substances were produced directly by God—being the indivisible, indestructible, non-extended atoms out of which the universe was constituted. But whereas in his earlier presentations, including the 'New system', these substances are arrived at through an analysis of the material world, there is a new emphasis in his later metaphysics on thinking of the material or phenomenal world as a construction out of the basic atoms or substances. Instead of working back from the public world and common assumptions about material substances, an objective space, and so on, as he had previously tended to do, Leibniz was more inclined to work from the other end, with the radically simplified ontology implied by the thought that all God created were monads. He was now committed to a programme of analysis that he sketched in his reaction to Berkeley:

We do not need to say that matter is nothing, only that it is a phenomenon like a rainbow. Nor do we need to say that matter is a substance, only that it is a result of substances, and that space is no more real than time, namely, just the order of coexisting things as time is that of successive things. The true substances are monads.[56]

Leibniz's detailed analyses of these topics in other later writings are amongst his best work of that period. They are the fruits of a radical ontology which he shared in large measure with the cabbalists.[57]

The fact that little more of van Helmont's cabbalistic philosophy was published in the eighteenth century indicates how short-lived was the favourable reception given to his ideas. Nor is this surprising, if it was as a discussant of philosophy rather than as an author that he was valued by Locke and Leibniz. It was, in any case, the style of his philosophizing that commended his conversation to Locke. Leibniz liked many of van Helmont's ideas, and he was by no means alone in trying to put such ideas on a solid

---

[56] Translated from Leibniz's notes at the end of his copy of Berkeley's *Principles of human knowledge* (1710). The notes were transcribed by W. Kabitz in 'Leibniz und Berkeley', *Sitzungsberichte der preussischen Akademie der Wissenschaften* 24 (1932), 636.
[57] For further details of what Leibniz shared with van Helmont, as well as with More and Conway, see Brown, 'Leibniz and More's cabbalistic circle'.

footing. Thus, if van Helmont seems to us to be a residual figure who belongs more to the age of Paracelsus and Agrippa, his connections with Locke and Leibniz may suggest that we do not yet well understand the late seventeenth century.

Department of Philosophy
The Open University

5

MECHANIZING ARISTOTLE: LEIBNIZ AND REFORMED PHILOSOPHY

CHRISTIA MERCER

I. LEIBNIZ'S WALK IN THE WOODS

There is a well-known passage in which Leibniz describes a critical point in his early philosophical development. He writes to Remond in 1714:

After finishing the Ecoles Triviales I fell upon the moderns, and I recall walking in a grove on the outskirts of Leipzig called the Rosental, at the age of fifteen, and deliberating whether I should keep the substantial forms [*si je garderois les Formes Substantielles*]. Mechanism finally prevailed and led me to apply myself to mathematics. (G iii. 606, L* 655)[1]

Leibniz scholars have made much of this passage. First, they use it as evidence of Leibniz's youthful conversion from scholasticism to mechanism. Second, they sometimes attribute to him a memory lapse and insist that the walk must have occurred at least two or three years later than Leibniz says; that is, in 1663–5 and not in 1661–2.

The two claims are related in an interesting way. According to Willy Kabitz, in his influential book, *Die Philosophie des jungen Leibniz*, Leibniz's decision could not have taken place before 1664. Kabitz's argument for the later date is based on the assumption that, when Leibniz completed his walk, he had converted from the scholasticism of his youth to mechanism. Kabitz maintains that *De principio individui*, which is an exemplary piece of

© Christia Mercer 1997

[1] Citations from *Die philosophischen Schriften von Gottfried Wilhelm Leibniz*, ed. C. I. Gerhardt (7 vols, 1875–90; repr. Hildesheim 1960–62), are signified by 'G' followed by volume and page numbers; from *G. W. Leibniz: Philosophical essays*, trans. and ed. R. Ariew and D. Garber (Indianapolis 1989), by 'AG' followed by page number; and from *Gottfried Wilhelm Leibniz: Philosophical papers and letters*, trans. and ed. L. E. Loemker, 2nd edn (Dordrecht 1969), by 'L' followed by page number. An asterisk is used to indicate a deviation from the Loemker translation. Numerical references to the Leibniz corpus occurring with no initial prefix are to the still incomplete German Academy (formerly Prussian Academy) edition of Leibniz's *Sämtliche Schriften und Briefe* (1923—), identified by series and volume numbers (upper and lower case roman numerals) followed by page numbers (arabic numerals).

scholastic philosophy and which was written in 1663, could not have been composed after Leibniz's transforming stroll and therefore that the walk must have occurred after its composition. Moreover, because Leibniz's next work, *Specimen quaestionum philosophicarum ex jure collectarum* of 1664, includes Aristotelian elements and hence is not a complete break with Aristotelian principles, and because his letter to Thomasius of February 1666 has no Aristotelian elements and so is such a break, we should postpone the walk and "his decision for the mechanical hypotheses until some time in 1665". Therefore, Kabitz concludes, Leibniz was mistaken in saying his decision occurred when he was fifteen: he was in fact at least three years older.[2]

Since its publication in 1909 Kabitz's book has remained the most complete account of the 1660s, and subsequent commentators have on the whole accepted its conclusions.[3] While the exact date of Leibniz's decision is not so important, the assumption made by Kabitz and his followers is, namely, that one cannot be an Aristotelian and a mechanist at the same time and that, in Stuart Brown's words, these philosophies "confronted him as stark alternatives".[4]

This is of course a perfectly reasonable assumption. When Leibniz rejects the substantial forms in favour of mechanism, there is every reason to believe that he has thereby put aside the Aristotelianism of his youth. The conception of individual substance, as a union of matter and an organizing substantial form, stands at the centre of Aristotle's metaphysics. As he claims in the *Categories*, "substances . . . are entities which underlie everything else" and "are the subject of everything else" (2b 15–37). The rest of Aristotle's philosophy assumes this notion. Therefore, when standard mechanists like Descartes and Gassendi replace Aristotle's account with a view of corporeal substance as merely extended stuff, and when they insist that all the qualities of a body can be explained wholly in terms of the subtle motion of its parts, they reject the very foundations of the Aristotelian

[2] W. Kabitz, *Die Philosophie des jungen Leibniz* (Heidelberg 1909), 50–51.

[3] In the fifty years before the publication of Kabitz's book, there were several studies written on Leibniz in Germany, some of which consider the influence of Aristotle. For two of the most interesting of these, both of which treat Leibniz's early years, see J. Jasper, *Leibniz und die Scholastik* (Münster 1898–9), and especially F. Rintelen, 'Leibnizens Beziehungen zur Scholastik', *Archiv für Geschichte der Philosophie* 16 (1903), 157–88; for the entire list, see K. Müller and A. Heinekamp, *Leibniz-Bibliographie* (Frankfurt 1984). During the same period, G. E. Guhrauer compiled his biography of Leibniz which remains helpful: *Gottfried Wilhelm Freiherr von Leibniz: eine Biographie* (2 vols, Breslau 1846). Since the publication of Kabitz's book in 1909, there has been only one systematic study of the period. Besides Kabitz's monograph, the most complete studies remain K. Moll, *Der junge Leibniz* (2 vols, Stuttgart 1978) and A. Hannequin's 'La première philosophie de Leibnitz', *Études d'histoire des sciences* 2 (1908). There has been virtually no work done in English, although E. J. Aiton's impressive biography of Leibniz contains a good summary of the period: see his *Leibniz: A biography* (Bristol 1985), chs 1–2.   [4] S. C. Brown, *Leibniz* (Brighton 1984), 30.

philosophy. Descartes, for instance, well understood that the core of his metaphysics was incompatible with that of Aristotle. He wrote to Mersenne that the Aristotelian philosophy "is so absolutely and so clearly destroyed by means of the establishment of my philosophy alone, that no other refutation is needed".[5]

It is therefore perfectly sensible to interpret Leibniz's Rosental decision as a rejection of the Aristotelian philosophy. In another much quoted passage, Leibniz writes:

I had penetrated far into the territory of the Scholastics, when mathematics and the modern authors made me withdraw from it, while I was still young. I was charmed by their beautiful ways of explaining nature mechanically, and I rightly despised the method of those who use only forms or faculties, from which one can learn nothing. (G iv. 478, AG 139, L* 454)

Such passages and the fact that Leibniz remains committed to mechanical physics throughout the period have been taken to provide ample evidence of his youthful rejection of the Aristotelian philosophy. For most interpreters of the 1660s writings, the only question that remains is one of influence: Leibniz presents the views of several modern authors as though they were his own, so that it has been very difficult to make out whether it was Bacon, Gassendi, Hobbes, or Weigel who was the major source of his philosophy. Some commentators have presented plausible stories for the primary influence of one of these authors;[6] others have taken the sheer number of views expounded and the long list of references as proof that Leibniz is merely an enthusiastic convert to the new philosophy without any clear ideas of his own. In Catherine Wilson's words, Leibniz's early philosophy is "characterized by uncertainties and reversals".[7] Scholars have often noted that Leibniz's early texts are strewn with references to Aristotle, but they have mostly agreed with Hannequin, who described Leibniz's use of the Peripatetic philosophy as a "perpetual violence made on Aristotle". Because of Leibniz's obvious abuse of key features of the ancient philosophy, these

---

[5] *Oeuvres de Descartes*, ed. C. Adam and P. Tannery (11 vols, Paris 1974–83), iii. 470 (henceforth cited as 'AT' followed by volume and page numbers).

[6] Concerning Hobbes's influence on the young Leibniz, see H. Bernstein, 'Conatus, Hobbes, and the young Leibniz', *Studies in the history of science* 11 (1980), 25–37; D. Garber, 'Motion and metaphysics in the young Leibniz', in *Leibniz: Critical and interpretive essays*, ed. M. Hooker (Minneapolis 1982), 160–84. Concerning Bacon, see especially Y. Belaval, *Leibniz: Initiation à sa philosophie* (Paris 1962), ch. 2. For the influence of Gassendi and Weigel, see Kabitz, 53–4; P. Petersen, *Geschichte der aristotelischen Philosophie im protestantischen Deutschland* (Leipzig 1921), 347–8; and especially Moll, vols i–ii. Brown, 31–2, credits Leibniz with Gassendian atomism between 1666–8, as do M. Čapek, in his 'Leibniz's thought prior to the year 1670', *Revue de métaphysique et de morale* (1966), 249–56, and Hannequin, ch. 1.

[7] C. Wilson, *Leibniz's metaphysics: A historical and comparative study* (Manchester 1989), 45.

references have been considered mostly rhetorical and his rejection of that philosophy sincere.[8]

From a survey of the youthful writings, then, it would appear that around 1664 Leibniz rejected the Aristotelianism of his youth and accepted the mechanical philosophy; that he was undecided about the details of that philosophy and hence had no coherent philosophical offering of his own until he produced the two-part *Hypothesis physica nova* and *Theoria motus abstracti* of 1670–71, his first significant publication on topics concerning metaphysics and physics. This is the story that Kabitz first proposes and that most subsequent commentators accept.[9] It is a plausible story, based on reasonable assumptions and careful scholarship.

But it is false. In what follows, I shall claim that when Leibniz emerged from the Rosental grove he was not a mechanist but an eclectic Aristotelian, and that during the 1660s he was engaged in a very definite enterprise, namely, to attempt a synthesis of the ancient and new philosophies, something he managed to do in a brilliant way by the end of the decade.[10] More specifically, I shall argue that in the early 1660s Leibniz did not turn from the Aristotelian philosophy to mechanism, but rather from scholastic to mechanical physics; that his intense (and apparently haphazard) study of the mechanical options during the mid-1660s was motivated by a desire to discover the common denominator of the "new" philosophies so that he could intelligently combine it with the philosophy of Aristotle, and that in 1668–9 he finally achieved the conciliatory goal to which he committed himself

---

[8] See esp. Wilson, 47; Čapek, esp. 254–5; Hannequin, 49.

[9] The vast majority of commentators who discuss the 1660s and who mention the decision in the Rosental after the publication of Kabitz's book agree with him both on the date of the walk and on the nature of Leibniz's decision. See A. Robinet, *Architectonique disjonctive, automates systémiques, et idéalité transcendantale dans l'oeuvre de G. W. Leibniz* (Paris 1986), 8–9; Brown, ch. 3; L 4, 660 n. 2; K. Müller and G. Krönert, *Leben und Werk von Gottfried Wilhelm Leibniz* (Frankfurt 1969), 6; G. Stieler, *Gottfried Wilhelm Leibniz: Ein Leben* (Paderborn 1950), 13–14; D. Mahnke, *Leibnizens Synthese von Universalmathematik und Individualmetaphysik* (Halle 1925), 371–2; K. Fischer, *Gottfried Wilhelm Leibniz: Leben, Werte, und Lehre* (Heidelberg 1920), 38ff. There are some exceptions: e.g. Petersen, 349ff., accepts Kabitz's dating of the walk, but takes the conversion to be less dramatic; while Wilson, 46, AG vii, and H. W. B. Joseph in his *Lectures on the philosophy of Leibniz* (Oxford 1940), 9–10, see Leibniz's decision as a rejection of Aristotelianism, but none the less accept that it occurred when he was fifteen. The most important exception is Belaval, ch. 2, who accepts neither the date nor the conversion. For more on Belaval's position, see note 11.

[10] A few scholars have noted Leibniz's comments about reconciling the Aristotelian and modern philosophies and have credited him with a youthful eclecticism according to which he is collecting ideas. However, none of these studies has attempted an analysis of the 1660s in this light, nor has any articulated the result of Leibniz's eclecticism. See Moll, vols i–ii, *passim*; L. E. Loemker, 'Leibniz's conception of philosophical method', in *The philosophy of Leibniz and the modern world*, ed. I. Leclerc (Nashville, Tenn. 1973), 135–57; E. Hochstetter, 'Leibniz-Interpretation', *Revue de métaphysique et de morale* (1966), 174–92; Belaval, ch. 2; A. Foucher de Careil, *Mémoire sur la philosophie de Leibniz* (Paris 1905), ch. 1.

during his walk in 1661.[11] Moreover, I shall show that Leibniz's first published presentation of his original metaphysics and physics is not the two-part work of 1670–71, but rather his letter to Thomasius of 1669 which he published in 1670 and which contains a presentation of his original theory of substance, one that has previously gone unnoticed and one that Leibniz considered to be thoroughly Aristotelian.[12]

In order to grasp the real significance of Leibniz's Peripatetic decision, we must see it and his subsequent writings in their proper philosophical and historical context. In section II, I set this context; in section III, I show that against this background we can discern in the letter to Thomasius of 1669 Leibniz's real philosophical goals and his first theory of substance; and in section IV, I re-evaluate both the walk in the woods and the texts of the 1660s in this light. I argue that the vast number of references, the wide range of proffered ideas, and the apparent shift in views in Leibniz's early writings have acted as a camouflage of his real intentions; and finally I suggest that his early commitment to a conciliatory philosophy within an Aristotelian framework continues unabated and forms the foundations for the philosophy of the *Discourse on metaphysics* of 1686.

II. MECHANIZING ARISTOTLE

However foreign the landscape may appear to us, when Leibniz emerged from the Rosental grove he was on ground well trodden by his contemporaries. In this section we shall explore that little-known area of overlap between the Aristotelian and mechanical philosophies. Once we recognize that Leibniz, like many seventeenth-century philosophers, intended to reconcile the new mechanism with the thought of Aristotle, the philosophical richness of his early works becomes apparent.

The tradition that is most relevant to Leibniz's philosophical development is that of reformed philosophy. But that tradition itself is best understood in the context of Renaissance humanism and eclectic Aristotelianism. Before turning to the former, it is appropriate to present the relevant facts about the latter.

---

[11] Both Belaval and Hochstetter recognize that, when Leibniz rejects the substantial forms, he has not thereby cast aside the Aristotelian philosophy. But neither author articulates how Leibniz goes on to use the ancient thought.

[12] Both Garber and Moll have presented the outlines of a system in the period of 1668–9, but their interpretations differ significantly from the one I argue for here. Garber, 162ff., takes Leibniz to be a Cartesian, while Moll, vol. ii, *passim*, sees him as a Gassendian atomist. I shall argue in what follows that the original theory of substance is an Aristotelian one; it is this theory that has gone unnoticed.

(a) *Renaissance humanism and eclectic Aristotelianism*

The nature and extent of humanism as a method, tradition, and philosophy have been much discussed.[13] We may bypass these complications and move directly to the two features of that movement that are particularly relevant to our discussion of Leibniz. First, many humanists made a distinction between the philosophy of Aristotle and that of the scholastics. From Petrarca on, they insisted that the thought of the ancient was superior to that of his uncomprehending followers.[14] Second, many humanists practised and preached conciliatory eclecticism. For such philosophers, the assumption was that the diverse philosophical traditions were not as incompatible as they at first appear; the goal was to forge a reconciliation among the worthy schools; the result was a mixture of ancient and modern ideas; and the hope was that the proper synthesis would effect peace among conflicting philosophers. Giovanni Pico della Mirandola (1463–94) is one of the earliest and most important examples of this humanist syncretism. Pico maintained that each philosophical tradition has a share of the truth and that, once that truth is discovered, we will be able to reconcile those traditions into one comprehensive philosophy.[15] For thinkers like Pico, two doctrines that at first seem incompatible may often, after careful study and full analysis, be made to cohere. To twentieth-century sensibilities, the resulting coherence may seem no more than a perversion of the original tenets; to the sincere Renaissance conciliator, the coherence was a step towards philosophical truth and intellectual peace. Such humanists thought nothing of adapting philosophical doctrines to fit their own interests, ideas, and prejudices.[16]

---

[13] For standard accounts of Renaissance humanism, see P. O. Kristeller's *The classics and Renaissance thought* (Cambridge, Mass. 1955) and *Studies in Renaissance thought and letters* (Rome 1956); E. Gilson, 'Humanisme médiéval et Renaissance', in *Les idées et les lettres* (Paris 1932); and E. Garin's *Ritratti di umanisti* (Florence 1967). For the most important recent discussions and for references to the vast intervening literature on the topic, see A. Grafton, *Defenders of the text* (Cambridge, Mass. 1991); *The transmission of culture in early modern Europe*, ed. A. Grafton and A. Blair (Philadelphia 1990); and *The impact of humanism on western Europe*, ed. A. Goodman and A. Mackay (London 1990). For a lengthy discussion of the humanist background to Leibniz, see L. E. Loemker, *Struggle for synthesis* (Cambridge 1972), chs 1–4.

[14] See Petrarca's *De sui ipsius et multorum ignorantia*, a translation of which (by Hans Nachod) appears in *The Renaissance philosophy of man*, ed. E. Cassirer and others (Chicago 1948). In the latter edition, see pp. 53–4, 77, and esp. 136–7.

[15] See especially his *De hominis dignitate* and *Apologia*, in *Opera omnia* (Hildesheim 1969), i. 313ff. and 115ff.

[16] The young Leibniz was familiar with Giovanni Pico and with another widely known Renaissance syncretist, Agostino Steuco (1497/8–1548), whose most important syncretic work, *Perennis philosophia*, he cites. See VI. ii. 137 and also II. i. 176. The mature Leibniz had books by each in his private library: see G. Utermoehlen, *Studia Leibnitiana, Suppl.* 23 (1983), 221–38. For an interesting discussion of the similarities between the methodological assumptions of Leibniz and Steuco, see C. B. Schmitt, 'Perennial philosophy: From Agostino Steuco to Leibniz', *Journal of the history of ideas* 27 (1966), 505–32.

Conciliatory eclectics often had their favourite author, and the favourite of many was Aristotle. Aristotelianism, like Platonism, was very adaptable and formed the core of a wide variety of eclectic philosophies. In this context, it is important to remember that scholastic Aristotelianism was itself eclectic in that it was based on a reconciliation between Aristotelian philosophy and Christian doctrine. L. W. B. Brockliss describes it well when he writes:

it was an Aristotelianism carefully accommodated to the needs of Christianity. Not only were specific Aristotelian assertions such as the eternity of the world rejected on Scriptural grounds, but also Aristotle's general explanatory principles were interpreted in such a way as to fit spiritual as well as material action; the movement of grace as well as the movement of bodies.[17]

With the rediscovery of ancient texts and intellectual traditions, humanist Aristotelianisms multiplied at a rapid rate. One can hardly over-emphasize the variety of uses to which the ancient thought was put during the Renaissance.[18] For example, in his *De intellectu* the Italian Aristotelian, Agostino Nifo (1469/70–1538), forged a complicated synthesis of Aristotelian, Platonic, and Christian doctrines in an attempt to argue that the immortality of the soul could be defended on grounds both of Christian revelation and of philosophical demonstration;[19] and the Cambridge Aristotelian, Everard Digby (1550–92), proposed in his *Theoria analytica* a combination of Platonic, cabbalistic, Hermetic, and occult ideas within a generally Aristotelian framework. According to eclectics like Digby, the goal was to "save" the truth in Aristotle, but also to add to it.[20]

In the Protestant Germany in which Leibniz grew up, the thought of Aristotle was combined with a number of philosophical and theological doctrines. Owing to the anti-Aristotelianism of Luther and the early reformers, the scholastic philosophy of the universities had to be radically reformed. The important sixteenth-century educational reformer, Philipp Melanchthon (1497–1560), managed to forge a synthesis of the writings of

---

[17] L. W. B. Brockliss, 'Aristotle, Descartes, and the new science: Natural philosophy at the University of Paris, 1600–1740', *Annals of science* 38 (1981), 33–69, at 39.

[18] Historians of science and philosophy are beginning to document the complicated history of Renaissance Aristotelianism. For the most important of these, see B. P. Copenhaver and C. B. Schmitt, *Renaissance philosophy* (Oxford 1992), ch. 2; C. B. Schmitt, *The Aristotelian tradition and Renaissance universities* (London 1984), *Aristotle and the Renaissance* (London 1983), *John Case and Aristotelianism in Renaissance England* (Montreal 1983), 'Towards a reassessment of Renaissance Aristotelianism', *History of science* 11 (1973), 159–93; J. McConica, 'Humanism and Aristotle in Tudor Oxford', *English historical review* 94 (1979), 291–317. For related literature, see Schmitt, *Critical survey and bibliography of studies on Renaissance Aristotelianism* (Padua 1971), and the extensive bibliographies in the above texts.

[19] Agostino Nifo, *De intellectu* (1503), I. i. 10.

[20] Everard Digby, *Theoria analytica* (1579), 48. For a discussion of Digby, see Schmitt, *Case*, 47ff.

Aristotle and those of Luther by carefully selecting those bits of Aristotle's writings that did not directly confront reformed theology. The result was an educational programme where theology had replaced metaphysics as the central point of focus and where unthreatening Aristotelian works like the *Ethics* were retained. By the next century the *Metaphysics* had resurfaced and more serious attempts were being made to construct a coherent metaphysical system that also conformed to Protestant theology.[21]

The enormous complexity of the philosophical debate during the second half of the seventeenth century is due to the fact that philosophers inherited both Renaissance humanism and the variety of philosophical sources promulgated by the humanists, while they also had to contend with the new natural science and its mathematical method. There evolved an impressive array of philosophical options and a startling group of eclectic mixtures. One of Leibniz's correspondents, Johann Christoph Sturm (1635–1703), nicely represents eclectic Aristotelianism in seventeenth-century Germany. In his *Philosophia eclectica*, Sturm describes the proper critical eclecticism and claims that a true and coherent system will be constructed out of the most significant authorities.[22] According to Sturm, in order to find what is "most true" we must rid ourselves of sectarian philosophy and seek the knowledge "of the many" (5). Because the proper eclectic philosophy will be constituted of the best part of every philosophical school, only eclecticism can be the "source of true wisdom" (22). Once the wisdom of Plato, Gassendi, Descartes, and "other geniuses" was acquired, the result would be a coherent and true system, and one fundamentally based in the philosophy of Aristotle. As the texts of Sturm and others make clear, seventeenth-century Aristotelians were perfectly capable of accepting many of the new developments in natural philosophy and conforming Aristotelian ideas to them.[23] By the mid-century, at the very time that philosophers like Descartes and Gassendi were crying

---

[21] For the relation between Aristotelianism and Protestantism in northern Europe, see, e.g., M. Wundt, *Die deutsche Schulmetaphysik des 17. Jahrhunderts* (Tübingen 1939), 141–4, and *Die Philosophie an der Universität Jena* (Jena 1932); Petersen; J. Bohatec, *Die cartesianische Scholastik in der Philosophie und reformierten Dogmatik des 17. Jahrhunderts* (Leipzig 1912), esp. 127ff.; E. Lewalter, *Spanisch-jesuitische und deutsch-lutherische Metaphysik des 17. Jahrhunderts* (Darmstadt 1967).

[22] Johann Christoph Sturm, *Philosophia eclectica* (1686), esp. 44–5, 185–6. Sturm's works were widely read. Leibniz refers to him (e.g. I. i. 80) and his works (e.g. VI. i. 186, G iv. 399, 504) throughout his life, but he does not specifically refer to *Philosophia eclectica*.

[23] Recently historians of science and philosophy have begun to document the progressive elements in early modern Aristotelianism and the important role the Aristotelian philosophy played in the development of modern science. See, e.g., C. Mercer, 'The vitality and importance of early modern Aristotelianism', in *The rise of modern philosophy*, ed. T. Sorell (Oxford 1993), 33–67; Brockliss, 'Aristotle, Descartes, and the new science'; I. Düring, 'The impact of Aristotle's scientific ideas in the Middle Ages and at the beginning of the Scientific Revolution', *Archiv für Geschichte der Philosophie* 50 (1968), 115–33.

for the demise of the Aristotelian philosophy, others were calling for its transformation.

(b) *Reformed philosophy*

There evolved throughout Europe, and especially in the Protestant areas of the north, a loosely knit group of intellectuals, whose members often referred to themselves as the "reformers" (*reformatores*) and their philosophy as "reformed philosophy" (*philosophia reformata* or *emendata*). These thinkers were committed to reforming the Aristotelian philosophy in order to make it (or at least their version of it) consistent with the new natural philosophy. The reformed philosophers are best understood in the context of Renaissance humanism and eclectic Aristotelianism with the additional variable of the new mechanical philosophy.[24] Like the early humanists, they were inclined to look at the ancient himself, to distinguish him from his scholastic followers, and to combine Aristotelian ideas with those of other traditions. But, unlike their predecessors, they had had time to digest fully the new proposals in physics and to face squarely the abundance of ever new discoveries (e.g. sun spots) that often seemed to contradict their cherished Aristotle. Many early modern intellectuals had turned to the new philosophy because they were displeased with the scholastic philosophy of the schools[25] and because the new discoveries did seem to argue against Aristotelian principles. But this alternative was considered too extreme by others. For many seventeenth-century thinkers, mechanism was not only a first step towards atheism; it was unacceptable just because of its total rejection of traditional philosophy, most particularly of Aristotle.[26] They maintained that the Aristotelian philosophy did not need to be rejected; it just needed to be reformed. In typical humanist fashion, the need to reform Aristotle often

[24] In the seventeenth century there was a wide range of philosophical options which were called new and modern, but were not versions of atomism or corpuscularianism (e.g. the Paracelsian tradition). For a nice survey of the more important of these, see A. G. Debus, *Man and nature in the Renaissance* (Cambridge 1988). My concern here however is with the new mechanical philosophy.

[25] For a discussion of scholastic education in seventeenth-century universities, see especially L. W. B. Brockliss, *French higher education in the seventeenth and eighteenth centuries* (Oxford 1989); Schmitt, 'The rise of the philosophical textbook', in *Cambridge history of Renaissance philosophy*, ed. C. B. Schmitt and others (Cambridge 1988), 792–804; J. A. Trentman, 'Scholasticism in the seventeenth century', in *Cambridge history of later medieval philosophy*, ed. N. Kretzmann and others (Cambridge 1982), 818–37; P. Reif, 'The textbook tradition in natural philosophy, 1600–1650', *Journal of the history of ideas* 30 (1969), 17–32.

[26] The desire on the part of many philosophers, even those who accepted the mechanical philosophy, to retain as much as possible of the tradition was quite strong. In his fascinating book, *Descartes and the Dutch* (Carbondale, Ill. 1992), T. Verbeek offers several examples of Cartesians who were not prepared to start "from nothing" as Descartes himself proposed, but rather hoped to prove their affiliation with traditional philosophy. Although some were politically motivated, most were sincere (8–9).

took on a moral tone, with suggestions that the teachings of the master must be purified of the degradations to which they had been submitted by his unfaithful and uncomprehending followers. Everyone in this camp agreed that the babbling of the schoolmen must be rejected while the truth of Aristotle be retained.[27]

During the 1660s, Leibniz praises the works of several reformed philosophers, but he is most enthusiastic about the thought of Joannes de Raey (1622–1707).[28] In a letter to his teacher Jakob Thomasius, Leibniz writes that, in the same way that Thomasius had saved Aristotle "from the smoke of the Scholastics", so De Raey in his *Clavis philosophiae naturalis Aristotelico-Cartesiana* shows that "Aristotle wonderfully conforms" to the philosophy of "Galileo, Bacon, Hobbes, Descartes, and Digby" (II. i. 10). Thomasius's response is noteworthy: he criticizes his student for having been too taken by the philosophical opinions of De Raey (II. i. 12).

For our purposes, De Raey's introduction to his *Clavis* is especially interesting.[29] According to De Raey, after the Europeans "lost the works of Aristotle" their understanding of him was due entirely to the translations and commentaries imported from the Arab world. Because the Arabs (and especially Averroes) misunderstood Aristotle and because (at that time) "the Greek language was lost" to Europeans who therefore could not consider "the true Greek codex", the latter unwittingly accepted these bad translations and interpretations. By such means, according to De Raey, Aristotle's philosophy became lost behind the "most perverse and corrupt words of the Arabs". Not only did this general misunderstanding of Aristotle continue among the scholastics; the prejudice against him continued even after the ancient philosophy "was brought to light" and "the thought of Plato, Cicero, Plutarch, Seneca, and similar authors" was understood. Even now, many philosophers reject Aristotelian philosophy without knowing Aristotle's real views. According to De Raey, the great importance of Cartesian philosophy is that it reveals the true meaning of Aristotle's principles. De Raey concludes his introduction by saying that in his book he will uncover the real views of the ancient and show that they are both consistent with Cartesian philosophy and quite unlike what the scholastics have claimed.

---

[27] For Leibniz's most explicit comments on this, see the preface to his edition of Nizolio's *De veris principiis*, esp. VI. ii. 414–27, L 124–8. Like Leibniz, most seventeenth-century philosophers distinguished not just between Aristotle and the scholastics, but also between the good and bad scholastics. For the importance of these distinctions, see Mercer, 'Vitality', 41ff.

[28] Although Leibniz thought of De Raey as a reformer, I do not know that De Raey himself ever used this designation. Verbeek, 8, rightly classifies him as a Cartesian, but also notes that according to De Raey himself his most significant insight is the discovery of the profound similarity between the philosophies of Aristotle and Descartes. For a much fuller discussion of De Raey, his other works, and his influence, see Verbeek, esp. 71ff.

[29] Joannes de Raey, *Clavis philosophiae naturalis Aristotelico-Cartesiana*, 2nd edn (1677). The introduction or *Epistola dedicatoria* contains no page numbers.

The most fascinating feature of De Raey's introduction is that he not only claims that the scholastics and others have misconstrued the real nature of Aristotle's philosophy; he also presents a neat explanation of how such a general misinterpretation came about and why it is now possible to discover Aristotle's real meaning.[30] However incompatible modern mechanism and Aristotelian physics may seem, the incompatibility is only apparent, an unfortunate result of the systematic misunderstanding of Aristotle's thought. In order to discover the correspondence between Cartesian and Aristotelian philosophies, all one has to do, De Raey suggests, is to penetrate through the layers of misinterpretations to the real philosophy of Aristotle. Not surprisingly, De Raey thinks that he has accomplished this task.

De Raey's method in the remainder of his book is to describe what "the schoolmen" say about a crucial element in Aristotle's philosophy (e.g. substance, form, matter), to quote Aristotle (rendered in Latin) on the topic, and then to explain what Aristotle really means. De Raey's chapter on substantial form, entitled 'On substantial form and the soul of man, out of Aristotle, against the Aristotelians', offers a significant example. In this chapter, he argues that the original notion of substantial form is quite different from what it has generally been taken to be. According to De Raey, a substantial form is simply that which is essential, i.e. something that can act as a reason (*ratio*) or essence of a thing, and therefore a substance is simply that which has an essence. Since matter has an essence, it follows that matter is a substance (473–5). In other chapters, De Raey treats the doctrines of Aristotle in a similar way: he begins with a lucid and accurate account of an important Aristotelian notion and then uses it to argue for a position unlike anything accepted by the ancient. Concerning the chapter just noted, for example, while it may be true that a substantial form is most basically an essence, that a substance is by definition that which has an essence, and even (for some scholastics) that matter has an essence, it by no means follows that matter is itself a substance.[31] It is important to emphasize, however, that De Raey does manage to construe intelligently and then put to interesting use

---

[30] As early as Petrarca we find thinkers blaming "the Arabs" for the misunderstanding of the philosophy of Aristotle in the Latin west. See, e.g., Petrarca, in Cassirer and others, *Renaissance philosophy of man*, 140–43. Petersen, 351, maintains that many philosophers in Germany believed that Aristotle had correctly understood what the moderns were putting forward. De Raey's addition to this point is that it is the Cartesian philosophy that allows us to regain the proper understanding of the ancient's thought.

[31] The schoolmen disagreed as to whether matter had its own essence and hence could exist without form. Aquinas thought matter was pure potency and could not (*Summa theologiae*, lib. I, qu. 66, art. 1); Scotus thought matter had a reality distinct from form and could exist without it (*Opus oxoniense*, lib. II, disp. 12, qu. 1); and Eustachius agreed with Scotus with a few added thoughts of his own (*Summa philosophiae quadripartita*, Physica, lib. I, disp. 2, qu. 9). For those seventeenth-century philosophers who wanted to make Aristotle more compatible with the new natural philosophy, the position of scholastics like Scotus and Eustachius was far more attractive than that of Aquinas.

genuine elements of Aristotle's metaphysics in his honest attempt to reconcile the ancient's thought with Cartesian mechanism.[32]

Leibniz refers favourably to other reformed philosophers during his youth, and it is interesting that those whom he mentions range from the somewhat conservative Jean-Baptiste du Hamel to the more radical Kenelm Digby. These reformers differ among themselves concerning the degree to which Aristotle represents the truth and the extent to which they are willing to transform his ideas. Du Hamel, for example, was so committed to the metaphysics and physics of Aristotle as traditionally interpreted that he was prepared to use the mechanical philosophy only in fairly restricted ways. According to Du Hamel, the best the moderns can do is help to "illuminate the ancients". Although he is willing to admit that the mechanical explanations of some natural phenomena are useful, he insists that such mechanical explanations can only go so far. Natural bodies are still composed of matter and substantial form (as traditionally interpreted), and their properties ultimately have to be explained in such terms. Du Hamel remains committed to the *ratio* of Aristotle although he is willing to confirm it by "experience and observation".[33]

At the other end of the spectrum is the English philosopher, Kenelm Digby, who mixes his Aristotelianism with a large dose of atomism. Although he insists that his philosophy is "built upon the same foundations" as Aristotle, who was "the greatest Logician, Metaphysician and universal scholar . . . that ever lived", Digby's Aristotelianism requires a radical transformation of fundamental doctrines of the ancient. Digby apologizes for his departure from Aristotle on a "few points", but insists that he follows in the steps of that "great oracle of nature" and that "the way we take is directly the same solid way, which Aristotle walked before".[34]

---

[32] Verbeek, 72, also thinks De Raey is sincere in his attempt to integrate the Cartesian philosophy "into the philosophic tradition".

[33] My discussion of Du Hamel is based on his *Philosophia vetus et nova ad usum scholae accommodata, Astronomia physica, De meteoris et fossilibus libri duo*, and *De consensu veteris et novae philosophiae*, published together in 1681. See especially *De consensu*, 323–4, 542–3, 718. Leibniz writes about one of Du Hamel's books: "In it he brilliantly explains the hypotheses of some of the best known ancient and recent thinkers and often criticizes them with discernment" (II. i. 15, L 94).

[34] Kenelm Digby's major work is his *Two treatises in the one of which the nature of bodies; in the other, the nature of mans soule; is looked into: in a way of discovery, of the immortality of reasonable soules* (1644; repr. London 1978). Quotations here are from 343ff. The young Leibniz speaks well of Digby (VI. ii. 246, 426) and mentions him in letters to Thomasius of 1663 (II. i. 3) and 1668 (II. i. 10), but clearly thinks of him as a mechanical philosopher more than as a reformer (see, e.g., VI. ii. 161, 302, 433). This is important, for it suggests that the young Leibniz was prepared to disagree with those reformers that he did not think were Aristotelian enough. For a slightly more detailed discussion of the views of both Digby and Du Hamel, see C. Mercer, 'The seventeenth-century debate between the moderns and Aristotelians', *Studia Leibnitiana, Suppl.* 27 (1990), 18–29.

As we shall see in the next section, Leibniz is himself a reformed philosopher, set upon reconciling the ancient and the modern philosophies. But before turning to Leibniz's original conciliatory proposals, it is worth noting that, among the reformers whom he mentions, he bears the closest resemblance to De Raey. Like De Raey, he believes that the proper understanding of Aristotle's metaphysics and physics will reveal that the ancient philosophy could comfortably conform to mechanism. Whereas Digby often seems more wedded to Aristotelian terminology than to the philosophical doctrines that lay behind it and Du Hamel does not attempt a full integration of the two, De Raey is committed to preserving key elements of Aristotle's metaphysics while constructing his synthesis of ancient and modern ideas. Although the result of Leibniz's synthesis is different from that of De Raey, his attitude toward the ancient system is similar.

III. THE LETTER TO THOMASIUS

In April 1669, Leibniz wrote a letter to Jakob Thomasius in which he argues at length for the reconciliation of the Aristotelian and mechanical philosophies. He thought highly enough of the letter to attach it, with only a few minor changes, to the preface of his edition of a text by the Renaissance humanist, Mario Nizolio, published early in 1670.[35] Leibniz's introduction to Nizolio's *De veris principiis et vera ratione philosophandi contra pseudophilosophos* of 1553 thereby became the first piece that the youthful Leibniz published on a contemporary metaphysical topic.[36] The letter to Thomasius is significant: it offers the key to Leibniz's original metaphysics and eclectic methodology; it sets the stage for his later philosophical investigations; and it reveals the real importance of his walk in the woods. The text is obscure and worth working through in some detail.[37]

[35] Nizolio is one of the anti-Aristotelian humanists who (like Peter Ramus) wanted to reform logic teaching and to replace scholastic logic with a form of rhetoric. For a brief account of Nizolio and references to secondary literature, see Copenhaver and Schmitt, 207. For a helpful discussion of the relationship between the thought of Leibniz and Nizolio, see V. Waldemar, 'Leibniz, Nizolius et le nominalisme moderne', *Studia Leibnitiana, Suppl.* 18 (1983), 151–6.

[36] Although Leibniz made very few additions and deletions to his original letter to Thomasius before its publication, they indicate a dramatic shift in his views about substance. Compare the original version, II. i. 14–24, with the published version, VI. ii. 433–44. (Gerhardt does not note all the changes in G iv.) For a detailed discussion of these changes and the reasons behind them, see my *Leibniz's metaphysics: Its origins and development* (Cambridge, forthcoming); for a summary of that material, see C. Mercer and R. C. Sleigh Jr, 'The early metaphysics to the *Discourse on metaphysics*', secs 2–3, in *The Cambridge companion to Leibniz*, ed. N. Jolley (Cambridge 1995). Because the second version of the letter is slightly clearer at times, I shall refer to it here, noting those cases when the difference between the versions is relevant to my discussion.

[37] In the scholarly literature to date, there appears to be no systematic analysis of the letter to Thomasius, though several scholars have discussed it briefly. For the fullest account, see Moll,

Leibniz's letter may be divided into three parts of increasing specificity: in the first, he draws a rough sketch of the contemporary philosophical and methodological terrain and indicates where on the proposed map he stands; in the second, he presents an argument for the particular methodological strategy he accepts; and then, in the third, he explicates the metaphysical conclusion that he thinks that strategy produces, namely, his theory of substance. I shall treat each of these in turn.

(a) *The general method and goal*

Leibniz begins his letter by congratulating Thomasius on his *Origines historiae philosophicae et ecclesiasticae*, the second edition of which appeared in 1669.[38] Thomasius's book is an extremely concise discussion of the origins of certain philosophical and ecclesiastical doctrines, in which he attempts to trace present opinions back to their ancient origins. He typically explains how one or more ancient author solves a particular problem and then lists the solutions proposed by more recent thinkers. His sources range from Plato, Pythagoras, Aristotle, the Manichees, and the Apostles, to the Church Fathers, Scotus, Agricola, and Luther. It is important to note that they do not include "modern" thinkers. One of the longest discussions concerns the question of whether the subject of metaphysics is *ens* or *prima substantia*. In this case, Thomasius presents a variety of opinions (the majority of which are presented in one-sentence summaries) and then accepts the opinion he attributes to Aristotle (12–13).

Leibniz congratulates his teacher because the latter has given "profound reasons" for the "interconnections among doctrines" and has not given a "mere enumeration" of ideas. As opposed to other (humanist) authors who are "skilled more in antiquity than in theory [*ars*] and have given us lives rather than doctrines", Leibniz says that Thomasius has given us a "history of philosophy and not of philosophers" (VI. ii. 433, L* 93). He adds: "I wish, indeed, that you would produce both a style and mode of expression [*stilum filumque*] for this new age and warn our unseasoned youth that it is wrong to give our renovators [*novatores*] credit either for everything or for nothing". Leibniz then lists a number of philosophers "among whom the mantle of philosophy is torn apart" and tells Thomasius that it "will be play for you, but fruitful for the public, to warn the world about them".

---

vol. ii, *passim*; also S. C. Brown, 'Leibniz: Modern, scholastic, or Renaissance philosopher?', in *The rise of modern philosophy*, ed. T. Sorell (Oxford 1993), 213–30, esp. 217ff.; Wilson, 47ff.; Robinet, 8, 128–9; Belaval, 63ff.; Hannequin, 41ff.; Kabitz, 60ff.

[38] It was popular enough to go through a third edition in 1699. References are to that edition. The book seems to have been well received. Sturm, for example, in his *Philosophia eclectica*, 72, refers to Thomasius as "most celebrated".

This introductory paragraph is important because it presents the proper context in which to see the letter. Leibniz makes three requests of Thomasius, each of which is supposed to fulfil a need of this "new age" and each of which Leibniz *himself* goes on to satisfy. First, Thomasius is supposed to warn the naive youth against taking the innovators (*novatores*) to be either wholly right or wrong. That is, according to Leibniz, while the new natural philosophers offer much that is important, they do not offer the whole truth. It is ironic that Leibniz makes this request of his esteemed teacher: the young Leibniz knew perfectly well that his mentor "despises" the "new philosophers" (see II. i. 13). But if Thomasius was not prepared to fulfil this first request, Leibniz was.

Second, Leibniz asks his teacher to caution the public about the tearing apart of philosophy by recent philosophers. Interestingly enough, Leibniz's examples of philosophers who are sundering philosophy include Aristotelian philosophers (Sennert and Sperling), humanists (Nizolio), and the whole range of natural philosophers and mechanists (from Campanella, Galileo, and Telesio, to Hobbes, Gassendi, Digby, and Descartes). In short, the people on Leibniz's list have nothing in common except the fact that they are all fairly recent authors who have expressed their own philosophical opinions. But that is surely the point: what Leibniz proposes here is that these intellectuals are destroying philosophy in that each chooses to argue for his own position without proper regard for the views of others. The unfortunate result of their approach, Leibniz suggests, is a wide variety of divergent views which have little or nothing to do with one another.

It is worth noting that Leibniz makes a very similar point many years later, when he proclaims in 'Specimen dynamicum' (1695) that we must curb "the passion of sects, which is stimulated by the vain lust for novelty". He writes in that work: "we must guard against being more eager to destroy than to construct, and against being tossed about uncertainly, as if by the wind, among the perpetually changing teachings put forth by certain freethinkers".[39] In the letter to Thomasius, Leibniz suggests that such freethinkers are destroying the "seamless garment" of philosophy.[40] This and the related claim that the new philosophy is neither wholly right nor wholly wrong is an implicit advertisement for Leibniz's style of conciliatory eclecticism. That is, instead of arguing for such a variety of incompatible

---

[39] *G. W. Leibniz: Mathematische Schriften*, ed. C. I. Gerhardt (7 vols, 1849–63; repr. Hildesheim 1962), vi. 235, AG 119, L 436.

[40] Leibniz's metaphor of the "mantle of philosophy" that is being "torn apart" echoes the Biblical account of Jesus's "seamless garment" at John 23: 19. In Biblical criticism and analysis, much is made of the fact that because Jesus's robe was seamless it was not torn into parts by those dividing up his possessions after his death. Among other things, the seamless garment becomes a metaphor of the singleness and wholeness of Christianity. Leibniz seems to want to claim that philosophy is similarly seamless and should also not be divided.

views, Leibniz would have his contemporaries look for what is true in conflicting sects and try to compose some harmonized system out of them. That Leibniz intends to construct such a system is clear from what follows.

Leibniz's third request of Thomasius is to create "a style and mode of expression" to suit this new age. Leibniz suggests that his teacher is particularly well suited for this task because he, unlike other humanists, is capable of presenting the "profound reasons for the interconnections among doctrines". The implication is that the new age needs a style that is different from the one used by the majority of Leibniz's contemporaries and that someone like Thomasius, who is skilled enough to "uncover and unite the truth buried and scattered under the opinions of all the different philosophical sects",[41] ought to create one. In his preface, Leibniz had described Thomasius as "the most celebrated Peripatetic in Germany", and one who has "the most accurate understanding of philosophy" as well as the "most exquisite" erudition (VI. ii. 426). The suggestion in the letter, then, is that the requested style of presentation will be one based on a proper understanding of the thought of Aristotle. Leibniz goes on to use such a style in his letter.

The full importance of Leibniz's introductory paragraph becomes evident at this point. By asking Thomasius to fulfil three specific needs of this "new age", Leibniz implicitly presents his own concerns in the letter. He easily fulfils his first and second requests: the inclusion of this introductory paragraph in the preface to his edition of a text by the Renaissance humanist, Nizolio (whose treatise is about the proper way of doing philosophy), itself constitutes a public cry for a conciliatory style of philosophy and a warning against the sundering of philosophy by the various conflicting sects. In short, by warning the public against the danger posed by these conflicting philosophers and by suggesting that what is needed is a more conciliatory approach, Leibniz argues here for the sort of conciliatory eclecticism that he goes on to use. He also thereby presents the correct context in which to see the remainder of his letter: he proceeds to forge a reconciliation of two different (and seemingly opposed) philosophical sects by showing their interconnections. In such a way, Leibniz goes on to satisfy his third request in that he attempts just such a reconciliation.

A question arises at this point: why does Leibniz present the goals of his letter in such an indirect way? Why not just state his intentions instead of disguising them as requests for Thomasius? The answer to this question is both difficult and far-reaching. As the careful student of his philosophy well knows, Leibniz frequently neither states his real intentions nor fully articulates his own views. One often has to discover them beneath the surface

---

[41] In his letter to Remond of 1714, Leibniz uses the quoted phrase to describe what he has tried to do during his life. See G iii. 606, L 654.

and piece them together from scattered suggestions. A satisfactory explanation of Leibniz's persistent hesitancy cannot be given here, but it is worth noting that his conciliatory method constitutes at least part of its motivation. He does not want to be yet another philosopher lusting "for novelty" and pronouncing the truth of his opinions; rather, he hopes to lead his readers quietly to the "interconnections among doctrines".[42]

Once Leibniz has properly introduced his letter, he distinguishes among the most important contemporary thinkers and explains where he stands among them. He thinks that it is important to note the difference between the Cartesians (who, he says, are "those who follow the principles of Descartes") and other philosophers who "though often confused with Cartesians are not". In the process, he lets us know where he stands:

As to myself I confess that I am anything but a Cartesian. I maintain the rule which is common to all these renovators [*restauratores*] of philosophy, [namely that] *nothing ought to be explained in bodies except through magnitude, figure, and motion.*[43] Descartes himself, I hold, merely proposed this rule, for when it came to actual issues, he completely abandoned his strict method and jumped abruptly into certain amazing hypotheses. . . .

Hence I do not hesitate to say that I approve of more things in Aristotle's books on physics than in the meditations of Descartes; so far am I from being a Cartesian. *In fact, I venture to add that the whole of Aristotle's eight books can be permitted without violating the reformed philosophy.* (VI. ii. 434, L* 94, Leibniz's emphasis).

Leibniz could not be clearer. He is a renovator in that he wants to explain corporeal properties wholly in terms of magnitude, figure, and motion, although he is not in the Cartesian half of this group because he does not follow the principles of Descartes (unfortunately, he never states which principles he has in mind). It is important that at the outset of his letter Leibniz distances himself from the Cartesians and from any other particular mechanical sect.[44] He is not interested in the metaphysical underpinnings which the mechanists offer for their philosophy (and the various debates surrounding them), but only in mechanical explanations of corporeal properties. Besides this, he tells us that he is an enthusiastic reformer and believes that Aristotle's physics can be permitted without violating the reformed philosophy. He goes on to explain a bit more about what his position involves:

---

[42] It should be obvious that Leibniz's constant attempts to define and redefine terms and to construct deductive arguments fall well within the scope of this conciliatory eclecticism. His *De transubstantiatione* of 1668 is a nice example of his use of precise definition and deductive argumentation within an eclectic context. See VI. ii. 508–10, L 155ff. Loemker's translation does not include all of this text.

[43] The emphasis is found only in the 1670 version.

[44] He also thereby distances himself from eclectics like De Raey who explicitly construct their reconciliation around the philosophy of Descartes.

For the most part Aristotle's reasoning about matter, form, privation, nature, place, infinity, time, and motion is certain and demonstrated (except what he said about the impossibility of a vacuum). . . . Scarcely any sane person can doubt the rest of Aristotle's arguments.[45] . . . Who would disagree, for instance, with his theory of substantial form as that by which the substance of one body differs from that of another? Nothing is truer than his view of primary matter. (VI. ii. 434, L* 94)

Of course, in the second half of the seventeenth century, Leibniz's comment here is a bit of an exaggeration. The recent philosophers whom Leibniz has just mentioned question exactly these Aristotelian doctrines and do so precisely because they accept the rule Leibniz attributes to them. What could Leibniz possibly have in mind here? He continues:

The one question is whether Aristotle's abstract theories of matter, form, and change should be explained by magnitude, figure, and motion. This is what the Scholastics deny and the Reformers [*Reformatores*] affirm. The latter opinion seems to me to be not only the truer but also the more in agreement with Aristotle. (VI. ii. 434, L* 94–5)

Besides the *recentiores* (all of whom accept the stated rule), there is a group of *reformatores* who propose to explain Aristotle's most basic physical principles in terms consistent with mechanism. Those principles, as interpreted by the scholastics, cannot be so explained. The pressing question is, therefore, whether the scholastics or the reformers are correct in their interpretation of Aristotle's physical principles. Leibniz thinks that a reformed philosophy can be constructed that would fully "explain" the relevant principles, and that such a philosophy would be more in agreement with Aristotle than are the opinions of the scholastics. Moreover, Leibniz suggests, if this reformed philosophy successfully explained Aristotle's abstract theories of matter, form, and change, in terms of magnitude, figure, and motion, then most philosophers would accept the resulting "Aristotelian" views about, for instance, prime matter. After all, these views would be a synthesis of Aristotelian and mechanical principles and would appeal to the modern philosophers and to the Aristotelians, or so Leibniz seems to believe. Leibniz's intention is to formulate just such a reformed philosophy.

The context that Leibniz sets in the first few paragraphs of his letter is enormously important. He neatly displays his general philosophical concerns and his precise location on the seventeenth-century philosophical map. He acknowledges the humanists (those "skilled in antiquity"); the traditional

---

[45] Note that in the first version of this letter Leibniz states that "no sane person can doubt the rest of the contents of Aristotle's physics, metaphysics, logic, and ethics". According to Gerhardt, Leibniz crossed out this entire statement in his manuscript (see G iv. 164). But the young author obviously changed his mind and decided to leave it, as quoted here, in the version to be published. It is interesting that he was indecisive about whether or not to include this strong statement. Compare VI. ii. 434 and II. i. 15.

scholastics (e.g. Scaliger, Sennert: see VI. ii. 433, L 93–4); the mechanists, among whom some are Cartesian and some not; and the reformed philosophers. By placing himself in the latter group, Leibniz tells his readers exactly where he stands within the philosophical alternatives. In these few paragraphs, he also reveals his keen interest in conciliatory philosophy and the precise form his eclecticism would take. The proclamations he makes for a conciliatory method place him squarely within the tradition of Renaissance humanism, while his constant preference for Aristotle and the use he made of Aristotelian concepts expose him as a reformed philosopher. He will now attempt to argue for this philosophy.

(b) *The reformed philosophy of the letter*

Leibniz introduces the conclusion for which he will argue by asserting that, as a variety of philosophers have noted, the scholastics perverted Aristotle's meaning in metaphysics, logic, and law. Leibniz proposes to demonstrate that the schoolmen did this in physics as well. In other words, he will argue that the reformers and not the scholastics are correct about Aristotle's physics. This, he says, can be done in two ways:

> It can be shown either that the reformed philosophy [*Philosophia Reformata*] can be reconciled with Aristotle's and does not conflict with it or, in addition, that the one not only can but must be explained through the other, nay, that the very views which the moderns [*recentiores*] are putting forth so pompously flow [*fluere*] from Aristotelian principles. By the former way, the possibility of the reconciliation is confirmed; by the latter, the necessity. But if the reconciliation is shown to be possible, it is by that fact accomplished. Even if the explanation [*explicatio*] of both Scholastics and moderns [*recentiores*] were possible, the clearer and more intelligible of two possible hypotheses must always be chosen, and without any doubt this is the hypothesis of the moderns, which conceives no incorporeal entities within bodies but assumes nothing beyond magnitude, figure, and motion. (VI. ii. 435, L* 95)

Leibniz presents here, in his typically terse fashion, the assumptions and structure of his argument. The two crucial issues are, first, whether the scholastics or the reformers interpret Aristotle's physics more properly and, second, whether the physical explanations offered by the scholastics or those offered by the reformers can be shown to be true.

Leibniz's argumentative strategy is clever. In the mid-seventeenth century, the most damaging criticism levelled against the Aristotelians concerned the use of substantial forms in explaining physical phenomena. The ridicule to which the Aristotelians were subject is well known. It was common for philosophers to claim, as Descartes had, that the schoolmen explain "that which is obscure through that which is more obscure" (AT iii. 507). Leibniz intends to deflect this criticism. If he can show that such complaints do not apply to the ancient thought itself but only to those scholastics who perverted its meaning, then he will have saved Aristotle himself from the flames of ridicule.

According to Leibniz, the scholastics posit the existence of "a kind of immaterial being" which is "insensible" within bodies, namely, substantial form, in terms of which corporeal properties are to be explained. But "Aristotle seems nowhere to have imagined any substantial forms" of this kind (VI. ii. 440, L 99). Leibniz explains that, because the reformers have properly understood the thought of Aristotle, they deny both the existence and the intelligibility of any sort of immaterial form and maintain instead that all corporeal properties are to be explained in terms of matter in motion. According to Leibniz, then, the reformers do not want to explain the properties of (say) fire as the traditional scholastics had done, namely, in terms of some immaterial form in the fire. Rather, they agree with the mechanists that the heat in fire can be fully and intelligibly explained by simple reference to the movement of the matter which makes up the fire; there is no need to posit any other entity.

It is important to understand that the context here is one of physical explanations and that, according to Leibniz, the reformers and the moderns offer one explanatory model while the scholastics offer another. Within this context, Leibniz wants to convince us (1) that the position of the reformers is consistent with the thought of Aristotle and therefore that the scholastics' interpretation of Aristotle's physics is incorrect; (2) that the reformers' position in fact *follows* from the fundamental principles of Aristotle's philosophy, once that philosophy is properly understood; and (3) that, even if the physical explanations of corporeal phenomena offered by both the scholastics and the reformers were "possible", the former would have to be rejected because of its lesser intelligibility and because (as he goes on to say) of the "manifest truth" of the reformed philosophy. A final point to note about Leibniz's strategy here is that, although the discussion is at present focused on physical explanations, it is ultimately about the metaphysical foundations of physics. Leibniz asserts that "the views of the moderns" about physics "flow from Aristotelian principles"; that is, from the basic constituents of Aristotelian metaphysics.[46]

Having stated the conclusion for which he will argue and outlined his argumentative strategy, Leibniz turns his attention to the proof that the reformers and not the scholastics are correct about Aristotle's physics. He writes: "I cannot better show this . . . than by asking for any principle of

---

[46] In the same way that Aristotle's notion of cause (*aitia*) is quite different from our own, so is his notion of principle (*archē*). The exact meaning and uses of '*archē*' have been much debated, but it is fair to say that, for Aristotle (and for Leibniz), a principle is an origin or source. For a clear discussion of the differences between our notions of principle and cause and those of Aristotle, see C. Witt, *Substance and essence in Aristotle* (Ithaca, NY 1989), esp. 15–19.

Aristotle which cannot be explained by magnitude, figure, and motion" (VI. ii. 435, L 95). He then proceeds to treat Aristotle's principles of matter, form, and change in turn. In each case, he takes one of these fundamental principles and transforms Aristotle's original notion into a mechanistic one. Prime matter becomes continuous mass (*massa*), "which fills the world while all things are at rest" and "from which all things are produced by motion and into which they are reduced through rest". As such, the "essence of matter or the very nature [*forma*] of corporeity consists in antitypy or impenetrability" (VI. ii. 435, L 95).

With this notion of matter in place, Leibniz proceeds to the crux of his mechanization of Aristotle, namely, his account of form. According to Leibniz, the substantial form of a body is its *figura*, which is an "organized arrangement of parts" of matter produced by motion. He writes: "For division comes from motion, the bounding of parts comes from division, their *figurae* from this bounding, and forms from *figurae*; therefore, forms come from motion" (VI. ii. 435–6, L* 96).[47] At first glance, this seems quite un-Aristotelian. For Aristotle, the form is the cause of the being of the thing, that which makes the thing what it is. As such, it is metaphysically prior and cannot itself be caused. What Leibniz has done here is to make motion the cause of the being of a thing and thereby deprived substantial form of its causal and metaphysical priority.

When it comes to change, Leibniz reduces the various kinds of change (e.g. generation, corruption) to local motion. He thereby appears to deny what Aristotle considers the essentially purposive aspect of nature. Once Leibniz shows to his satisfaction that "all changes can be explained by motion", he happily concludes that "there is obviously almost nothing in Aristotle's physics which cannot be readily explained and made clear through the reformed philosophy" (VI. ii. 437–8, L 97).

Thus far, Leibniz points out, he has only shown that these positions "can be reconciled; it still remains to show that they ought to be" (VI. ii. 438, L 98). As previously proposed, he will now demonstrate that they ought to be reconciled by showing how the views of the moderns about physical explanations "flow from Aristotelian principles". But Leibniz's present task is not a very difficult one. The first part of his demonstration virtually accomplished it: because Leibniz has mechanized Aristotle's basic principles

---

[47] The Latin '*figura*' is ambiguous as between the shape and the nature of a thing. Although Leibniz does not give a complete account of *figura* in the present letter, he does in an earlier letter to Thomasius. He writes in October 1668 that the *figura* arises from "a combination of motions" and "comprises an orderly arrangement of parts" of matter (II. i. 10). In short, it is an organized arrangement of parts of matter. From the present context, then, it is clear that Leibniz has the latter meaning in mind. It seems appropriate, however, not to translate the term. For a much more detailed account of Leibniz's notion of *figura* and the other elements of his early conception of substance, see my forthcoming book.

of matter, form, and change, and because Aristotle's fundamental principles are the origins or sources of everything else in nature, the position shared by the reformers and moderns (namely, that all corporeal phenomena can be explained by matter in motion) will follow from those principles. Leibniz explains:

For what does Aristotle discuss, in the eight books of the *Physics*, besides figure, magnitude, motion, place, and time? If the nature of body in general can be explained in terms of these, then the nature of a particular body must be explained in terms of a particular figure, a particular magnitude, etc. In fact, he himself says in the *Physics*, Book iii, Section 24, that all natural science concerns magnitude (with which figure is, of course, associated), motion, and time. . . . Everything in nature must therefore be explained through these. (VI. ii. 438, L 98)

In this context, Leibniz's earlier comment about reconciling the reformers and Aristotle is not surprising: he wrote that "if the reconciliation is shown to be possible, it is by that fact also accomplished" (VI. ii. 435, L 95). By so neatly mechanizing the Aristotelian principles, he has shown that the physical explanations proposed by both the moderns and the reformers really do follow from Aristotelian principles.

With the proof of the reconciliation completed, Leibniz goes on to show that some of the more important details of Aristotle's physics can also be shown to conform to the position of the moderns. Leibniz's discussion here is reminiscent of De Raey: he presents a statement from Aristotle's writings of a fundamental tenet and interprets it so that it conforms to his analysis of the ancient.[48] The details of Leibniz's discussion need not concern us; what is important is that he manages to fit the recalcitrant parts of Aristotle's physics into the scope of his reformed philosophy. He concludes: "the Aristotelian Philosophy has been reconciled to the Reformed Philosophy" (VI. ii. 441, L* 100).

Leibniz is not yet satisfied. He now turns his attention to the final part of his demonstration and attempts to show "the manifest truth of the Reformed philosophy itself".[49] He maintains that nothing is needed to explain the phenomena of the world besides magnitude, figure, and motion. Again, the details of his discussion are not particularly relevant. What is important is the fact that Leibniz here makes use of nominalist principles and thereby incorporates "the nominalist sect, the most profound of all the Scholastics" into his reformed philosophy (VI. ii. 420, L 127).

---

[48] It is important to note that although De Raey and Leibniz are quite similar in their methodology, they differ both on details and in their general goal. De Raey accepts many of the doctrines and much of the terminology of Descartes and considers himself a Cartesian; Leibniz rejects the Cartesian philosophy and accepts merely "the rule" of the moderns.

[49] Loemker does not include this sentence as it appears in the 1670 version: compare VI. ii. 441 and II. i. 21 with L 100. In fact, at this point in the translation, Loemker combines statements from each version without noting which is which.

In the preface to his edition of Nizolio, Leibniz praises the nominalist tradition, gives a brief history of its greatest members, and then writes:

The general rule which the nominalists frequently use is that *entities must not be multiplied beyond necessity* . . . which, though more obscurely stated, reduces to this: *the simpler a hypothesis is, the better it is.* And in accounting for the causes of phenomena, that hypothesis is the most successful which makes the fewest gratuitous assumptions. . . . The same thing is true of all the reformers of philosophy today; if they are not supernominalists, they are almost all nominalists. (VI. ii. 428–9, L 128)

In his letter to Thomasius, he now claims that "there are no entities in the world except mind, space, matter, and motion" and therefore that:

the hypotheses of those recent thinkers [*recentiores*], who use only these to explain phenomena, are the better ones. For it is a defect in hypotheses to assume what is unnecessary. For truly all things in the whole world can be explained by these things alone. . . . And truly the human mind can imagine nothing other than *mind* . . . , *space*, *matter*, and *motion*, and what results from these things arranged [*comparatis*] among themselves. (VI. ii. 441–2, L* 100, Leibniz's emphasis)

Following the nominalists and reformers, Leibniz claims that everything in nature can be explained wholly in terms of mind, space, matter, and motion. There is no reason to admit the use of superfluous immaterial forms (or anything else) in natural explanations. Therefore, scholastic science ought to be rejected and reformed philosophy accepted.

By such means Leibniz has completed the tripartite demonstration originally promised. He has shown (1) that the position shared by the reformers and moderns is consistent with the physics of Aristotle and therefore that the scholastics' interpretation of Aristotle's physics is incorrect; (2) that the reformers' position follows from the fundamental principles of Aristotle's philosophy, once that philosophy is properly understood; and (3) that, even if the physical explanations offered by both the scholastics and the reformers were "possible" as accounts of corporeal phenomena, the former would have to be rejected because of its violation of nominalist principles. With impressive finesse, Leibniz has shown not only that the reformers interpret Aristotle's physics more properly than do the "uncultured" scholastics (VI. ii. 425, L 127), but also that they accept the insights of the nominalists. The materials are in place to formulate the "truth *per se*". Leibniz now goes on to erect the foundations for the true reformed philosophy.

(c) *The original theory of substance*

In the remainder of his letter to Thomasius, Leibniz presents a theory of substance that is supposed to constitute the foundations of the proper reformed philosophy. There are two closely related problems which arise at this point in the text. First, Leibniz does not reveal in the letter itself any good philosophical reasons for preferring the reformed philosophy to the mechanical one. The only criticism that Leibniz can muster against the moderns is to note that they play a part in the dismantling of philosophy. He does not criticize their view in the letter in any way. It is therefore very difficult to understand in the context of the letter why one ought to favour the reformed philosophy over mechanism, except for the fact that the Aristotelian language of the proposed reform might make it more palatable to traditional Aristotelians. To put the problem another way, if the mechanical philosophy is successful by itself, then there is little reason to contaminate it with anything out of Aristotle. Second, because it is difficult to see anything genuinely Aristotelian in Leibniz's proposals so far, there seems little reason to take Leibniz's proclamations of the virtues of Aristotle seriously. This part of the letter is so obscure and Leibniz's views so difficult to make out that commentators have taken Leibniz's conception to be a version of mechanism merely translated into Aristotelian terminology.[50]

For a solution to the first problem we need not go far. At least as early as 1668, Leibniz had decided that the standard metaphysical foundations of mechanism were inadequate. In his essay entitled 'Confessio naturae contra atheistas', he explains that as far as can be done "everything should be derived [*deducere*] from the nature of body and its primary qualities— magnitude, figure, and motion". He then goes on to ask:

> But what if I should demonstrate that the origin of these very primary qualities themselves cannot be found in the nature of body? Then indeed, I hope, these naturalists [mechanists] will admit that body is not self-sufficient [*sibi non sufficere*] and cannot subsist without an incorporeal principle. (VI. i. 490, L* 110)

The point here is that, according to the mechanical philosophy, all corporeal qualities are derivable from the primary qualities of body (here considered magnitude, figure, and motion). But Leibniz thinks there is a problem in that motion is not derivable from the nature of body itself. That is, there is nothing in extended stuff that can act as the source and explanation of motion. Therefore, Leibniz concludes, bodies are not self-sufficient and cannot subsist without an incorporeal principle that can act as the cause of motion.

Leibniz's point is both important and subtle. On the face of it, his argument against the mechanical philosophy fails miserably. Mechanists like

---

[50] It is not surprising that even those commentators who have understood Leibniz's account of bodies in the letter have balked at this point and felt justified in disregarding Leibniz's claims of Aristotelian authenticity. See Aiton, 28ff.; Wilson, 47–8; Robinet, 129ff.; Moll, vol. ii, *passim*; Hannequin, 45–6; Kabitz, 61–2; Petersen, 351; and M. Gueroult, *Dynamique et métaphysique Leibniziennes* (Paris 1934), 4ff.

Descartes and Gassendi were well aware of the fact that motion could not be derived from the nature of body *qua* extended stuff. Each philosopher had his own way of bringing mind, as a source of motion, to *res extensa*. That is, Gassendi and Descartes in fact agreed with Leibniz that God is required to account for the motion of bodies. Descartes maintains that God adds motion to body by continual re-creation, while Gassendi thinks that God infuses motion into atoms at their creation. Descartes and Gassendi were perfectly happy to let God be the cause of the motion of bodies. They saw no problem in the fact that the full account of motion did not rest in the nature of body *qua* extended stuff.[51] But this, according to Leibniz, is their fundamental mistake: if the account of a primary quality like motion cannot be found in the nature of body *qua* extended stuff, then body is not self-sufficient "and cannot subsist without an incorporeal principle". Leibniz's criticism cuts fairly deep. If one agrees with the Aristotelians that a substance is the cause and explanation of what a thing *is*, then mere extended stuff does seem somehow inadequate as a substance. A body, as an extended thing, is after all a thing that moves, a thing that has shape and size. Those properties are themselves a result of matter's being arranged or organized in a particular way. If that arrangement or organization does not have its source, cause, or explanation in the nature of body itself, then that nature does seem incomplete. It needs something external to it to give it its primary qualities and, in that sense, to complete it. In short, because Leibniz assumed that any substance worth the name ought to be self-sufficient, at least with regard to its primary qualities, he found material substance as defined by the mechanists wanting.[52] It was an attempt both to make corporeal substances self-sufficient and complete and to retain mechanical physics that led Leibniz to the position in his letter to Thomasius.[53]

[51] For example, Gassendi writes in 1658: "It may be supposed that individual atoms received from God . . . the force [*vis*] requisite for moving, and for imparting motions to others . . . All this to the degree that he foresaw what would be necessary for every purpose he had destined them for". See C. B. Brush, *The selected works of Pierre Gassendi* (New York 1972), 400–401. Descartes is also clear about the original source of motion (although the precise relation between God and the motion of a body at a particular time is less easy to discern). He writes, for example, in *Principles of philosophy*, II. 36, "*God is the primary cause of motion*. . . . Thus, God imparted various motions to the parts of matter when he first created them, and he now preserves all this matter in the same way, and by the same process by which he originally created it". See AT viii. 61–2; *The philosophical writings of Descartes*, trans. J. Cottingham and others (3 vols, Cambridge 1985–91), i. 240.

[52] Of the many scholars who discuss the 'Confessio naturae', only Hannequin and Moll have recognized the subtlety of Leibniz's position. See Hannequin, 32ff.; Moll, vol. ii, esp. 179. Although he does not discuss this essay, C. D. Broad grasps Leibniz's fundamental reasons for rejecting a mechanical conception of body in his extremely helpful book, *Leibniz: An introduction* (Cambridge 1975); see esp. 54ff.

[53] Leibniz's rejection of the metaphysical foundations of the standard mechanical physics was also motivated by theological concerns. On Leibniz's concern to explain the Eucharist, see D. C.

Against the background of Leibniz's criticism of mechanism, the genuine Aristotelian flavour of the theory he proposes in his letter is discernible. He constructs a corporeal substance that is appropriately self-sufficient and properly Aristotelian by demoting *res extensa* to a mere constituent of substance and distinguishing between a primary form and the form or *figura* in an individual substance. For Leibniz, prime matter is extended stuff which functions as the potential principle and thereby plays exactly the same *role* as Aristotle's matter: it is that "from which all things are produced" (VI. ii. 435, L 95). Although *res extensa* is not a substance by itself, Leibniz has neatly made it the passive element in substance. When *res extensa* is joined with the active principle or primary form, it becomes a constituent of a self-sufficient corporeal substance.[54] Like the Aristotelian notion, Leibniz's matter is indeterminate and must be made into something by form.

The primary active constituent of corporeal substance is God, the principle of motion, and what Leibniz calls the "primary form" (VI. i. 440, L 99). As such, God plays the role of Aristotle's substantial form, the determining principle, the principle that makes the thing what it is. When the primary form individuates matter, the result is an individual corporeal substance. God causes the motion that produces the individual substance. As noted above, the individual substance's form or *figura* does not conform to Aristotle's requirements, but we now have something that does. Leibniz writes: "For [divine] mind supplies motion to matter. . . . Matter is devoid of motion *per se*. Mind is the principle of all motion, as Aristotle rightly saw" (VI. ii. 439, L* 99).

It is significant that the individual substance here is composed of indeterminate matter and a determining form (i.e. God) and that, once this "organized arrangement of parts" of matter (VI. ii. 436, L* 96) or "secondary form" is created, it is itself a principle of motion. God may cause the organization of the parts of the substance, but once those parts are so organized the secondary form will be a cause of motion. For example, when it strikes another body, it is the cause (along with the organization of the other body) of the resulting motion.[55] If we understand this secondary form to be

---

Fouke, 'Metaphysics and the Eucharist in the early Leibniz', *Studia Leibnitiana* 24:2 (1992), 145–59. For an excellent discussion of the relation between Leibniz's theology and his metaphysics, see D. Rutherford, *Leibniz and the rational order of nature* (Cambridge 1995).

[54] See especially Leibniz's essay *De transsubstantiatione*, where he writes, for example, that "no body apart from concurring mind [*mente concurrente*] is to be taken as substance. . . . Substance is union with mind, and so the substance of body is union with a sustaining mind" (VI. ii. 509, L* 116).

[55] Thus, this is not a version of occasionalism: although God causes the matter in the substance to move, once this *figura* or "organized arrangement of parts" of matter is formed it can itself act as the cause of the motion in another body, say, by striking it. In fact, Leibniz's secondary form here is an example of what medieval scholastics called a secondary cause. For an

the arrangement or organization of primary matter, then it has some of the features of the Aristotelian notion: it constitutes the nature of the substance and the cause and explanation of its essential properties (II. i. 11; VI. ii. 443, L 102). While it remains perfectly clear that much of what Leibniz says about matter and (secondary) form in this letter is inconsistent with anything the ancient accepted, these un-Aristotelian elements fit neatly within a theory of substance that has the structure of Aristotle's. For example, although God is the principle and cause of individuation and matter has a well defined nature, the fact that they combine as active and passive elements to form a union that constitutes the cause and explanation for substantial properties is recognizably Aristotelian.[56] With admirable finesse, Leibniz has placed a version of mechanical physics firmly upon an Aristotelian foundation. In the process, he has made corporeal substances self-sufficient and saved the Aristotelian system from ridicule.

IV. THE WOODS REVISITED

Against both the historical background displayed in section II and the argument in the letter to Thomasius presented in section III, we are now in a position to re-evaluate Leibniz's youthful philosophy. The key to understanding Leibniz's thought in the 1660s (and much of what he did later) is to recognize that he practised a form of critical eclecticism which fostered the accumulation and consideration of a wide variety of diverse ideas, which assumed an underlying truth beneath the various conflicting schools, and whose only stipulation was that the resulting collection be made consistent with certain Aristotelian principles.

There are seven salient features of Leibniz's writings in the 1660s which even a quick perusal of the period affords. Previous scholars have attended almost exclusively to the first two of these:

1. Leibniz accepts a mechanical account of corporeal properties.

2. In articulating his views about bodies and their properties, he relies more heavily on ideas out of Gassendi and Hobbes than on other mechanists.

The other five features, though equally prominent, have been mostly ignored. They are as follows.

3. In presenting his views on bodies and their properties, Leibniz never

---

excellent discussion of secondary causes, occasionalism, and their philosophical differences, see A. J. Freddoso, 'Medieval Aristotelianism and the case against secondary causation in nature', in *Divine and human action*, ed. T. V. Morris (Ithaca, NY 1988), 74–118.

[56] Leibniz's proposal here is somewhat like that made by Suárez and some other scholastics, namely, that the figure (*figura*) or form of a body is something like "the determination of magnitude" (Disp. XLII, sec. iii. 15).

gives the same account twice and never combines his Hobbesian and Gassendian ideas in exactly the same way. In short, he does not stay with any one analysis; he seems to be constantly regrouping and recombining his ideas.[57]

4. Jakob Thomasius played a significant role in the development of Leibniz's philosophical ideas throughout the decade.[58] Leibniz was greatly impressed by Thomasius from the beginning of his university studies[59] and, like many of his German contemporaries, considered him an important conciliatory philosopher. We can glean from Thomasius's books and published lectures the philosophical and methodological lessons he taught his students.[60] He encouraged the serious study of the history of philosophy, which he said must always be well founded in the thought of the ancients; he taught that, in order to solve a philosophical problem or clarify an idea, one must first understand its historical source. His own lectures display a familiarity with an impressive range of philosophical schools and doctrines and a propensity to collect ideas from a wide variety of sources, both contemporary (e.g. Luther) and ancient (e.g. the Stoics). He often takes an idea or a problem (e.g. 'De amore virtutis', presented in August 1662) and discusses it in terms of its origins. Although he clearly has some knowledge of the "moderns" (e.g. Hobbes), he does not take the mechanical philosophy seriously. When he mentions or argues against the "recent philosophers" (*recentiores*), he has in mind the scholastic philosophers of his own time: Soner, Dreier, and Dannhauer.[61] The single most important feature of Thomasius's philosophical concerns, however, is his belief in the superiority of Aristotle and the need to understand him on his own terms.[62] As he wrote to Leibniz in 1668, "I think no one in the history of philosophy has hit the mark better than Aristotle" (II. i. 13). From his first letter to Thomasius of 1663 (II. i. 3) to the publication of the April 1669 letter in 1670, the young Leibniz's admiration for his teacher is obvious: he saves his best metaphysical

---

[57] Compare VI. i, nos 4, 7, 8; II. i, no. 3.

[58] In the notes by Leibniz which Foucher de Careil collected and published, but which have subsequently been lost, we learn a great deal about the young man's regard for Thomasius. See Foucher de Careil, *Mémoire*, 6ff., and *Lettres et opuscules inédits de Leibniz* (Paris 1854), 386–7. The materials collected by Foucher de Careil are important and it is worth noting that the editors of the Akademie edition treat them as primary sources.

[59] See, e.g., Sturm, *Philosophia eclectica*, 72–3.

[60] My discussion is based on his *Origines historiae philosophicae et ecclesiasticae*, 3rd edn (1699); *Physica, Logica, Metaphysica*, and *Rhetorica*, published together (1692); *Dissertationes LXIII varii argumenti magnam partem ad historiam philosophicam et ecclesiasticam pertinentes* (1693). The last is a collection of some of the lectures Thomasius gave in the 1650s, 1660s, and 1670s; they reveal a good deal about his attitudes towards philosophy and the proper philosophical method.

[61] *Physica*, 69–87; *Origines*, 14. On Hobbes, see *Dissertationes*, lect. VIII, entitled 'De statu naturali adversus Hobbesium', dating from Jan. 1661.

[62] See, e.g., *Dissertationes*, 466, 478–9.

and methodological ideas for his esteemed teacher and as a consequence his letters to Thomasius are the most important of the period.

Given the young Leibniz's commitment to his illustrious teacher, the other prominent features of the texts of the decade should not come as a surprise.

5. Leibniz almost always combines his "modern" views with ideas from a variety of other sources, especially from Aristotle. The only exception to this is a letter to Thomasius of February 1666 in which he refers to Hobbes and gives a Gassendian account of perception.[63] We need not, however, take this absence of Aristotelian elements as proof of Leibniz's whole-hearted mechanism, or of much else. In the first place, the letter reads very much like an exercise that the student prepared for his teacher. It consists, in its twenty-six line entirety, of a solution to a paradox first proposed by Anaxagoras about the possibility of black snow. Leibniz begins with the hypothesis that colour is only an idea and not a quality in things. He then uses this hypothesis, along with some Gassendian principles, to solve the paradox (II. i. 4–5). There would be reason to take this position as somehow representative if Leibniz continued to make important use of these same principles. He does not; and there is little reason to believe that Leibniz was particularly wedded to Gassendi's views on perception or to Gassendi's philosophy for that matter. A second reason for not generalizing from this one instance is that Leibniz was soon to publish his *De arte combinatoria*. Because this work uses the Aristotelian account of cause, analyses the four Aristotelian primary qualities in mechanical terms, and presents Aristotle's notion of the mean, there is little justification for thinking that Leibniz had given up combining ancient or historical ideas with modern ones.

6. Another feature of the 1660s is that Aristotle is the single most important source of the young man's ideas. In his notes, writings, and letters between 1663 and 1672, Leibniz refers to Aristotle some 151 times, compared with 98 references to Hobbes and 33 to Gassendi. But what is more important than just numbers is the kind of references these are. To show the certainty of a principle or the truth of an opinion, Leibniz considers it sufficient simply to note that it was accepted by the "most profound Aristotle" (see, for instance, VI. i. 84). In humanist fashion, a reference to Aristotle seems to constitute its own kind of rhetorical argument. Although the vast majority of these concern ethical and legal topics, many pertain to issues in natural philosophy, the area where mechanism would naturally have its strongest influence. The most damaging criticism Leibniz can muster against the Philosopher during this time occurs in a passage we have already

---

[63] Scholars of the period have made much of this letter. Kabitz used it as evidence that by 1666 Leibniz had finally rejected his youthful Aristotelianism; Kabitz and many others have taken it as proof of his commitment to Gassendi. See, e.g., Čapek, 259; Belaval, 33; Kabitz, 51–2; Hannequin, 24ff.

seen from his letter to Thomasius: "For the most part Aristotle's reasoning about matter, form, privation, nature, place, infinity, time, and motion is certain and demonstrated, almost the only exception being what he said about the impossibility of a vacuum and of motion in a vacuum" (II. i. 15, L 94). But if Leibniz could not bring himself to criticize Aristotle, he had no such problem in disagreeing with philosophers like Hobbes.[64] Even Leibniz's letter to Hobbes of July 1670 exemplifies his greater regard for Aristotle. After noting some problems which he thinks Hobbes's conception of body may face, he defers to Aristotle on a topic concerning body (II. i. 57, L 107). Both here and in the other one hundred and fifty references to Aristotle, Leibniz takes the ancient to be the final word on most topics, even those concerning physical matters.

7. Finally, not only are Leibniz's texts full of references to Aristotle and, to a lesser extent, Gassendi and Hobbes; they are brimming with citations of a vast number of ancient, medieval, early Renaissance, and contemporary philosophers. He seems to have consumed books and ideas with a ferocious appetite and to have been happy to use them whenever possible. The preface to his edition of Nizolio's *De veris principiis* perfectly exemplifies the extent of his erudition (and his pride in it). It includes paragraph-long lists of references to philosophical doctrines and texts from a huge variety of contemporary and historical sources. Indeed, Leibniz's preface looks much more like a work by Thomasius or Sturm than one by Descartes, Hobbes, or even Gassendi.

These facts make one thing immediately clear: Leibniz was not just a mechanist during the period. To isolate his reflections on the mechanical philosophy is to miss the point of what he was doing. Even the quick survey of the 1660s offered here suggests that Leibniz's youthful philosophical evolution is both more complicated and more interesting than previously thought. On the basis of these and other facts, I would now like to present the general outline of Leibniz's philosophical development during the 1660s.[65]

Leibniz matriculated at the University of Leipzig in April 1661, three months before his sixteenth birthday and two years before he wrote *De principio individui*. Accordingly, the recollection of his walk as he describes it to Remond in 1714 places his decision at about the time he began his

---

[64] E.g. VI. i. 490, L 110; VI. ii. 428, L 128; VI. ii. 432, L 130.

[65] In fact, I am leaving out of my discussion a major concern of Leibniz's during the period, namely, the attempt to develop a universal characteristic. This topic has been much discussed and, although related, it is not crucial to an understanding of the development of his original metaphysics. For discussions of his early ideas on this important topic, see esp. Wilson, ch. 1; Moll, vol. i, *passim*; M. Mugnai, 'Der Begriff der Harmonie als metaphysische Grundlage der Logik und Kombinatorik bei Johann Heinrich Bisterfield und Leibniz', *Studia Leibnitiana* 5:1 (1973), 43–73, and D. Rutherford, 'Philosophy and language in Leibniz', in *The Cambridge companion to Leibniz*, ed. Jolley, 224-69, esp. sec. 1.

university study. Since Leibniz was of very sound mind in 1714, it is unlikely that he would forget whether something so noteworthy as the commencement of his university studies had happened at about the same time as the Rosental decision or three years before. Moreover, there is at least one other text in which Leibniz describes his meditative walk. He writes in 1697: "for I began very young to meditate and I was not quite fifteen years old when I wandered for whole days in a forest to choose a party between Aristotle and Democritus" (G iii. 205). It therefore seems very likely that Leibniz made his transforming stroll around the age of fifteen, at least two years before he wrote *De principio*.

It also seems clear that his Rosental conversion was only partial. Leibniz had rejected the immaterial substantial forms of the scholastics, but not the Aristotelian philosophy. That is, at the completion of his walk, mechanism had "prevailed" and he had chosen Democritus in a very limited way: he had decided to use mechanical principles and not scholastic substantial forms to explain the properties of bodies. In a fascinating passage written in the 1660s, Leibniz describes the crucial, next phase in his early development:

As soon as I arrived at the Academy, by a rare fortune I met, as a Master, the well-known J. Thomasius who, *although he did not accept my doubts and was very little disposed to let me do such a reform of the substantial, incorporeal forms of bodies*, engaged me very strongly to read Aristotle, announcing to me that, when I had read this great philosopher, I would have a wholly different opinion from that offered by his scholastic interpreters. I soon acknowledged the wisdom of this advice and saw that between Aristotle and the scholastics there was the same difference as between a great man versed in the affairs of state and a monk dreaming in his cell. I therefore took of Aristotle's philosophy another idea than the common one. . . . Aristotle seemed to me to admit, more or less like Democritus or, in my time, like Descartes and Gassendi, that there is no body which can be moved by itself.[66]

Leibniz could not be clearer: when he arrived at the academy he was already concerned to reform the scholastic notion of substantial form (he may also have had other doubts about the Aristotelianism he gleaned from his early education); under the encouragement and advice of Thomasius, he began a more serious study of Aristotle than he had previously made; the result of this study was that he went beyond the teaching of his master and discovered that Aristotelian physics could be made to conform with mechanism.

It was under Thomasius's tutelage that Leibniz wrote *De principio individui*. The dissertation shows the influence of the teacher in two interesting ways: it displays an impressive mastery of scholastic philosophy, especially of those schoolmen whom Thomasius deemed most valuable,[67] but

---

[66] Foucher de Careil, *Mémoire*, 6–7; my emphasis. According to Foucher de Careil, 5, the passage cited here was written during the 1660s.

[67] See, for example, Thomasius, *Dissertationes*, esp. lect. XLI, 'Adversus philosophos novantiquos'.

it also solves the problem of individuation in a way suggested by the master himself.[68] In other words, *De principio* is exactly the kind of work the admiring student would produce in an attempt to follow his mentor's advice.[69] As Leibniz was to write in the late 1670s, speaking of himself in the third person: "he fell first across the ancients, in whom at the beginning he understood nothing, and then something, and at last as much as was needed". He gained an understanding "not only of their language but of their thoughts" (G vii. 52).[70]

But at the same time that Leibniz was coming to understand the thought of Aristotle, he was also applying himself to the mechanical philosophy. The fact that he could make his Rosental decision in 1661, write *De principio* two years after that, and then compose both the Thomasius letter of February 1666 (in which he discussed the possibility of black snow in Gassendian terms) and *Nova methodus discendae docendaeque jurisprudentiae* (in which he makes use of Baconian and Aristotelian doctrines) a year later tells us a great deal about the complexity and variety of Leibniz's interests during this time.[71] He may have been interested in a mechanical account of body, but he was interested in many other things as well.

When Leibniz emerged from the Rosental woods, he had set himself a course on which he would remain throughout his youth: to construct a comprehensive and true metaphysics that would somehow be built out of the ultimate principles discovered beneath the various sects and within a generally Aristotelian framework. The reason his works are brimming with such a variety of references and the reason his views on bodies, for example,

---

[68] In Thomasius's preface to the piece, he introduces the problem of individuation and suggests what the right solution might be (see VI. i. 7). This is in fact just the sort of solution to the problem that Leibniz goes on to defend, i.e. one that rejects Scotus's *haecceitas* in favour of a Suarezian notion of complete entity.

[69] Leibniz's dissertation is a first-class piece of work. Kabitz, 49, describes it as a "virtuoso piece of scholastic philosophy" and Wundt, *Schulmetaphysik*, 143, maintains that its survey of scholastic literature is well done, even for the time.

[70] The remainder of this passage is interesting: Leibniz compares the ancients with the moderns about whom he felt "disgust" and says that what he learned from the ancients, as opposed to the moderns, was "always to seek for clearness in words". The picture he paints is rather different from those found in the later accounts of his development, or even in the letter to Arnauld of 1671 (II. i. 169–81). The lesson here is important: we should not take any one of the various (and often inconsistent) accounts he gives of his philosophical development too seriously. When describing his intellectual history, as he does in the letters to Remond and in 'A new system of the nature and the communication of substances' of 1695, Leibniz often paints in broad strokes. The point of these stories is not so much to present the actual steps in his intellectual autobiography as to give his reasons for accepting some philosophical doctrines and rejecting others. It is a mistake then to base one's history of Leibniz's philosophical development entirely upon such accounts, as many commentators have done. As the analysis offered here suggests, the *facts* of his development often suggest both a more complicated and a more interesting story. For more about his philosophical development, see my forthcoming book.

[71] In the preface of the latter work, he refers to Plato, Socrates, Galileo, Harvey, Descartes, Campanella, and a long list of lesser figures. See VI. i. 264–5.

are constantly being recombined and reconsidered is that he was casting about for the key to his conciliation. As a syncretist, he must search through the dominant philosophical options and attempt to find what is worthwhile in each; as a philosopher interested in combining the mechanical physics with Aristotelian metaphysics, he must discover the common denominator among the mechanical options in an attempt to achieve the proper mix. It is not surprising that the works of the mid-1660s are replete with a vast variety of differing opinions. For example, his comments of 1663–4 on Daniel Stahl's *Compendium metaphysicae* reflect his propensity to collect as opposed to reject.[72] These notes are particularly interesting because they reveal the energy with which he compared ideas from a wide variety of sources (VI. i. 21–41). Although Stahl's book is a commentary on Aristotle's metaphysics, Leibniz brings an impressive array of authors and doctrines to the text. He refers to Aquinas, Hobbes, and Honoratus Fabri regarding Stahl's discussion of *ens* and *essentia*, and mentions Hobbes in connection with the author's account of words. The young Leibniz obviously has opinions about Aristotle's views and is prepared to criticize both the completeness and the accuracy of Stahl's account (see, e.g., VI. i. 39). Another important example of the young man's eclectic tendencies is *De transsubstantiatione* of 1668. Here he compares his own account of substantial form with that of Zabarella, Averroes, and others, and contends that his notion of God is like that of Plato and the Stoics (VI. i. 510).

But we should not let the vast number of references and startling combinations camouflage Leibniz's genuine philosophical goal: he seeks to penetrate "into the harmony of these different realms" (G iii. 607). As we saw in section III (c), he has discovered the common denominator among the members of the mechanical sect by 1668: in his 'Confessio naturae', he treats "the naturalists" as a group and argues that their physics does not have the proper metaphysical foundation. Other works from the period, like his *De arte combinatoria* of 1666 (VI. i. 163–230) and his notes on a text by Thomas White of 1668 (VI. i. 501–7), also reveal his concern to find a common core within differing proposals and to combine ideas from a myriad of sources into a coherent mixture. As noted in section III (b), the reformed philosophy of the preface to his edition of Nizolio is one built out of Aristotelian, mechanical, and nominalist doctrines.

Nor should we doubt Leibniz's sincerity. There is ample evidence that he was ingenuous in his proposals. He was surely cognizant of the fact that some readers would not be sympathetic to his reformed philosophy and its interpretation of Aristotle. Thomasius had responded to an earlier (and less

[72] Stahl had been a well respected Aristotelian at Jena the generation before Leibniz and was well liked at Leipzig; this work reflects his scholarly Aristotelianism. For a discussion of Stahl, see Wundt, *Schulmetaphysik*, 126–9.

developed) version of Leibniz's conciliatory philosophy by warning his student that before there can be "any hope of harmony" among the philosophical schools "we need to examine a bit more fully the mind of the Philosopher". After suggesting that Leibniz has misunderstood Aristotle, his esteemed teacher goes on to point out that the substantial form cannot be identical to accidental things like the figuration and magnitude of parts "in whose agreement you seem to construct the harmony" (II. i. 12). Then Thomasius acknowledges that he is "aware of this way of talking" and that others may accept this way of making "peace". In other words, Thomasius does not find Leibniz's position shocking; he just wants to have nothing to do with the moderns "whose philosophy I plainly despise" (II. i. 13).

Even without his teacher's approval, Leibniz was proud of his original theory of substance and his first attempt at a conciliatory philosophy. In the writings of 1668–9, he frequently emphasizes his success at revealing the true sophistication of the philosophy of Aristotle (e.g. II. i. 15, 17; VI. i. 510); and in one of his most important early publications, *Hypothesis physica nova* of 1671, he proudly announces his reconciliation of Aristotle with the mechanists (VI. ii. 247). But the most vivid display of the motivation and sincerity behind his reformed philosophy occurs in a paragraph which he wrote to Thomasius in April 1669 but deleted from the published version of the letter. He tells his teacher that the "truth *per se*" of the reformed philosophy must be shown "in the same way that the Christian religion can be proved by reason and experience as well as from sacred scripture" (L 100).[73] He then continues the analogy:

The saintly fathers clarified the sacred scripture with the best interpretations; the monks soon obscured it with their superstitions. [Now] the reformed theology is threefold: there is heretical theology that rejects the scriptures themselves . . .; there is the schismatical theology that rejects the ancient fathers of the church . . .; there is the true theology that reconciles the teachers of the church with the sacred scriptures and the earliest church. . . . Similarly, the Greek interpreters clarified Aristotle; the Scholastics obscured him by means of idle talk. [Now] the reformed philosophy is threefold: the dull [*stolida*] philosophy, that of Paracelsus, Helmont, and others, that straightforwardly rejects Aristotle; the audacious philosophy that has little concern for the ancients, nay, open contempt for them, and replaces even the good ideas with suspicious meditations, as Descartes did; and the true philosophy that understands Aristotle to be both a great man and for the most part true. (II. i. 21; compare VI. ii. 441)

In this extraordinary passage, Leibniz compares Aristotle to sacred scripture and the Greek commentators to the Church Fathers. In the same way that "the monks" perverted the Bible, so the schoolmen obscured Aristotle.

---

[73] Loemker includes this sentence in his translation, but not the rest of the passage. In fact, the whole passage is deleted from the 1670 version. Loemker does not make this clear.

Analogous to the true theology, the true reformed philosophy will be one of reconciliation grounded in the philosophy of Aristotle. Leibniz's commitment to a reformed philosophy is clear, as is the fact that he had no taste for any philosophy (audacious or otherwise) that ignored the "great man".

Once we see the works of the 1660s as motivated by a conciliatory eclecticism and the published letter to Thomasius as an attempt to offer just such a philosophy, the importance of the period becomes clear. Not only do the texts of the 1660s display Leibniz's fundamental methodological assumptions; they contain his first attempt at original metaphysics. In particular, the letters to Thomasius of 1668-9 present Leibniz's first theory of substance and the first of several attempts to formulate an account of individual substance that is both fully self-sufficient and an adequate base for mechanical physics.

But the lessons from the period are more important than that. When Leibniz emerged from the Rosental grove, he was on a path that would eventually lead to the mature thought of the *Discourse on metaphysics*: he had rejected the use of substantial forms in physical explanations, but he had not rejected the philosophy of Aristotle; he had accepted mechanism as the source for physical explanations, but he had not accepted the modern metaphysical options that went with it (say, those of Descartes or Gassendi). By the late 1660s, this path had led him to his first account of substance and, after some important revisions, to the theory of substance assumed in the physical works of 1671, a theory also modelled on an Aristotelian conception.[74] In the 1670s, as Leibniz's interests and sources expand to match the intellectual fecundity of the period, it becomes more and more difficult to identify the myriad of sources for his eclectic system; but he none the less remains fundamentally committed to a conciliatory philosophy centred around the metaphysics of Aristotle.[75] However much the details of his metaphysics (and physics) evolve, Leibniz does not waver from his attempt to forge a synthesis of Aristotelian metaphysics and mechanical physics. And however much the sources of his doctrines multiply and vary, he continues to attempt to achieve a philosophy of reconciliation. Thus,

---

[74] In brief, he decided that his attempt to formulate a corporeal substance out of a union of the mind of God and matter was not adequately self-sufficient and would have to be changed. He came to believe that, in order to construct a truly self-sufficient substance, he needed to make the source of motion internal to the nature of substance in a way that the mind of God was not. For a complete account of the motivations behind this change in view and of the development of the theory of substance of the early 1670s, see my forthcoming book; for a summary, see Mercer and Sleigh, secs 2–3.

[75] To cite one particularly significant example, during his years in Paris (1672-6), he studied Plato more seriously than he previously had. He was particularly interested in neoplatonic accounts of the creation of the world; and there is good reason to believe that such ideas played a significant role in the development of his doctrine of pre-established harmony. For further details, see my forthcoming book.

Leibniz could write in 1714, in the same letter to Remond with which I began this paper: "I have tried to uncover and unite the truth buried and scattered under the opinions of all the different philosophical sects, and I believe I have added something of my own which takes a few steps forward" (G iii. 606, L 654).[76]

Department of Philosophy
Columbia University

[76] I would like to thank Daniel Garber, Stephen Grover, P. O. Kristeller, Donald Rutherford, Robert Sleigh, and Margaret Wilson for helpful comments on an earlier draft of this paper. I am indebted to Susan Roth for help with bibliographical matters. Because there has been a nine-year lag between the acceptance and publication of this paper, it does not reflect my most recent research on the development of Leibniz's early thought.

6

LEIBNIZ AND THE
ANIMALCULA

CATHERINE WILSON

Leibniz's theory of immaterial atoms or monads might well be described as a continuation of policy by other means. For although his theory is in line with the seventeenth century's generally favourable attitude towards atomism, his version, according to which atoms are sentient and even living, is highly unorthodox. It is now safe to say that his opposition to the theory of physical atoms, as well as his objections to the non-atomistic corpuscular physics of Descartes, are well understood. The problems of cohesion, division, composition, and the continuum, and the inadequacy of "matter" as a substratum for force, were sufficient to convince him that the substance of the world could not be composed of atoms or particles possessing only extension, figure, and motion. Less well understood are the developments in seventeenth-century natural science which suggested a different approach to the question of the nature of substance from that supplied by the mainstream of corpuscularian mechanists, and this paper is addressed to that issue. For, contrary to the conventional picture, which assumes that the problem of "form" was either banished with the reduction of structures to corpuscular complexes or survived only as a reactionary Aristotelianism, many of the major and minor writers of the second half of the century were specifically concerned with the morphology of living creatures and with what that suggested about the irreducibility of life to matter in motion.

This essay examines Leibniz's anti-corpuscularian ideas from the positive perspective, considering them not as reactions to the inadequacies of Cartesianism and its variants, but as an attempt to incorporate into metaphysics the new revelations of the microscope, revelations which brought the notion of form again into the centre of natural philosophy. I shall concentrate accordingly on two main themes: first, the interest of Leibniz and his near contemporaries in the subject of palingenesis, or the revocation of vanished form, and preformation, or the assertion of the pre-existence of the body, and all of its parts, of every living creature before its birth; second, the prominence of beliefs about the infinite distribution of living creatures of

© Catherine Wilson 1997

an inconceivably small size. The discussion should serve, I hope, to break down the impression that the subvisible world of the scientifically sophisticated seventeenth-century philosopher was simply one of inert particles subject to mechanical laws.

Leibniz's interest in the microscope has struck a number of scholars of the period. In his study of the microscopist van Leeuwenhoek, Clifford Dobell observed that "The great and learned Leibniz paid attention to his discoveries which were not without influence upon his own philosophy: indeed the abstract 'monads' of the *Monadology* are not altogether unrelated to Leeuwenhoek's concrete 'animalcules' ".[1] Heimsoeth, too, claims that the work of the early microscopists exercised "a particularly deep and permanent impression" on Leibniz and goes so far as to suggest that the fish-pond of the *Monadology* is perhaps only one of van Leeuwenhoek's water drops writ large.[2]

The historian faces a difficulty, however, in evaluating such well-intentioned claims about influences. The "little animals" smaller than any insects ever seen before, which van Leeuwenhoek, beginning in 1673, discovered in rain, snow, and various self-prepared infusions, were one of the most notable discoveries of the second half of the seventeenth century. And there seems to be some general analogy or similarity between monads and animalcules.[3] But what remains to be said? Did the discovery of animalcules inspire the theory of monads? Did it confirm it? What did Leibniz actually know and think about van Leeuwenhoek or his animalcules in the first place? Fortunately, the historical record of Leibniz's awareness of and attitude to the microscope is sufficiently detailed to permit some approach to these questions. First, however, a brief sketch of experimental microscopy in its early period is in order.

I. EXPERIMENTAL MICROSCOPY, 1665–1720

For convenience, we can divide early microscopical work undertaken in the

---

[1] C. Dobell, *Antony van Leeuwenhoek and his "little animals"* (1932; repr. New York 1960), 385.

[2] H. Heimsoeth, *Atom, Seele, Monade* (Wiesbaden 1960), 347.

[3] It is hard not to think of monads as very small, though according to *Monadology*, sec. 3, they are unextended and can have no size. See *Die philosophischen Schriften von G. W. Leibniz*, ed. C. I. Gerhardt (7 vols, 1875–90; repr. Hildesheim 1960–61), vi. 607.

Further references to this edition are identified by 'G' followed by volume and page number. References to Leibniz, *Philosophical papers and letters*, trans. and ed. L. E. Loemker, 2nd edn (Dordrecht 1969), are indicated by 'L' followed by page number; an asterisk indicates a deviation from Loemker's translation. References with no identifying prefix are to the German Academy edition of Leibniz's *Sämtliche Schriften und Briefe*, in progress, cited by series and volume numbers and page number.

twenty-five years between 1665 and 1690 into three main categories:[4] (1) Hooke's early studies of ordinary household and garden objects;[5] (2) Swammerdam and Malpighi's studies of human, insect, and plant anatomy;[6] and finally, (3) van Leeuwenhoek's discovery, by means of lenses of a matchless power and optical quality, of micro-organisms.[7]

Hooke looked through a lens of a power equivalent to that of a modern low-power dissecting microscope; he selected and examined a variety of insects and human parasites, plant parts, cloth, hair, mould, also needles and print; and, most important, he had what he had seen engraved and reproduced in his beautiful, widely admired, still admired *Micrographia*. Besides setting the standards for a scientific iconography, Hooke popularized the idea that nature is an artist more skilful than any human artist; the triumphs of human industry—woven cloth, polished points, solid print, and so on—are rough, coarse, and imperfect compared with the exquisite fabrication of negligible insects issuing from the hand of God. Secondly, Hooke made plain what had long been suspected and announced on a priori grounds to be the case: that what the ordinary naked human eye perceives is not the truth of things, but simply an image relative to our size and visual equipment. Colours, for example, change or disappear under the microscope, and so do textures; the insect eye focuses not one but thousands of images, and who can say what the bee or the fly perceives? In the course of the *Micrographia* Hooke gives us, in an incidental way, his theories of gravity, ether, and generation; and he discovers the "cellular" structure of cork. But there is no theoretical programme behind the book: it is a collection of more or less adventitious observations.

Swammerdam, by contrast, was gripped by a fixed idea, the theory of the nymph. He believed that all creatures are produced from a rudimentary form called the nymph which exists in the egg, not miraculously, not by metamorphosis or transformation, but by a process of growth, uncovering, and unfolding. This process, he thought, we can observe in the development

[4] The microscopical investigations of Francisco Redi into the generation of insects, Puget into the structure of the insect eye, and Grew into plant tissues could also be added to this abbreviated list: late sixteenth- and early seventeenth-century naturalists, such as Penny, Moufet, and Goedaert, also appear to have used lenses in their studies of insects.

[5] *Micrographia, or Some physiological descriptions of minute bodies made by magnifying glasses* (1665).

[6] Major works published during Swammerdam's lifetime included *Tractatus . . . de respiratione* (1667); *Historia insectorum generalis* (1669); *Miraculum naturae sive uteri muliebris fabrica* (1672); and *Ephemeri vita* (1672) on the mayfly. Malpighi's studies of the lungs, the structure of the viscera and glands, the anatomy of plants, the chicken embryo, and the anatomy of the silkworm were published through the assistance of the Royal Society in his *Opera omnia* of 1686.

[7] Notices of his investigations appeared originally in *Philosophical transactions of the Royal Society*, reprinted in the so-called *Opera omnia seu arcana naturae* (4 vols, 1722).

of larva to ant, worm to fly, tadpole to frog, and to some extent in the development of "wormlet" or "vermicle" into a human being. More consistently than either Redi or Harvey, Swammerdam denied that generation could proceed from anything except parents, via the production of eggs and nymphs.

Swammerdam was able to make his discoveries, reported first in *The history of insects* in 1669 and translated into French in 1682, by the extraordinary techniques he discovered for separating the layers of an insect's body. According to Boerhaave, he effected this by an ingenious process of blanching them in scalding water, peeling off the epidermis, and then solidifying the structures in a mixture of wine and distilled vinegar "which, by giving firmness to the parts gave an opportunity of separating them with very little trouble from the exuviae or skins, without any damage to the viscera, so that by this contrivance the Nymph could be shown wrapped up in the Caterpillar, and the Butterfly in the Nymph".[8] Examining the hive-bee, he discovered that larva, pupa, and imago "may at one stage of the life-cycle exist simultaneously one within the other like a nest of boxes". Examining the egg of the louse, he discovered in it the rudiments of the louse with a pair of dark eyes; examining the egg of the frog he found the rudiments of the tadpole. In *The history of insects*, a sketch of a preformationist theory of human generation is given in the most casual manner, under the title 'Man himself compared with insects and with the frog'. Here he says that "it is clearer than the light at noon, that man is, like insects, produced from a visible egg", and that "man, that rational animal, finds his first nourishment and represents, as it were, a Vermicle or Worm, or to use Harvey's words, a Maggot lying in the egg". Furthermore, it is plain "that these parts of the Man-Vermicle grow by degrees into a head, thorax, belly, and limbs".

[I]t is indeed very admirable to observe, how the limbs sprout about the shoulder blades, and at the lower parts of the body: for, in the beginning they resemble the small cups of flowers, or the bags and cases of the parts of insects; the former enclosing the flowers, and the latter the wings; and then, by degrees, just as the legs of the Frog, they grow out of the body and are divided into joints.[9]

Turning now to van Leeuwenhoek, we find a different kind of observer, with Hooke's omnivorousness, but with a forty-year field of action. Van Leeuwenhoek looked at everything which it could possibly occur to anyone to look at: insects, infusions, bodily organs, fluids, tissues, excretions,

---

[8] Herman Boerhaave, 'Life', in John Swammerdam's *Book of nature*, trans. T. Flloyd (1758; repr. New York 1978), p. xvi.

[9] *Book of nature*, 104. On Harvey's "maggot", see his *Disputations concerning the generation of animals*, trans. G. Whitteridge (Oxford 1981), 113. The young embryos of dog, horse, deer, ox, hen, snake, and man himself, Harvey says, "so exactly resemble the shape and consistency of a maggot that your eyes cannot distinguish between them".

scrapings, and so on. He was no draughtsman, and though he had some illustrations supplied, he mainly described what he had seen in long rambling letters, addressed for the most part to the Royal Society. Van Leeuwenhoek discovered forms of life which no one had known anything about. They were not insects. These were the true animalcula—the flagellates, the bacteria, the spermatozoa, the protozoa. He announced his discovery in a celebrated letter to the Royal Society of 1676:

In the year 1675, about half-way through September . . . I discovered living creatures in rain, which had stood but a few days in a new tub that was painted blue within. This observation provoked me to investigate this water more narrowly; and especially because these little animals were, to my eye, more than ten thousand times smaller than the animalcule which Swammerdam has portrayed, and called by the name of Water-flea, or Water-louse, which you can see alive and moving in water with the bare eye.[10]

These animalcula were to the barely visible cheese mite, van Leeuwenhoek says, as a bumble-bee to a horse, "for the circumference of one of these same little animalcules is not so great as the thickness of a hair on a mite".[11] A few years later, he discovered even smaller organisms, the bacterial parasites inhabiting the frog's intestines, the streptococcus which lives in the plaque between our teeth; in 1677, he confirmed the discovery by the Dutch student Ham of the spermatozoa.[12] The last put him into a priority dispute with Hartsoeker, who claimed to have made this discovery much earlier, though his propriety and astonishment, he said, had kept him from publicizing it.

II. THE INFLUENCE OF MALEBRANCHE

We can establish Leibniz's state of awareness of experimental microscopy and its results through attention to numerous references in his letters and essays. The correspondence of the late 1670s contains, for example, a number of references to Hooke's 1665 *Micrographia*,[13] a copy of which Leibniz obtained after many delays from his friend Schultze in 1678.[14] In *A new physical hypothesis* of 1671, he refers to the Jesuit Athanasius Kircher's *Scrutinium physico-medicum* (1658), where the author claimed to have detected microscopical worms in putrefying matter which he proposed as the cause of plague (VI. ii. 241). The following year, Leibniz was given a report on

---

[10] Letter to Oldenburg, 9 Oct. 1676, in *Philosophical transactions of the Royal Society* 12 (1677), 821–31; another translation in Dobell, 117–18. [11] Dobell, 123.
[12] *Philosophical transactions* 12 (1677), 1041.
[13] I. ii. 300, 302, 325, 341, and 377.
[14] Letter to Schultze, I. ii. 341.

Kerckring's lens-assisted finding of "eggs" in human females, including virgins (I. i. 202). 'De summa rerum' of 1675 presents speculations obviously derived from microscopy about infinite descending chains of creatures (VI. iii. 475). In the same year we find a brief comment on Swammerdam's physicotheological treatise on the mayfly, which formed part of his microscopical opus (VI. iii. 380). In 1676, in his notes 'De sede animae' discussing Boyle's pamphlet on the Resurrection, Leibniz refers to Borel's microscopical observations on cherry seeds (VI. iii. 478). And in 1678 he writes to Christian Phillip that Hudde invented the single-lens microscope in 1666, that it has been exploited by van Leeuwenhoek, and he observes that the latter has made a "big noise" in France with it (I. ii. 385).

These remarks show that Leibniz was *au courant* of microscopical work, especially during the years of his Paris residence. In view of his close friendship with Huygens, who personally designed and used microscopes, it is tempting to suppose that he had the opportunity to try one out, though he does not seem to say so. In any event, the doctrine of microscopical pan-animism, or pananimalculism for short, was actually furnished to him attached to the name of Swammerdam by 1678; Justel wrote to him to say that Huygens had brought some microscopes back from Holland with which one could see an infinity of little animals in a drop of water, "which has made people conclude", Justel says, "that everything in nature is animated" (I. ii. 354). Where both pananimalculism and preformation are concerned, however, the most important source for Leibniz was Malebranche, who not only conducted his own microscopical observations, but inserted his speculations on animalcula into his physics, his epistemology, and his theology.

One does not need to read far into *The search after truth* to find these references—they are present in the opening chapters on the science of vision—and we know that Leibniz was reading this book shortly after its appearance in 1675. Malebranche showed him how the microscope fitted in with metaphysics. Malebranche saw preformation as a necessary correction to strict Cartesianism, which was epigenetical, and as a way to christianize Descartes, which seemed to need doing. He recognized that mechanism had its limits: it could explain the formation of worlds, but not that of the simplest creature.[15] But the only other alternatives to Descartes's implausible account of the formation of the foetus by filters, sieves, and the process of

---

[15] "[T]here is a great difference between the formation of living and organized bodies, and that of the vortexes of which the universe is composed. . . . It would be wrong then to pretend to explain the formation of animals and plants and their parts, one after the other, on the basis of the simple and general laws governing the communication of motion" (*The search after truth*, VI. ii. 4, trans. T. M. Lennon and P. J. Olscamp (Columbus, Oh. 1980), 465: all further references are to this translation).

accretion were a pent-up Aristotelian potential from which the brakes had been removed—a theory not acceptable to the anti-scholastic Malebranche— or, equally unacceptable, an occult active force: the plastic nature or hylomorphic principle of Henry More, the "operative ideas" of Marcus Marci von Kronland, or Harvey's astral contagion.[16] Just as preformation saved the case for mechanism by dispensing with obvious counterexamples, so mechanism seemed to imply preformation. For a machine can only work when it is all there: the heart, for example, cannot beat without the stimulation of the brain, or pump blood without the existence of a circulatory system. Thus, when the heart is there and working, the organism—the whole machine—must already be "there".[17]

The biological theory of preformation is a fascinating topic because of the apparent conflict between the visual evidence for it, which was ambiguous, and the strong theory-driven insistence on its truth. Those who had observed most patiently were convinced that the parts of the animal were formed sequentially. For Aristotle, the organs seem to emerge from a formless mass in a definite order: first the heart, later the head, later the limbs, with the remaining internal organs being filled in later. Nature, he says, is like a painter who first makes an outline, then adds the colours and details (*Generation of animals*, II vi). Other writers might disagree on the order of the formation of the organs, but the consensus was that there was an order. Was preformationism then simply a denial of the ocular evidence?

Malebranche thought that he had some direct ocular evidence. "When one examines the seed of a tulip bulb in the dead of winter", he says,

with a simple *magnifying lens* or convex glass, or even merely with the naked eye, one easily discovers in this seed the leaves that are to become green, those that are to make up the flower or tulip, that tiny triangular part which contains the seed, and the six little columns that surround it at the base of the flower. Thus it cannot be doubted that the seed of a tulip bulb contains an entire tulip. (*Search*, 26)

The same thing is probably true of every tree, every plant, and every animal:

Nor does it seem unreasonable to believe even that there is an infinite number of trees in a single seed, since it contains not only the tree of which it is the seed but also a great number of other seeds that might contain other trees and other seeds, which will perhaps have on an incomprehensibly small scale other trees and other seeds and so to infinity. (ibid., 27)

With chickens, however, the ocular evidence is less compelling. Can the chicken really be all there and look nothing like a chicken? Malpighi— himself officially a preformationist—had depicted the ten-day-old embryo as

---

[16] On Harvey and Marcus Marci, see esp. W. Pagel, *William Harvey's biological ideas* (repr. New York 1967), 285ff.
[17] *Search*, loc. cit. The argument is revived in a vitalistic context by Bonnet: see J. Needham, *The history of embryology*, 2nd edn (Cambridge 1959), 213.

a kind of tube with huge eyes at one end, not very different from Harvey's maggot, and the preformationist Swammerdam endorsed that description. All Malebranche will say is: "a chicken that is perhaps entirely formed is seen in the seed of a fresh egg that has not been hatched", this germ being under the tiny white spot—the cicatrix on the yolk (ibid.). He is here restating his claim that nature's role is "only to unfold" these seeds. In the *Dialogues on metaphysics*, which devote a whole chapter to preformation, the character Theotimus admits that we cannot see every part of the plant in the seed, but "we may try to imagine them". Indeed, we are obliged to try to imagine them; reason demands that we envision what we cannot see.[18] And Régis, who argues that the germ is preformed in the female ovum and that its development is set in course by the male sperm which acts on it chemically to produce a fermentation which loosens it up and lets it expand, concedes that we cannot see the whole organism in its early stages.[19]

Thus the presence of the preformed organism might seem to involve no more than a sort of intellectual mandate to imagine it, and it might be consistent with a thoroughly indefinite appearance even under the lens. Nor was the position that the chicken was all there, even though nothing like a chicken could actually be seen, absurd or even unempirical; the transparency of most biological structures, the jelly-like consistency of parts, made the notion of an actually existing form which could not be seen with available techniques and lenses reasonable. The preformationist did not understand the concept to involve a mere reduction in scale, moreover: different parts and organs developed, expanded, unfolded, or lost their opaque coverings, at different rates.[20]

It is not clear whether a strictly naive form of preformation-as-miniaturization was held by any natural philosopher of the period. We are used to reading about Hartsoeker and Dalenpatius or De Plantade, who supposedly "saw" little human beings curled up in foetal position in spermatozoa, and drew what they saw. The case of Dalenpatius, however, involved a spoof and an error.[21] And when Hartsoeker, in his treatise on dioptrics, produced the famous engraving of the large-headed baby curled up in the spermatozoon, he did not pretend to be illustrating what he saw.[22] Van

---

[18] *Dialogues on metaphysics*, trans. W. Doney (New York 1980), dial. XI, p. 267. "We must conceive this. It can at any rate be conceived."

[19] P.-S. Régis, *Cours entier de philosophie* (1691; repr. London 1970), 64.

[20] See, for example, the statements of Albrecht von Haller quoted by Needham, 201–2.

[21] F. J. Cole, *Early theories of sexual generation* (Oxford 1930), 68ff.

[22] He employs the subjunctive to say: "If one could see the little animal through the skin which covers it, we would perhaps see something like this figure, unless the head were perhaps larger in proportion to the rest of the body than one has drawn it here" (Hartsoeker, *Essai de dioptrique* (1694), 229).

Leeuwenhoek, who formulated the principle *"omnis animal ex animalculo"* as early as 1679, says that, although he cannot see the form of the animal in the animalcule, he does not despair of doing so, and he has "often fancied" that he could see the head, shoulders, and other limbs of the foetus.[23]

It might, then, seem that preformation can better be defined by what it excluded—extra-mechanical agencies, or vague scholastic potentials—than by any stipulation about what microscopical observation would have to reveal. Thus, it is often seen as a "rationalist" position, contrary to the "empiricist" preference for epigenesis. But if preformation is consistent with empiricism—for Swammerdam and Malpighi were as good and diligent observers as Harvey—it is also consistent with mysticism, a fact which is not irrelevant when it comes to considering Leibniz's reception of the theory of preformation in its various aspects. When Henry Power, the microscopist, writes to his mentor Thomas Browne in 1659 describing his investigations with lenses, he says that he believes the whole plant to be epitomized in the seed; the seed containing not only the form of the plant—which is the standard Aristotelian theory—but the matter of the plant condensed or, as Power says, "capsulated & stradled up in severall filmes, huskes & shells".[24] "Some say that in the Cicatricula . . . you may see all the parts of a chick exactly delineated", he observes, expressing some caution here. Power, who is honest and a good observer, wonders whether it may be permissible to say that the parts of the organism are all delineated though not demonstrable to sense. This notion of "invisible delineation" is a philosophically powerful one. It embodies a kind of contradiction and is saved from outright incoherence only through what it offers the imagination; it lends itself to mysticism. Browne, writing in the era of the magnifying lens though not yet in the era of the microscope, has such an understanding of the presence of the tree in the seed: "In the seed of a Plant to the eyes of God, and to the understanding of man, there exist, though in an invisible way, the perfect leaves, flowers, and fruits thereof: (for things that are in *posse* to the sense, are actually existent to the understanding)."[25] Here, to be sure, preformation threatens to dissolve into Aristotelian potential. What holds it back is a religious metaphor; what human beings perceive only indistinctly and sketchily God sees in perfect unfolded detail.

[23] F. J. Cole, 'Leeuwenhoek's zoological researches', Pt I, *Annals of science* 2 (1937), 1–46, at 9–10.
[24] Power to Browne, 10 May 1659, in *The works of Sir Thomas Browne*, ed. G. Keynes (4 vols, London 1928), iv. 265–6.
[25] Thomas Browne, *Religio medici*, in *Selected writings*, ed. G. Keynes (London 1968), 58.

III. PALINGENESIS AND PREFORMATION:
LEIBNIZ'S CONCERN WITH THE PERSISTENCE OF FORM

It is unfortunate that we do not know exactly what form Leibniz's belief in preformation took; whether he preferred Régis's fermentation theory, or insisted upon a more literal, Malebranchian interpretation. But we do know that he makes broad use of the ideas of the reduction, unfolding, and persistence of animal form. We see this first in his account of death. Leibniz, who found the Cartesian idea of a separated soul "monstrous", argued that death, like birth, involves only a form of encapsulation. His might be called a "postformationist" account; its reliance on the revelations of the microscope is indisputable.

In the letter to Arnauld of 30 April 1687, for example, he observes that there is an infinity of animalcules in the smallest drop of water, and offers his opinion that—whether or not burned-up organisms actually will grow again in the cinders, a view which depends on some "doubtful experiments"—organisms cannot be destroyed. "When one realizes that generation is only the augmentation and development of an animal which is already formed, one will also be persuaded that death or corruption is nothing but the diminution and encapsulation of an animal which does not leave off subsisting and remains living and organized" (G ii. 123). These comments are further developed in a discussion of the revivification of hibernating swallows, drowned flies, and cocooned silkworms: creatures which look and act quite dead may nevertheless maintain their life—"sleep is an image of death". He notes that it is difficult to establish his position experimentally, for "generation goes forward naturally and little by little, which gives us time to observe it, but death suddenly reverses direction, by a leap . . . which prevents us from following the details of this retrogression" (ibid.).

It might at first seem, indeed, that Leibniz's views about the postformation and the persistence of the whole organism after death were simply extensions of theories of pre-existence. However, the situation is not so simple. Leibniz had been concerned with the problem of physical survival, and had developed a kind of encapsulation theory even before he became acquainted with biological preformationism. The explanation for this is that the invisible persistence of form was already understood in a chemical context, especially in connection with the operations of solution and recrystallization. When salt crystals are dissolved in water and made to recrystallize, a form seems to persist invisibly or potentially in some material substance. Indeed, the idea which tempted some preformationists, that "forms" need not be plainly visible and identifiable to be "there", may actually have been borrowed from chemistry and an associated "occult" literature.

The theme of resuscitation from ashes, to which Leibniz keeps returning, points irresistibly, despite the up-to-date reference to animalcula, back towards the fascination of the Renaissance with tombs, ashes, and relics, and the subject of the physical resurrection of the body. One finds in the literature dealing with these subjects—the literature of palingenesis—references to "sparks of life" and "seeds of immortality"[26] which their proponents believe must somehow reside in the ashes of the dead when they have lost even their skeletal integrity. As in the recrystallization case, or in the case of the recovery of a metal from an amalgam, the thing, the organism in ashes, is both "there" and "not there", and this in a "mystical" sense.[27]

The philosopher who turned to chemistry to explain the resurrection might be accused of having attempted to give a naturalistic explanation for a miracle, thereby destroying the religious meaning of the procedure. Thus palingenesis had both a positive and a negative dimension for the theologically-minded philosopher, and it was often unclear whether it was merely a case of proposing a symbolic analogue from, say, chemistry, or whether chemical processes were actually intended. Consider, for example, Browne's statement in *Religio medici*—a work, incidentally, which was known to Leibniz: "Those strange and mysticall transmigrations that I have observed in Silkewormes, turn'd my Philosophy into Divinity", Browne says, telling us how he has learned from the philosopher's stone "how that immortall spirit and incorruptible substance of my soule may lye obscure, and sleepe a while within this house of flesh" (*Selected writings*, 46).

I have often beheld as a miracle that artificiall resurrection and revivification of *Mercury*, how being mortified into [a] thousand shapes, it assumes againe its owne, and returns to its numericall selfe. Let us speake naturally, and like Philosophers: the formes of alterable bodies in these sensible corruptions perish not; nor, as wee imagine, wholly quit their mansions, but retire and contract themselves into their secret and inaccessible parts, where they may best protect themselves from the action of their Antagonist. (ibid., 55)

Browne continues by noting that, when a plant is burned up, the form seems to a school-philosopher "to have taken his leave for ever: But to a sensible Artist the formes are not perished, but withdrawne into their incombustible part, where they lie secure from the action of that devouring element", as is clear from the generation of plants from cinders. The contrast is between

---

[26] *Journal des savants*, Jan. 1716, 71–9. This review of J. H. Cohausen's book on ancient tombs and their contents mentions Robert Fludd's experiment in re-forming the figure of a man from the cinders of his head.

[27] Palingenesis is particularly associated with Kenelm Digby, Robert Fludd, and Kircher; it might involve either actual revivification of the organism, as in Kircher's experiments with drowned flies, or the reconstitution of its form in something wraithelike, as in Fludd's or some of Digby's experiments. See 'Palingénesie', in *Encyclopédie ou dictionnaire raisonné des sciences, des arts, et des métiers*, ed. Diderot and D'Alembert (1757), xi. 784–5.

school philosophy (read: heathenish, Aristotelian), which says that forms go out of existence, and mystical philosophy, which says that forms survive in a withdrawn, encapsulated state. So, Browne summarizes, the scholar or student of nature does not become an atheist, and he even "beholds not in a dreame, as *Ezekiel*, but in an ocular and visible object the types of his resurrection".

Leibniz himself seems to trace the path from a chemical preformation theory of "contraction" and "withdrawal" of Browne's type, to a biological theory of encapsulation of Malebranche's type. Before going on to consider when and why, I shall try to document this shift.

Leibniz's early interests in alchemy would have familiarized him with the phenomenon of the chemical tree of the philosophers, the *arbor Dianae*, with Paracelsus's recipes for the creation of *homunculi*, and with the palingenesis literature; and he was evidently aware of some of the most curious ideas about the generation and persistence of form of his time, such as Marcus Marci's theory of embryological development through the refraction and differentiation of something analogous to optical rays. One of his earliest statements about the persistence of the body in a subvisible form appears to draw on some combination of this literature; in his famous letter to Duke John Frederick of 1671, Leibniz states that the soul at death retires into a small part of the body, a "kernel", which is somehow an image or isomorph of it (G i. 53–4). The eclecticism of his early ideas about the persistence of forms, and their relation to non-biological mystico-chemical theories of preformation, is further illustrated by a text partially translated some years ago by Loemker: Leibniz's notes on Boyle's paper on the resurrection of the body from 1675.

Boyle tries in his paper to show that resurrection is no more impossible than many easily demonstrable physical and chemical transformations. He takes into account the usual objections and puzzles about identity which practices like cannibalism bring up. But he forces the reader to admit first that the human body "is in a perpetual flux or changing condition" anyway, since it grows "from a *corpusculum* no bigger than an insect to the full stature of a man, which, in many persons that are tall and fat, may amount to a vast bulk".[28] He recites numerous instances of chemical transformations and changes of form, especially involving mercury, and he describes Kircher's (characterized by Leibniz as "doubtful") and others' experiments of resuscitating plants from their ashes. These might, Boyle says, argue that "in the saline and earthy . . . particles of a vegetable that has been dissipated and destroyed by the violence of the fire, there may remain a plastic power, enabling them to contrive disposed matter so as to reproduce such a body as

---

[28] Robert Boyle, 'Some physico-theological considerations about the possibility of the resurrection', in *Selected philosophical papers of Robert Boyle*, ed. M. A. Stewart (Manchester 1979), 198.

was formerly destroyed".[29] Note that he is not arguing exactly that God does employ chemical principles or plastic powers to resurrect; his point seems to be, rather, that the wonderful transformations and recoveries that can be accomplished by ordinary physico-chemical means show that a resurrection of the whole human body by divine means is not out of the question.[30]

Leibniz's reactions to the paper are thoroughly approving; unlike Boyle, though, he seems determined to exclude both the direct action of God and the idea of a purely corpuscular bodily substratum. Instead, he reaches back to his old kernel theory, which here appears in the form of an idea about a "flower of substance":

I hold, namely, that this flower of substance is our body; that the flower of substance now persists perpetually in all changes; that this was foreshadowed through the Luz of the Rabbis. Hence it is easy to see why cannibals, in eating a man, have no power at all over the flower of substance. This flower of substance is diffused through the whole body; somehow comprises the whole form. Add to this what Borelli[31] says in his microscopic observations about the figure of the cherry tree in the shell of the seed or nut enclosed by its fruit; also about the tree of the philosophers; also what is found on plastic force in the French journal, from the English.[32]

Knowing something about Leibniz's later repudiation of plastic nature in favour of preformation makes this passage especially interesting. Here the theory of signatures, plastic natures, the rabbis' theory of the Luz, the "flower of substance", all seem to be aspects of the same thing. Plastic nature is said to be "this active substance, of a certain figure" which is capable of growth and which "exists before conception". Not surprisingly, he goes on to add the alchemical account: the resurrection of the body is here supposed to be something like the precipitation of a salt out of a solution. "[W]hat happens in any species of salt you choose may also happen more generally with any human individual you choose; in that more subtle solution and in a shorter time everything may be recomposed through crystallization." And he refers to the chemical tree of the philosophers, formed by the crystallization of metal salts, as though it had something to do with the image of a cherry

---

[29] Ibid., 196.

[30] The orthodox reacted strongly against experimental resurrections as well as the suggestion that resurrection might be a natural or non-miraculous process. See, for instance, Redi's criticisms of Kircher's resuscitation experiments: "The holy mysteries of our Faith cannot be comprehended by human reason" (*Experiments on the generation of insects* (1688), trans. M. A. Bigelow (1909; repr. New York 1969), 35–6).

[31] Read: Borel.

[32] 'De sede animae' (1676), translated by L. E. Loemker, 'Boyle and Leibniz', *Journal of the history of ideas* 16 (1955), 22–43, at 43. The references are to J. Schegk, *De plastica seminis facultate libri tres* (Strasburg 1680); to Davisson, a Paracelsian doctor; to the dispute between Perrault, the Cartesian, and Mariotte on the seat of the soul; and to an unknown Englishman—perhaps Henry More. The Luz of the rabbis, versified by Samuel Butler in his *Hudibras*, is the *os sacrum*, considered indestructible by water, fire, grinding, or smashing.

tree which the microscopist Borel saw delineated in the shell of a cherry seed. This eclecticism gives way to the more unified account which we see already emerging in the Arnauld correspondence. Postformation is, on this account, simply preformation read backwards, a contraction and enfolding, a diminution of function, a sleep of indefinite duration.[33]

IV. THE MICROSCOPE IN LEIBNIZ'S MATURE PHILOSOPHY

References to the instrument abound in Leibniz's work after 1686 as well as before, with this difference: Leibniz appears to lose interest in details of new observations and to become captivated by the idea, which he ascribes often indifferently to van Leeuwenhoek, Malpighi, and Swammerdam, that generation is really only development and augmentation of what is already there. We find multiple references accordingly in the correspondence with Arnauld (1686–7);[34] in 'A new system of the nature and the communication of substances' (1695);[35] and in numerous other works.[36] In the last two years of Leibniz's life he actually corresponded with van Leeuwenhoek, raising some doubts about the latter's spermaticism; he argued, repeating a standard objection of the ovist party, that the theory implied a wastefulness in nature.[37] He also tried unsuccessfully to persuade van Leeuwenhoek to open a school for training students to manufacture and use microscopes.

The persistence and invariance of these references lead one to wonder whether the metaphysical notion of invisible delineation in particular and the revelations of the microscope in general might have had other significant, if less obvious, points of application for Leibniz, beyond his theory of

---

[33] See 'The principles of nature and of grace' (1714), secs 4, 6 (G vi. 599–601, L 637–8).

[34] For example, at G ii. 122ff.

[35] In sec. 6, for example: "The *transformations* of Swammerdam, Malpighi, and Leeuwenhoek, the best observers of our times, have come to my aid" (G iv. 480, L 455).

[36] See, for example, the discussion in *New essays* of Kerckring and van Leeuwenhoek as ovist and spermaticist (VI. vi. 316). The essay of 1705, 'On vital principles and plastic natures', refers to "very exact observers who have already found that one may doubt that any animal is produced spontaneously, and that animals may already exist in miniature before conception, just as well as plants" (G vi. 543, L* 589). In 'The principles of nature and of grace', plants and animals are said not to come from putrefaction or chaos, as the ancients believed, but from preformed seeds. The same essay contains a probable reference to van Leeuwenhoek's (by then abandoned) curious theory of spermatogenesis through the mating of male and female sperm: "What has just been said about the larger animals applies as well to the generation and death of the spermatic animals; that is to say, they are the enlargements of other, smaller spermatic animals" (G vi. 601, L* 638). Finally, the Leibniz-Clarke correspondence of 1716 repeats Leibniz's long-held view that "the organism of an animal is a machine which presupposes a divine preformation" (G vii. 415–16, L* 715).

[37] For the text of the letters and van Leeuwenhoek's replies, see C. G. Ehrenberg, *Rede zur Feier des Leibnitzischen Jahrestags* (Berlin 1845).

immortality. As noted at the start, Leibniz's basic ontology, highly distinctive for the period, consisted in an immaterialist, dynamicist, organicist atomism. In the *Monadology*, section 66, he depicts the world as a plenum of living beings: wherever you look "there is a world of creatures, living beings, animals, entelechies, of souls in the smallest portion of matter" (G vi. 618, L* 650). The bodies of these living beings are themselves inhabited by smaller animals, and perhaps even composed of smaller animals. And these animals in turn are, at least in one version of the theory, compounded out of immaterial monads—active perceiving mirrors of the universe—together with bodies which "belong" to them or are "attached to them". The more usual position, represented by the corpuscularians Descartes, Boyle, and Locke, is that life is somehow a function of the mutual interrelation of the individually inanimate parts of a particular organism to one another, even if consciousness and perception cannot be a matter of functional relationships. Leibniz for his part retains the central idea that the phenomena of life—growth, respiration, digestion, etc.—are explicable by "mechanical" laws. But living means perceiving, for Leibniz, and thinking is only a kind of perceiving (sec. 14); he thus rejects the Cartesian suggestion that animal or vegetable life could be synthesized, i.e. that material particles could ever be assembled in order to replicate the processes of life and so perception. There can be no unensouled animals or plants, nor can there be thinking substances which are not somehow "attached" to organic bodies.

The same pattern of appropriation and rejection is apparent in his attitude towards the corpuscularian view that the apparent continuity of material substances disguises an underlying division into discrete units which are the original products of creation. Leibniz agrees that analysis comes to an end with simple units. He thus remains an atomist who regards the Aristotelian continuum as an illusion. But indivisible particles can never be demonstrated by physical analysis, no matter how refined. Refined metaphysical analysis, by contrast, reveals indivisible units; but, surprisingly, these turn out to be animate beings rather than inanimate particles.

Given that Descartes had worked out his scientific ontology before 1665 when the microscope achieved its sudden burst of popularity, is there any reason to suppose that Leibniz's abandonment of Aristotelianism and his subsequent deviations from Cartesianism, these representing the two alternatives of his youth, were connected in any way with the introduction of the microscope? Earlier I noted that microscopical observations furnished him with a weapon against the form-matter metaphysics of the Aristotelians, and evidence in favour of the two-level scheme according to which sensory qualities are appearances of underlying arrangements of particles not possessing these qualities. This is the substance of the letter to Thomasius, which draws specifically on Hooke's work rather than on that of Boyle, who was not at the time known to Leibniz. And the microscopists' distinction between the everyday world of smooth surfaces and qualitative differentiation, and the different world which enhanced vision shows within and underneath it, is certainly carried over into Leibniz's distinction between the phenomenal world and the metaphysically real world which underlies and produces it.

It is safe to say, however, that the dominant interpretations of the origins of Leibniz's monadology do not assign much importance to the microscope. One reason for this silence is the widely shared belief that Leibniz arrived at his monadological views by 1686 and thereafter did not change them, and that he arrived at them by one or both of two routes: through a consideration of subject-predicate logic or through reflection on the nature of the continuum. As there is no mention of microscopes or microscopical animals in the *Discourse on metaphysics*, representing Leibniz's 1686 description of his system, his unorthodox stance has seemed to be sufficiently well explained without their help.

Against this claim two points need to be made, in addition to the methodological point that the subjectively-felt lack of any need for appealing to some additional explaining factor does not show its objective historical irrelevance. The introduction of explicit references to animalcules in the explanatory Correspondence which followed the *Discourse*, and later in Leibniz's exoteric writings generally, suggests either that he was already drawing on the revelations of the microscope and had decided that he could bolster his case by being more explicit, or else that he acquired some new ideas about the microworld in 1686–7.[38] These data later became urgently needed as justification after Leibniz's confidence in the acceptability of his logical-conceptual determinism was shaken.

In section 8 of the *Discourse*, Leibniz states that "there are from all time in the soul of Alexander traces of everything that has happened to him and marks of everything that will happen to him and even traces of all that happens in the universe, though only God can know them all"; and the same is true correspondingly for every other individual substance (G iv. 433, L* 308). It is often said, following indeed Leibniz's own explanation of the matter, that this view originated in his subject-predicate logic: a proposition is true when and only when the predicate is "contained in" the subject; thus, for it to be possible for that set of statements (including future contingent statements) about a person which are true of him to be true of him, he must "contain" all his predicates. However, the ascription of predetermined future acts and sufferings to historical persons, and the ascription of marks and traces of past actions and sufferings to existing persons—the notion that past and future are marked, stamped, or impressed in the individual substance— is what makes the containment theory non-trivial. Observe that the logical

---

[38] Perhaps through an encounter with Fontenelle's *Conversations on the plurality of worlds* (1686): see C. Wilson, *The invisible world* (Princeton 1995), ch. 6.

theory of containment is ontologically indifferent; Caesar's future actions can be contained in the "notion" of Caesar no matter what kind of thing Caesar is. But for marks and traces to be impressed in Caesar he must be a substance of a certain type. As Leibniz tells Arnauld in 1687, "it is indeed through the ideas of substance that the evidences of the future are formed in advance and that the traces of the future are preserved for ever in everything".[39] To say that the logical subject Caesar "contains" his future assassination says no more than that it is now irrevocably the case that Caesar will be assassinated. But the claim that marks and traces of his future assassination can now be visible to an ideal intelligence in his substance, but will only later be revealed to posterity, is a stronger claim. These "marks" and "traces" which Leibniz refers to repeatedly are actual modifications of the person's substance.[40] It is therefore not just the case that the notion of an individual substance is that of a being which is determined to, and will inevitably experience, a certain sequence of perceptions, and whose body will be found in a sequence of positions and locations in the neighbourhood of various other things, as Leibniz's parallelist language sometimes suggests. The emphasis is rather on an internal set of invisible delineations, and is best brought out with the help of Leibniz's own analogies. Ordinary names contain their predicates invisibly, in the sense that the ocular inspection of an ordinary name will never reveal any specific properties of the referent. But if ordinary names were replaced by the logically and scientifically perspicuous names of the Universal Characteristic, ocular inspection would reveal to the reader all the actual properties of the referent. Seeds contain their organisms invisibly in the sense that unassisted ocular inspection will not reveal the whole organism; but if our apparatus were good enough, we would see all of its parts. The comparison between the word and the seed is not forced, as Leibniz's own description of the characteristic as like an optical instrument shows.[41] Substances, finally, contain their future states and actions invisibly, in that most of them are unknown to the subjects themselves and only fully apparent to God. Individual substances are thus somewhat like names—they are associated with "concepts" which have analyses; but they are also somewhat like seeds, in that they are inscribed with signs of their future states.

---

[39] G ii. 98. For other references to "marks" and "traces", see G ii. 39, 45, 57.

[40] See Seneca in *Quaestiones naturales*, III. 29: "In the seed are enclosed all the parts of the body of the man that shall be formed. The infant that is borne in his mother's wombe hath the rootes of the beard and hair that he shall weare one day. In this little masse likewise are all the lineaments of the bodie and all that which Posterity shall discover in him" (quoted by Needham, 66). It was exactly the idea that God knows the future through his inspection of concepts that Arnauld found objectionable.

[41] C. Wilson, *Leibniz's metaphysics: A historical and comparative study* (Manchester 1989), 34.

An individual mind, Leibniz says in the *Discourse*, restricting the discussion now to minds rather than "substances", contains marks of the future production of all its thoughts and a disposition to produce them. The production of a thought, or the passage from one thought or experience to another, takes place in accord with some internal logic of development into which we have only a partial insight, and, in this sense, all our thoughts and experiences are innate to us (G iv. 454, L 321). Elsewhere, however, he shows himself attuned to the normal distinction between ideas which come to us from "outside" and those which arise as the mind reflects on itself. This more restricted version of innatism also borrows from the theory of preformation. Our innate ideas, like our physical bodies, as far as Leibniz is concerned, have no true beginnings; the problem of their origins is solved by saying that they were always there. Our knowledge of necessary truths, and of concepts like "being", "substance", and "unity", exists within us in invisibly delineated form: it is both "there" and "not there", for any one of us may be and remain ignorant of the formulation of some necessary truth, or fail to reflect on the concepts (*New essays*, VI. vi. 51–2). So Leibniz insists against Locke that both the concepts and the propositions of all of arithmetic and geometry, along with practical and speculative principles, are innate (ibid., 77). And he says that this does not mean that we have a pure disposition to think of them, or a pure power of thinking of them. This would mean that the mind possessed an epigenetical formative capacity. They are really there, just as the wings of the butterfly are already marked out in the larva.

Leibniz compares the bringing up of an idea into consciousness with the growth and development of an organism only once, to my knowledge; but the comparison is noteworthy. To Bayle's objection in his dispute with Jaquelot that we have no control over our bodies or over the formation of our ideas, because such control would imply a knowledge of hidden processes in our bodies and an artistic ability to represent the forms of everything we can imagine, and would imply an omnipotence of the will which is empirically refuted,[42] Leibniz answers that our freedom consists in spontaneity and our spontaneity does not require knowledge or the formation of intentions. "Are salts, metals, plants, animals and a thousand other animate or inanimate bodies aware how that which they do is done, and need they be aware? . . . [W]e do not form our ideas because we will to do so, they form themselves within us, they form themselves through us, not in consequence of our will, but in accordance with our nature and that of things." As the foetus, because of its divine preformation, is formed according to mechanical laws in the animal, so the soul, which is "a spiritual automaton that is still more

---

[42] Pierre Bayle, *Réponse aux questions d'un provincial*, in *Oeuvres diverses* (5 vols, 1737; repr. Hildesheim 1966), iii. 786–7.

admirable", produces through divine preformation "these beautiful ideas, wherein our will has no part and to which our art cannot attain".[43]

There is nevertheless a certain reluctance on Leibniz's part to over-use such a powerful analogy. Indeed, if the process of generating an idea were like the development of an organism, our minds would be strangely passive: mere matrices and nests for ideas. There is a charm in the notion that our most brilliant ideas are precisely those to which "our art cannot attain", but only because it is obviously a paradox. It is we, after all, who by our own efforts seem to arrive at a full awareness of logical, mathematical, metaphysical, and moral ideas, by struggling to recollect them, to deduce them, or simply to meditate concentratedly upon them. When Leibniz suggests as an alternative that ideas are within us as the veins in a block of marble mark out a statue, he must seemingly fall back on a weaker notion of preformation; for the veins underdetermine the form of the finished statue as the embryo does not underdetermine the form of the future animal. He can allow for what is active in thinking—arriving at a truth is like labouring "to expose the veins and to polish them into clarity"—but at the price of weakening the claim that our knowledge of moral, metaphysical, and mathematical truths is already there (*New essays*, VI. vi. 52).

V. FROM ANIMALCULA TO MONADS

Leibniz's theory of the existence of an infinite descending chain of creatures, together with his seemingly independent thesis that each possible perspectival *situs* is occupied by a perceiving being, points again to a favourable reception of the microscopical literature. Again, the pathway here was marked out by Malebranche, who had stated in the *Search* that the sequence of creatures goes on for ever: "What a mite is compared with us, these animals are to a mite; and perhaps there are in nature things smaller and smaller to infinity, standing in that extreme proportion of man to mite." God might have made animals to infinity: "there are always tiny animals to be found with microscopes, but not always microscopes to find them" (*Search*, 26).

Though one might suspect here that Malebranche did not really know what he meant by 'infinity', Leibniz came to these statements in 1676 with fresh interest in and experience with the theory of infinitesimals and indivisibles. And it is these passages which seem to be echoed and dramatically extended in the Paris Notes in which the possibility of an infinitesimal creature is raised; a creature which is divisible yet less than any finite size. "We must see whether it can be demonstrated that there is something infinitely small yet not indivisible; from the existence of such a

[43] *Theodicy*, sec. 403 (G vi. 356); trans. E. M. Huggard (La Salle, Ill. 1985), 364–5.

being there would follow wonderful things about the infinite; namely, if we assume creatures of another, infinitely small world, we will be infinite in comparison with them."[44]

This picture of harmonious coexistence with and within a world of tiny unseen beings is one expression of Leibniz's plenist optimism. But we need only recall Pascal's portrayal of the disorienting effects of imagining the world as both infinite and present, as shrunk to a point or blown up to a cosmos,[45] to see that a range of responses is possible. Malebranche's interlocutor in the *Dialogues on metaphysics* confesses in a Pascalian mood that, although the theory of *emboîtement* reveals the wisdom and skill of the Creator, it "frightens the imagination", implying that it interferes with his religious satisfaction. He is reassured by the philosopher, who urges him to let his wonder only please and not terrify him (Dialogue XI, pp. 251–2). Like other spectacles, the microscope's display could be experienced as sublime— or as devoid of pathos. We might contrast here the cheerful imperturbability of van Leeuwenhoek with the "ardent imagination of passionate sadness" (in his editor Boerhaave's words) of Swammerdam, the "founder and martyr of his science", whose religious melancholy, according to Michelet, was fed by his horror before the abyss of life, with its millions upon millions of unknown beings and bizarre forms of organization.[46] That God had made so much of life showed that it must be dear to him; on the other hand, was there not a certain expendability implied in this over-production, a certain casualness in the free hand with which it had been dispensed? The philosopher could equally well conceive himself at the pinnacle of creation, or become persuaded that it was all there by chance or thanks to the power of nature. For while the microscope tended to refute the doctrine of spontaneous generation in insects by disclosing the true cycle of generations, it left the possibility at least temporarily open for the lesser animalcules which appeared from one day to the next in any backyard puddle of standing water. Leibniz's position excludes this possibility a priori. The *infusoria*, which are naturally immortal like all other creatures, must represent specific products of an original creation.

We are left with two unsolved problems, one historical, one systematic. First, can Dobell's claim that Leibniz was influenced by the discovery of microscopical organisms specifically by van Leeuwenhoek really be upheld? Were the observations of van Leeuwenhoek critical or, given the fact that many other observers saw very small animals, were they definitive in any way? Second—a systematic question—what are the relations of the animal-cules to the monads?

---

[44] 'De summa rerum', VI. iii. 475, L* 159.

[45] Pascal, *Pensées*, ed. F. Kaplan (Paris 1982), 153–4.

[46] J. Michelet, 'Swammerdam', ch. 8 of *L'Insecte*, in *Oeuvres complètes*, ed. P. Viallaneix (Paris 1986—), vol. iii.

Where the first question is concerned, it seems to me that van Leeuwenhoek's observations were decisive for Leibniz. It was not simply the smallness of what van Leeuwenhoek saw, but the unfamiliarity of those non-insect forms of life. Animals, one would have thought before van Leeuwenhoek, need at least some of the following: limbs, mouths, eyes, sensory organs, etc. Van Leeuwenhoek showed—though he did ascribe nerves and muscles to his animalcules—that it is possible to be an active, living, mobile, and so perceiving thing without resembling a creature of ordinary experience.

It is perhaps the answer to the first question—what was the importance of the empirical discovery of animalcula?—which is the key to the second, what did they have to do with Leibniz's immaterialist metaphysics? My suggestion here is that we need to see the monads as to some extent modelled after the animalcula—they have perception and appetition, and can exist at very low degrees of awareness and general competence—but also as a way of escape from the difficulties their existence presented.

The idea of an "atom of an animal" or a "living atom", a term which appears in Swammerdam and van Leeuwenhoek as well as in Malebranche,[47] coexists in the latter's thought with the explicit statement that there are smaller and smaller animals to infinity. But either there are smallest animals or there are not. Now, atomic animals would be arbitrary: why should nature stop with just that size? A complicating feature is that both Leibniz and Malebranche were attracted to yet another theory of infrastructure which excluded material atoms: that of miniature fluid vortices. Leibniz first advanced these ideas in his 'De summa rerum' in 1676 (VI. iii. 508ff.); Malebranche in 1690 in the sixteenth Elucidation to *The search after truth* (*Search*, 697). Claiming that the smaller the circle a body is revolving in, the greater its centrifugal force, Malebranche tries to show that the solidity of ordinary matter follows from the smallness of the vortices which compose it. If the sequence of creatures proceeds to infinity, so must the smallness of vortices; or else there are creatures whose life and development cannot be explained. For physiological processes depend on physical mechanisms (ibid., 688–9).

There is no evidence that either Malebranche or Leibniz worried about how an ontology of vortices and an ontology of animalcules were related. But the problem might have presented itself as an obstacle whose presence is

---

[47] The *Journal des savants* for 1668, for instance, reports on Eustachio Divini's discovery of an animal smaller than any known, many-footed, with a white back and scales. "If a grain of sand were the size of a nut, this animal would be as small as a grain of sand, which led one of the spectators present to call it 'atom of an animal'." For earlier mentions of animal atoms, see C. Singer, 'The development of the doctrine of *contagium vivum*, 1500–1750' (brochure, London 1913).

sensed rather than acknowledged. The theory of monads might be considered as a detour around it. We know that Leibniz did worry about the problem posed by Aristotle in *On generation and corruption* (I. ii); namely, how to get substance composed out of something infinitely divisible. That is the most general form in which the problem of the labyrinth of the continuum can be stated. An ontology based on the idea of a perfect fluid in motion—a fluid which could not be decomposed into particles—might have served. And vortices were conceived, in Leibniz's earliest tentatives, as animated by a mind or minds. Still, it would have been difficult to interdigitate the actuality of animalcules with the theory of vortices, and Malebranche's determination that centrifugal forces become indefinitely large as vortices become indefinitely small was not promising in this respect. Leibniz's eventual recourse to an immaterialist atomism in the form of a theory of monads was perhaps the solution which led him out of the dilemma of solids versus fluids.

This leads to the question whether the theory of monads is, in the last analysis, a theory of animals and animalcules which recede into the regions of indefinite smallness, or a theory of non-spatial, immaterial, perceivers. On the former view, every substance has an organic body and so a place relative to other organic bodies, and even seemingly inanimate objects like stones and planks are colonies of living creatures. On the latter, phenomenalistic theory, the objects encountered "in" space are the representations of perceivers, each of whom experiences its own "world" as a more or less adequate version of the world perceived by God.

That the animalcula were so obviously and interestingly "there" was perhaps, however, one reason why Leibniz would not embrace a pure phenomenalism in which it would have made no literal sense to speak of a natural world within which a subject was situated. From the formal-systematic point of view, he did not need anything to play the role of external object in his system. He had worked out his ideas about the harmony and convergence of perceptions in the '70s and, if logical consistency had been his only aim, he might well have rested with the group-solipsism they entailed. However, at many junctures, Leibniz asserted that perceptions were not simply "intentional" mental presentations to or of a monad, but had "extensional" objects which were aggregates of substances.

As several commentators have observed, Leibniz did for a time believe that all objects were aggregates of animalcules.[48] They were like the pond whose fish can only be seen when one approaches it closely, and the fish-pond is in turn like van Leeuwenhoek's pepper-water infusion, which can be seen to be swarming with life only when it is viewed with the microscope. "Each part of

---

[48] See D. Garber, 'Leibniz and the foundations of physics', in *The natural philosophy of Leibniz*, ed. K. Okruhlik and J. R. Brown (Dordrecht 1985), 29ff. This view was originally suggested by C. D. Broad, *Leibniz: An introduction* (Cambridge 1975), 83.

matter can be thought of as a garden full of plants or as a pond full of fish. But each branch of the plant, each limb of the animal, each drop of its humors, is also such a garden or such a pond." And although the air and water which surround visible creatures "are neither plant nor fish, they contain such, though usually of a smallness which makes them imperceptible to us" (*Monadology*, secs 67–8, L* 650). Leibniz did not want to give that fish-pond, the most arresting image of the whole *Monadology*, up, and who can blame him? That it was apparently irreconcilable with his immaterial atomism troubles his modern commentators; Leibniz himself seemed to combine a confidence that his two systems really did converge with an anxiety about the details required to work this convergence out.

To conclude the discussion, it is evident from the works of Malebranche and Leibniz that the rationalist philosophers—those who denied most forcibly the exercise of occult agents and insisted on the regularity of the course of nature and its transparency to human reason—accepted the revelations of the microscope most eagerly. In Malebranche's case, the microscope induced a profound modification of his underlying Cartesianism; in Leibniz's case, it provided a platform from which to launch a revised ontology. The main outlines of Leibniz's theory of substance were not derived solely from his logico-linguistic projects, nor from his understanding of the conflict between the Aristotelian theory of the continuum and the atomism of the Moderns. The "living atoms" of the *Monadology*, the pre-delineated experiences and actions of individual substances, the innateness of thoughts, ideas, and principles, and even his substitution of the modern theory of preformation for the occult theory of palingenesis, testify to Leibniz's favourable reception of a post-Cartesian technological development, the introduction of the microscope into seventeenth-century science.

Department of Philosophy
University of Alberta

7

BAYLE, LOCKE, AND THE METAPHYSICS OF TOLERATION

THOMAS M. LENNON

An argument against the toleration of dissenting (and therefore presumptively false) beliefs is that they not only upset the common interest, but also run contrary to the individual interest of those holding them. The argument is found, in one form or other, in a long tradition beginning with Plato and extending through much of the history of religious strife to various totalitarian regimes of our own time. The most cogent version of the argument is based on a theory of human nature, of what it is essentially to be human. The familiar linkage goes as follows. To know the good is to do the good, because doing the good is always in one's interest; because of what we are, doing the good satisfies our essential needs. Thus the importance of, and the justification for, constraining the individual's beliefs about the good. An intuitive illustration of the argument can be extracted from Book I of *The republic*: it is wrong to return a borrowed knife to a crazed owner, because to do so would be contrary to his interest; but beliefs can be more harmful than knives, and no less care should be taken with them.

Locke and Bayle are the two best-known proponents of toleration in the early modern period. Both, of course, reject the argument against the toleration of dissenting beliefs, and in particular the metaphysics on which its most cogent version rests. A comparative investigation of their metaphysics, which is anyhow of intrinsic interest, will introduce their views on toleration. In particular, Locke's doctrine that matter might possibly think is of obvious relevance to the question of a human nature, and around it cluster several issues for Bayle, including occasionalism, immortality of the soul, innate ideas, and, obviously, dualism. With respect to the issue of toleration, what emerges from it for Bayle is a conception of conscience, which in turn can be used to illumine both his and Locke's views on the topic. Because Bayle's position is in the end the more interesting one, the investigation here will be conducted largely from the perspective of his relation to Locke rather than conversely, and will cover four areas—biobibliography, metaphysics, toleration, and sources and influence.

© Thomas M. Lennon 1997

I. BIOBIBLIOGRAPHY

Soon after the suppression of the Protestant academy at Sedan, and with it his teaching position, Bayle fled France to Holland, never to return. Thus he was in Holland for the whole of Locke's exile there (1683–9), and according to Bayle's testimony the two actually met.[1] Without much evidence, it has been inferred that there was "genuine friendship" among Bayle, Locke, Shaftesbury, and the Furlys, father and son (Benjamin, the Quaker refugee whose extensive library was open to both Locke and Bayle; and Arent, who carried some of Bayle's letters to Coste).[2] The inference is not altogether implausible. Bayle wrote to Coste on 8 April 1704 that he speaks often with (the third Earl of) Shaftesbury, and with him often of Locke, to whom he asks that his respects be conveyed.[3]

Whatever the personal relationship between them, there seems to have been a mutual intellectual respect between Locke and Bayle. Locke wrote to Benjamin Furly on 12 October 1702 complaining that Bayle had not yet expressed his views on the *Essay*: "I value [Bayle's] opinion in the first rank of those who have got my book, yet he will not doe me the favour to let me know what he thinks of it, one way or other."[4] As for Bayle, he describes Locke as a man of *beaucoup d'esprit* and, in a typical epithet, refers to Locke as "one of the most profound metaphysicians of the century". Bayle says that Locke has very fine views on everything he undertakes, and that he is happy that Locke's thoughts are being translated (the *Essay*, by Coste) into French (*OD* iv. 695).

---

[1] Pierre Bayle, *Oeuvres diverses* (5 vols, 1737; repr. Hildesheim 1966), iv. 696; hereafter cited as '*OD*', with volume and page numbers.

[2] P. J. S. Whitmore, 'Bayle's criticism of Locke', in *Pierre Bayle: Le philosophe de Rotterdam*, ed. P. Dibon (Paris 1959), 81–96.

[3] *OD* iv. 841. A small fly in the ointment is Locke's complaint at being referred to as 'Doctor' in the first edition of Bayle's *Dictionnaire historique et critique* (1697). Bayle responded that he too was unhappy with the designation, which in England seemed to be, like 'Abbé' in France, one of civility only (letter to Coste, 15 May 1702: *OD* iv. 816). Bayle was not so unhappy or so attentive to Locke's concern, however, as to ensure that the designation did not appear in following editions. See 4th edn (1730), 'Sainctes' [F]; 'Dicéarque' [M]. Future references to the *Dictionnaire* are to this edition, citing article title and, where appropriate, letter designations of the 'Remarks'.

[4] *The correspondence of John Locke*, ed. E. S. de Beer (8 vols, Oxford 1975–89), vii. 688. On 15 March of the same year, Coste had written to Bayle, perhaps at Locke's instigation, with the same request, which led Bayle on 20 July to criticize Locke's arguments concerning extension (*OD* iv. 831). Here Bayle identifies with the Cartesian account, but he himself is no disciple of Descartes, for the idea-sensation distinction that he invokes in its support is hardly Cartesian. Moreover, many passages, both early and late, show that for Bayle the infinite divisibility of matter and its identification with space lead to insuperable difficulties. See, e.g., *Systema totius philosophiae*, *OD* iv. 306; 'Zénon d'Elée' [G].

Bayle's reading of Locke was complicated by his having no English—a handicap of which he complained, since he saw English as a language which "contains many books that would be useful" to him.[5] He was familiar to one degree or another with at least the following works of Locke: (1) the First Treatise on government;[6] (2) an extract from the First Reply to Stillingfleet;[7] (3) the Third Reply to Stillingfleet in Le Clerc's translation, from which he quotes in the *Dictionnaire* Locke's response to an objection concerning the immortality of the soul;[8] (4) the *Letter on toleration*, which originally appeared in Latin and of which Locke sent Bayle a copy at his request;[9] (5) among the posthumous works, Bernard's account of the *Paraphrases and notes on the Epistles of St Paul*.[10] Until Coste's translation of the *Essay* (1700), Bayle would have had only Le Clerc's *abrégé* of it in the *Bibliothèque universelle* (1688). The *Dictionnaire* quotes approvingly from *Essay* II. xi on the difference between men and beasts with respect to the bestial soul controversy, and says of the *Essay* that it is "an excellent work that deserves to be translated into French as well as it has been done by M. Coste" ('Rorarius' [K], note). Bayle's attention was focused by Coste at least on Locke's criticism of the Cartesian theory of extension. But despite his expressed intention to read the *Essay* with some care, Bayle seems to have done so only for parts of the work—for example, Book I on innate ideas, which he found convincing. The great pressures attending the second edition of the *Dictionnaire*, it seems, and problems of health[11] posed an obstacle.

II. METAPHYSICS

In an early work of problematic authorship,[12] Bayle at least flirts with what was later to be Locke's view on thinking matter. He grants the inconceivability of matter's thinking as a direct result of its mechanical properties; but this

---

[5] To Desmaizeaux, 3 Jan. 1702: *OD* iv. 803.

[6] To Minutoli, 14 Sept. 1693: *OD* iv. 803.

[7] *Nouvelles de la république des lettres*, Nov. 1699, 695ff.

[8] See below. Bayle followed the Locke-Stillingfleet controversy in *Nouvelles de la république des lettres*, and perhaps in reviews by Basnage de Beauval in *Histoire des ouvrages des sçavans* (May 1697, March 1698, Sept. 1699).

[9] To Coste, 29 Oct. 1704: *OD* iv. 850. Bayle had in the meantime obtained a copy from a friend.

[10] In *Nouvelles de la république des lettres*, April 1705, 448: letter to Coste, 30 April 1705.

[11] These eventuated in his death from tuberculosis, which Locke could have unwittingly precipitated but in fact did not. "Throughout his stay in Holland, Bayle had caught a cold every winter, which lasted, with spells of coughing, until spring. Friends had told him about 'Locke's principle that it is bad for one's health to cover up one's head', but he did not dare leave off the wig he always wore" (E. Labrousse, *Bayle* (Oxford 1983), 46, citing letter to Coste, 15 May 1702: *OD* iv. 820).

[12] See E. Labrousse, *Pierre Bayle* (2 vols, The Hague 1963–4), ii. 145–6.

does not mean, according to Bayle, that God cannot join thought to matter *upon occasion of* certain shapes and motions, so that the Cartesians may continue to hold that these mechanical properties are formally distinct from thought. Now, this is an interesting suggestion by Bayle. At a minimum, it means that despite Bayle's claim to the contrary Cartesianism is undermined, for it makes thought a mere quality attaching to a bare substance.[13] On this view, thought cannot be the determinable essence of the thinking thing of which specific thoughts are the determinates.

On the other hand, thought could be construed as the essence of the thinking thing, in the hypothetical case of a material thinking thing, if there were laws according to which God determines Himself to act upon certain occasions. That is, what occurs with nomological necessity might, on this hypothesis, be regarded as essential. But Bayle does not even regard what is actually the case in these terms. "What we experience of the reciprocal action of our body on our soul and conversely is an arbitrary determination [*établissement*] by the good pleasure of the Author of all things; He therefore could have established a different connection."[14] What this amounts to is very close to Locke's position that thought is an epiphenomenon, a superaddition by God rather than the essence of the thinking thing.

As it happens, Bayle came to a philosophical rejection of thinking matter. He had done so by 1699 in a letter that tied the issue to that of the void and related ontological issues. According to Bayle, had Locke adopted the Cartesian plenum and not followed Newton's hypothesis of the void, he would have more easily explained the hardness and weight that he then found an incomprehensible mystery, and he would not have compared them to thought "which he supposed God might have given to certain bodies. On this topic, I fully agree with his adversary [Descartes]. I do not believe it possible for any body, still less an assemblage of bodies, or an atom of Epicurus, to be susceptible of thought."[15]

In his *Réponse aux questions d'un provincial* Bayle gives the issue as careful and sophisticated a treatment as is to be found in his work. According to Bayle, in allowing the possibility that matter might think Locke returns us to the "chaos of the scholastics"; for he reintroduces the eduction of forms (thought and extension) from substance and the real distinction between substance and accident. If matter is not extended due to its substance or essence, it can acquire extension only in the way that Roman Catholics suppose, which is to say that forms are drawn from the potency of matter although they do not exist in it. Thus matter is treated as a mathematical point, a bare substrate as we might say, and quantity is somehow drawn out

[13] E. Labrousse, *Pierre Bayle*, ii. 177.
[14] *Réponse aux questions d'un provincial* (1705–7), ch. 140: *OD* iii. 786.
[15] To Mylord Ashley [Shaftesbury], 23 Nov. 1699: *OD* iv. 786.

of it. He does not use the expression here, but Bayle's criticism is that Locke has made extension an occult quality, which is open to all the familiar objections that it provides no explanation. Extension can be drawn (educed) only from what has extension, and hence its occurrence is always a true creation, or, alternatively perhaps, a miracle. "But of what use will the creation of three inches of extension be in making extended what is not extended? How join or mix together what is extended and what has no extension? How would matter become extended through an extension from which it is really distinct?" (*OD* iii. 942).

A second argument is based on the nominalism that Bayle in fact shares with Locke and he charges Locke with arguing *obscurum per obscurius*.

Were we led to something clear in abandoning this principle, many people would be patient; but we are cast into shadows all the more obscure since we know that the essential attributes of a substance do not numerically differ from each other, and thus we cannot believe it possible for matter to join with extension by one attribute and with thought by another. Numerically the same attribute must serve these two functions; i.e. matter, the essence of which is nothing else but its essential attributes really identical both with themselves and with it, must be joined by its whole substance to thought and extension. Spinoza, who taught that the eternal and necessary Being had the attributes of thought and extension together, recognized that this composite was incomprehensible and was the weakest and most incomprehensible spot in his system. (ibid.)

By allowing matter to think, Locke violates the ontological principle, one kind one job; that is, the material and thinking worlds cannot be grounded by extension and thought if both are properties of the same thing, because, given nominalism, both are identical to that thing and thus to each other.

Bayle also criticizes, specifically and at length, Locke's view that we do not know the nature of substance. While on Locke's view impenetrability, extension, divisibility, and mobility are properties of matter, they are not of its essence; which is to say, according to Bayle, that Locke holds the Catholic view that they are but *accidents* of it. The upshot of this is that matter may exist without extension and there is nothing to prevent it from thinking; and, *mutatis mutandis*, if thought is not the essence of the thinking thing, we cannot conclude that if a thing thinks it is immaterial (and presumably therefore immortal). There are two problematic aspects to Bayle's argument. Most obviously, criticism of the view that we do not know the nature of substance is strange criticism indeed from one who is supposed, as Bayle generally is, to be a sceptic. The very example should be a paradigm of the case in which a Pyrrhonian would suspend judgement. Secondly, Bayle here essentially repeats what had been Stillingfleet's objection to Locke in the form of a *reductio*. Now, this is even stranger, because a *reductio* is effective, obviously, only if it produces an inadmissible conclusion; yet Bayle was aware, as will be seen, that Locke admitted that the possibility of thinking matter upset a principal argument for the soul's immortality. Indeed, Bayle delighted in this result and defended Locke against Stillingfleet.[16] So what is going on here?

We know that Bayle took an interest in the Locke-Stillingfleet debate. He used material from this debate in the *Dictionnaire* in a way that illumines the questions just raised ('Dicéarque' [M]). Stillingfleet had argued that matter cannot think, given the "philosophical orthodoxy" that it is incomprehensible how it should. Locke replied that God's power extends beyond the limits of our conception, and that, although it is incomprehensible to us, He might have communicated to matter the faculty of thought. According to Bayle, Locke's position is rather like that of the scholastics who allow matter an *obediential potency*, whereby God can make a stone capable of the beatific vision or a drop of water capable of erasing original sin. Now, Bayle thinks he can refute this obediential potency with an argument that extension and thought cannot be in the same subject.[17] The argument, as related in *Nouvelles de la république des lettres*, is to the effect that our judgements comparing different things must be referred to a simple soul, which is thus immortal but which cannot be material. Another version of this argument appears elsewhere in the *Dictionnaire* ('Leucippe' [E]). There Bayle considers the hypothesis that, since no assemblage of atoms can have the property of thought if that is lacking to individual atoms, these latter individually have the property—a hypothesis no more unreasonable, he believes, than the hypothesis of eternal and eternally moving atoms. This would mean that there are as many thinking things in each thinking thing as it has atoms. "But each of us knows through experience that there is in him only one thing that [thinks]." In addition, according to Bayle, "to contend that, since man's soul thinks, it is immaterial, is in my view good reasoning and also establishes a very solid foundation for the immortality of our soul, a dogma that must be considered as one of the most important articles of good philosophy" ('Dicéarque' [M]).

Yet Bayle is no deist in this comment, arguing rationally on behalf of religious doctrines; for the point of his remark is to *defend* what he takes to be Locke's position against deism. Stillingfleet may have philosophical orthodoxy on his side, but Locke bases immortality of the soul on Scripture, "which is all the Christian, evangelical, and theological orthodoxy there can be". Immortality, heaven, hell, etc. are matters of Revelation, and, while there

---

[16] Although he elsewhere emphasizes the differences between Bayle and Locke, H. M. Bracken here allows their apparent convergence ('Bayle not a sceptic?', *Journal of the history of ideas* 45 (1964), 171 n. 7; see also his 'Berkeley on the immortality of the soul', *Modern schoolman* 37 (1960), at 89–90).

[17] The argument, derived from the Abbé de Dangeau, *Quatre dialogues* (Paris 1648), was reported in *Nouvelles de la république des lettres*, Aug. 1694, art. VI.

may be good philosophical arguments for the immortality of the soul, "those who believe in the immortality of the soul only because of philosophical ideas furnished by reason are no more advanced on the Kingdom of God than those who believe that the whole is greater than its part". Elsewhere he continues in the same vein ('Perron' [L]), quoting at length Locke's Third Reply to Stillingfleet, whose objection is that denying that the soul's immortality can be demonstrated by reason lessens its credibility. Locke's reply is that the objection itself would lessen the credibility of Revelation, for it would indicate that divine trust is insufficient for belief.

The tension in Bayle on the topic of thinking matter is released, if it is viewed as an instance of what he takes to be reason's general failure ever to arrive at definitive truth. The effect of philosophical reason on such important topics as the infinite divisibility of matter, the void, the distinction between real and sensible qualities, etc. is always destructive, leading to the conclusion that no view can be defended. In a favourite passage among readers of Bayle, reason is compared to a corrosive powder that eats not only the wound, but also sound flesh, and finally the bones themselves to their very marrow ('Acosta' [G]). The situation is the exact opposite to the much-discussed view attributed by Harry Frankfurt to Descartes: for Bayle, reason consistently applied leads to the *distrust* of reason. Such arguments that Bayle may appear to endorse, for example against thinking matter, are always in a context that itself is never definitively endorsed. Locke's failure to establish the possibility of thinking matter, or anything else about a human nature, is thus only to be expected.

III. TOLERATION

Such scepticism is sufficient to block the argument against toleration, for reason is never in a position to justify interference on the basis of a defensible conception of the individual's essential interest. Bayle is clear about his rejection of the Platonic view. The *Dictionnaire* article 'Abdas' [C] concerns toleration and seems aimed against Jurieu, who like Plato is an arch-opponent of toleration, believing that obligation is grounded in definitive truth of the matter. Bayle argues that Abdas should have restored the temple that he had demolished, just because it was the property of another. That the temple was to be put to an illicit use, namely idolatry, did not excuse him. We are obliged to restore a stolen purse, he says, even to a man who will use it in debauchery, for which the responsibility before God lies not with us but with him.[18]

But the view as developed so far does not amount to a positive endorsement

---

[18] The Kantian, deontological thrust of Bayle's views has been noted in the literature. For another example, see 'Acosta' [G].

of toleration. The clue to the positive view may be found in Bayle's recognition of the simple non-philosophical faith that he sees espoused by Locke, which may well be what both he and Locke called conscience. The concept is surrounded by a great deal of noise—theological in Bayle's case, political in Locke's—but it may initially be understood simply as belief in what appears to be true and acting on what appears to be good. While Plato might nominally endorse this concept, its value for him is *instrumental*; it is a means to truth, in particular about essences. For Locke and Bayle, the value of conscience is *intrinsic*. Regardless of the value of Locke's arguments, Bayle is attracted to his position because of his admission that the possibility of thinking matter, however real, is philosophically incomprehensible. The parallel is exact with belief in the Trinity, for example; so the issue is not the ground for belief—faith as opposed to reason. Rather, the concern with belief is that it be one's own, that it be authentic or autonomous. (As will be seen, sheer wilfulness is ruled out, because beliefs still need content.) We do the best we can with respect to truth, but we properly believe without ultimate guarantees—of the Cartesian sort, for example. This statement of the view is philosophically more interesting than the theological definism it would otherwise be (believe and do as God instructs); and, as will be seen, it also extends the coverage of toleration to groups otherwise excluded by it.

Bayle's direct arguments on behalf of the inviolability of conscience are not very convincing, at least not in isolation. He argues, for example, that

> if the true Church had the right to oppress others, it could base that right only on the conviction it had of being the true religion; this seems evident, because if it were possible for it to be the true religion without it being convinced of it, it would then, far from attempting to convert others, have to join some other communion. It follows from this that if the true religion has any right to oppress others, every religion has this same right, provided that it is convinced of being the true Church of God; since this is false and impious, it follows that God has given His Church only the way of persuasion by peaceful instruction to lead others to the true faith.[19]

The argument equivocates on the sense in which the true Church might base its right to oppress. If it means that only conviction could put the Church in a position actually to exercise the right, Bayle is trivially correct; for nothing follows concerning the Church's justification in doing so according to someone like Jurieu, who thinks that only objective truth can ground rights and duties. But if the argument means that conviction alone would provide the justification, then the question is begged against Jurieu, according to whom, whatever it may believe of itself, only the true Church is permitted—indeed it is obliged—to act as if it were the true Church (i.e. in oppressing others).

---

[19] *Critique générale de l'histoire du Calvinisme de Mr. Maimbourg* (1682), XXIII. iv: *OD* ii. 105.

Bayle is perhaps at his most persuasive when he generalizes from carefully articulated examples, such as that of the wife of Martin Guerre, who, according to Bayle, discharged her duties.[20] We nowadays would be inclined to analyse such cases in terms of the distinction between agent and act morality. In yielding to her husband's impostor, the wife performed an act contrary to her duty, but, since her ignorance was not culpable, she as an agent was not culpable. Bayle is inclined to run together this distinction, and to claim simply that "the erroneous conscience procures for error the same rights and privileges that the orthodox conscience procures for the truth". In any event, the failure to perform some prima facie duty which none the less suggests praise for the agent (or the performance of it which none the less suggests blame) is the common feature of the examples that Bayle multiplies. From them he generalizes as follows:

1. Willing to disobey God is a sin.

2. Willing to disobey a fixed and determinate judgement of conscience is the same thing as willing to transgress God's law.

3. Consequently, everything done contrary to the dictates of conscience is a sin.

4. All other things being equal, the turpitude of sin varies directly with one's knowledge that one sins.

5. An act that would be incontestably good (giving alms, for example) if done at the direction of conscience becomes worse, when done contrary to conscience, than an incontestably evil act (insulting a beggar, for example) is if done according to conscience.

6. Conforming to a fundamentally mistaken conscience in doing a thing we call evil makes an act much less evil than an act we call good that is done contrary to conscience in conformity with truth.

The upshot is that "the first and most indispensable of all our obligations is that of not acting against the inspiration of conscience, and that every act contrary to the lights of conscience is essentially evil".[21]

Acting according to conscience may be a necessary condition for a right action; but conscience cannot be sufficient, for it is without content. By itself, conscience provides no guidance. As doubts about her putative husband grow, the wife of Martin Guerre, for example, may well look for

---

[20] Popularized today by a recent film, the case was not unknown in the period. Montaigne, for example, was present for the verdict of the trial and discusses the case in his *Essays*. Bayle, who was raised in the next village from the site of the events, would have known about the case from the local retelling of it, which has been constant from the fifteenth century to the present. The short of the story is that Martin Guerre leaves wife and child to go off, appropriately enough, to war, and is replaced eight years later by an impostor claiming all his rights. For the fuller story, see N. Z. Davis, *The return of Martin Guerre* (Cambridge, Mass. 1983).

[21] *Commentaire philosophique sur les paroles de Jésus-Christ, 'Contrains-les d'entrer'* (1686–7), II. viii: *OD* ii. 425.

principles, rules, or at least considerations relevant to her decision about how to respond to his demand. To tell her to follow the lights of conscience does not offer much help, for conscience is not an independent voice within one that offers such direction. But this conception of conscience as having no content may be precisely Bayle's point. A necessary condition for the morality of an action, he may be saying, is its autonomy, and his injunction to obey conscience may be nothing more than a rejection of authority.[22] (Thus the negative formulation of it standardly given by Bayle, the sense of which is: do not act contrary to what you believe, i.e. do not let yourself be imposed upon by others. The content of the judgement, meanwhile, remains open, to be decided upon in all the various ways that Bayle elsewhere discusses: grace, education, and even reason.)

Bracken is importantly right in claiming a positive, if unspecified, relation between Bayle's doctrine of conscience and the Calvinist "way of examination", which insists upon the judgement of the individual in religious knowledge, as opposed to the Catholic "way of authority" which cedes judgement to the Church.[23] The interpretation offered here would in fact make the way of examination *an instance of* conscience. Previously, Rex had claimed that the two are opposed: Bayle argues, according to him, in the way of examination that Scripture cannot be interpreted to allow persecution (*Commentaire philosophique*, Pt I), and then argues the primacy of conscience (Pt II), with the (acknowledged) paradoxical result that those who believe themselves right in persecuting are obliged to do so.[24] But arriving at what one takes to be truth, as Bayle does in Part I, even if it is the truth, obviously does not guarantee that others will agree, and does not relieve them of acting on what they take to be the truth. Concern with the truth, about toleration for example, is certainly relevant; for otherwise moral judgements would be without content. But truth does not ground obligation, which is precisely the case that Bayle argues against Jurieu, and, incidentally, against the whole anti-toleration tradition.

Notably excluded from coverage by Bayle in his conception of toleration

---

[22] John Kilcullen has made an important, related point. (Perhaps it is the same point.) Conscience for Bayle is not an infallible agency distinct from the person, but just the person judging what is right and enforcing that judgement. Not irrelevantly, he makes the point while elucidating Bayle's fundamental moral commandment, "follow conscience", which Kilcullen takes to be satisfied "if we act on whatever *seems* true about what we ought to do" (J. Kilcullen, *Sincerity and truth* (Oxford 1988), 76).

[23] H. M. Bracken, *Mind and language* (Dordrecht 1984), 83–4. Bracken reintroduces a metaphysical element, however, by grounding the primacy of conscience for Bayle in Cartesian dualism. But Cartesianism or any other metaphysics, for Bayle, is exceedingly problematic to say the least, given the destructive nature of reason for him. Such Cartesianism as is to be found in the *Commentaire philosophique*, for example, seems to be assumed *ad hominem* in an argument to show that, quite apart from faith or religion, reason and philosophy do not lead to persecution.

[24] W. Rex, *Essays on Pierre Bayle and religious controversy* (The Hague 1965), 180–81.

are atheists. This exclusion is anomalous if the secular reading of conscience above in terms of autonomy is at all plausible. But Bayle's exclusion of atheists is without enthusiasm and is supported by only two arguments, one weak and perhaps offered only ironically, the other obviously fallacious. In response to objections, in particular from Jurieu, concerning his view of conscience, Bayle found himself arguing that the preachments of atheists can be suppressed, first, because magistrates are obliged to protect society by punishing those who would upset its fundamental laws, "among whom are customarily placed all those who remove Providence and all fear of God's justice".[25] But a major theme of his *Pensées diverses* (1682) is that atheists are in this and other respects no worse than idolaters (despite Bayle's claim to the contrary, read: Catholics), and that in some respects a society of atheists would be more viable than one composed of Christians. In any case, it is an empirical question, not a matter of principle, for him whether atheists can be good citizens.

Secondly, according to Bayle, atheists are precluded from appealing to St Peter's dictum that it is better to obey God than man, which is to say for Bayle that they cannot appeal to conscience.[26] But (1) this argument would strip from the atheist an appeal that is relevant only when he breaks the law, and it is not clear that in such circumstances anyone else is any better off. For Bayle, the atheist's punishment is just if the law he breaks is just; but if the law is just, it applies to everyone, regardless of conscience. Otherwise, the only issue is the empirical one above. (2) To obey conscience is to obey God. Thus, either the atheist as a matter of fact is unable to appeal to conscience, which Bayle does not say and in fact seems to deny; or, if the atheist appeals to conscience, his appeal seems justified.[27] (3) In any case, even if the atheist cannot claim the right, he none the less has it. The atheist who appeals to conscience before the Christian magistrate is like a property owner who though unable to produce a deed is yet known to be the owner. Although the atheist may not be in a position to claim the right, the Christian should know him to have it.

While there are significant similarities between Locke and Bayle on all of the above, there are also important differences that might first be noted in their moral and political outlooks. Locke grounds freedom in the individual's *rights*; Bayle grounds freedom in the individual's *duties*. In the civic sphere,

---

[25] *Commentaire philosophique*, II. ix: *OD* ii. 431.

[26] "An atheist, deprived as he is of the protection [of St Peter's dictum], properly remains exposed to the full rigour of the laws; and when he would spread his views contrary to prohibition, he will be punished for sedition, believing nothing above the laws which he none the less tramples under foot" (ibid.).

[27] Sometimes, however, Bayle indicates that to act according to conscience one must know that one is acting according to the will of God, but he gives no argument as to why this knowledge is necessary (*Commentaire philosophique*, I. vi: *OD* ii. 348).

freedom for Locke is primary; for Bayle it is order, which is a condition for freedom, that is primary.

Haunted by his knowledge of the Wars of Religion, Bayle was hostile to the idea of a social contract and the theories of the monarchomachists. He was, however, influenced by Hobbes, whose concept of the state of nature was in accordance with his own pessimism about man. While Locke looks to the future and is the theorist of a victorious revolution, Bayle's eyes are turned to the past; what he is seeking is a theoretical basis for the religious pluralism which the Edict of Nantes, no longer operative, had for a time made possible in France.[28]

While Locke anticipates the optimism of the Enlightenment, Bayle is very much in the tradition of Calvinist pessimism that throughout the seventeenth century had legitimated the unrestrained exercise of political authority by the monarch. In this tradition, all change is *ipso facto* a deterioration. The *status quo* must be preserved, then, at all costs, and *a fortiori* as efficiently as possible, and thus, as Bayle sees it, by an absolute monarch where one is in place. Thus Bayle's unswerving support for the French monarchy despite his exile and the persecution of himself and his family; for such ills were preferable to the alternative, namely, the horrible strife of civil war.[29] In addition, a monarch is best in a position to distinguish moral from political matters and to prevent the encroachment on the latter by ecclesiastical authorities. This clear division into the things that are Caesar's and those that are God's means that there are no theologically endorsed policies of state. It also means, on the other hand, that the state cannot restrict the fundamental moral principle, namely, to follow one's conscience. And here Bayle and Locke begin, from opposite directions, to converge.

It looks as if the key to Locke's position in *Epistola de tolerantia* (1689) is the separation of church and state.[30] Some human faults, he says, are so ineradicable that probably not all persecution can be eliminated; but the separation of church and state is necessary to the elimination of the one form of it that can be eliminated, namely, persecution based in law. Once the proper concerns of church and state are distinguished, no law can be made to control religious belief. The concern of the Church is the salvation of souls; the concern of the state is the safety of the commonwealth, a society designed in the interest of civil good: life, liberty, and property. The jurisdiction of the magistrate is fenced from the salvation of souls by three, not obviously distinguishable, considerations. The magistrate's control of religious belief

---

[28] Labrousse, *Bayle*, 85.

[29] Thus also the legitimacy of censorship of the press in the eyes of this hero to the Enlightenment. See Labrousse, *Pierre Bayle*, ii. 549.

[30] John Locke, *Epistola de tolerantia: A letter on toleration*, ed. R. Klibansky, trans. J. W. Gough (Oxford 1968), 65–71.

would be *inappropriate*, anyhow *impossible*, and, even if possible, *improbable* in achieving its intended effect.

Authority over religious belief has not been entrusted to the magistrate by God (presumably, this is a matter of empirical fact for Locke); nor can it be entrusted to him by man, who would thus be acting without faith, the inner persuasion which alone is relevant to salvation. To embrace a worship under compulsion would in fact aggravate salvation by adding hypocrisy to men's sins. What is more, application of the magistate's specific power, namely compulsion, is futile: "such is the nature of human understanding that it cannot be compelled by any outward force". Finally, even if belief could be constrained, men would have little hope of salvation in blindly accepting the religion imposed on them by the magistrate. For there is one true religion, says Locke, and that anyone should embrace it would thus be an improbable accident of birth.

It is important to notice that in his last consideration Locke seems to reject the key premise in anti-toleration arguments, that true religion is necessary for salvation.[31] For the individual conscience engaged in the way of examination will be no more likely than the magistrate to find the one true religion, and on the whole will be less likely to find it given the greater resources at the disposal of the magistrate. Instead, Locke must be assuming that the value of exercising individual conscience lies not in arriving at truth, but in the exercise itself.[32] None of this is as clear in Locke as it is in Bayle; but no other interpretation seems plausible, once it is realized that the same considerations proscribing state interference in religious belief apply to interference by any church in religious belief, or to interference by individuals. Locke does not apply them, but, on whatever grounds, he does make the relevant connections. As "no private person ought in any way to attack or damage another person's civil goods because he professes another religion or form of worship", so also "of particular churches, which stand in the same kind of relation to one another as private persons" (*Epistola*, 79–81).

Indeed, the considerations apply to everyone's beliefs, of every kind.[33] For

---

[31] On the same sort of grounds more thoroughly, eloquently, and cogently presented, Bayle agrees with Locke at least to the extent that not everyone can be expected to arrive at the true religion. All that God can expect is that one embrace what appears to be true, having done all that one can to discover it (*Commentaire philosophique*, x. iv: *OD* ii. 436–7).

[32] Locke had earlier shown an inclination toward viewing conscience as both inviolate and of intrinsic value: "speculative opinions and divine worship, are those things which have an absolute and universal right to toleration"; and, "in speculations and religious worship every man hath a perfect uncontrolable liberty which he may freely use without, or contrary to, the magistrate's command, without any guilt or sin at all, provided always that it all be done sincerely and out of conscience to God, according to the best of his knowledge and persuasion" ('Essay on toleration' (1667), in H. R. Fox Bourne, *The life of John Locke* (2 vols, London 1876), i. 175–6, 178).

[33] Such is the upshot of, for example, Locke's *Essay concerning human understanding*, IV. xvi. 4.

all belief, belief contrary to behaviour is hypocritical; all attempts to impose belief are bound to fail; and no *per impossibile* imposition of belief would have any better an outcome than the imposition of religious belief.[34] Moreover, the only relevance of Locke's church-state separation is to restrict the exercise of force to the civil domain; but, *even without that restriction*, the state is in no position to impose religious or any other kind of belief.

To be sure, there is an important difference between state interference and all other forms of it, for only the state has a rightful monopoly on the exercise of force. But, as Locke argues elsewhere, this exercise is a right voluntarily ceded to the state just by living within its jurisdiction. The state is no less a voluntary society than the Church or any other, *and conversely*; thus Locke also discusses the grounds for toleration within churches and implicitly in all societies. Throughout this discussion, Locke's arguments over and over again take the form of rebuttals of attempts to limit conscience, which he even more obviously than Bayle takes to be a primitive, unargued-for value. However much we may remonstrate with a man in an attempt to persuade him of what we take to be the truth, "in the end he must be left to himself and his own conscience" (*Epistola*, 101). Nor is the claim of conscience ever superseded. If the magistrate's decree is contrary to conscience, we are obliged to disobey, suffering the punishment for doing so if the decree, however mistaken, concerns the good of the commonwealth, but revolting if it intrudes upon the province of religion. Once again, the state-church distinction is invoked not to secure conscience, but, in this case, to determine the proper response when it has been violated (ibid.).[35]

Like Bayle, Locke excludes atheists from the provisions of his theory; simply, "they are not to be tolerated at all". One argument is Bayle's in the *Commentaire philosophique*: an atheist "cannot in the name of religion claim the privilege of toleration for himself" (*Epistola*, 135). All three considerations against Bayle's version of this argument above apply as well to Locke's version of it here. An additional argument from Locke is that "promises, covenants, and oaths, which are the bonds of human society, can have no

---

[34] The last point is rather an exaggeration, for Locke is not an epistemological anarchist and is prepared to admit some forms of expertise. But the need remains even in these cases to internalize the belief.

[35] Bayle views the obligation to obey in this situation as without exception. It is the sovereign's right to inflict injustice even if he is culpable in exercising the right, and his subjects have no right to disobey. *Nouvelles lettres de l'auteur de la Critique générale* (1685) IX. ii: *OD* ii. 225. Unlike Jurieu, who was prepared to foment rebellion among the Huguenots in France, Bayle evokes an earlier attitude of Calvinism. "Even in the period of severest repression, Calvin preached fidelity to the sovereign, and unequivocally condemned the spirit of revolt. Until the St. Bartholomew's Day massacre in 1572, this loyalty was a distinguishing characteristic of French Calvinism. Only after the massacre did the pamphleteers finally sound the call to revolt." (C. Fauré, *Democracy without women*, trans. C. Gorbman and J. Berks (Bloomington, Ind. 1991), 32.)

hold upon or sanctity for an atheist; for the taking away of God, even only in thought, dissolves all". Locke's concern is with oaths of allegiance, the ceremonial occasions for declaring membership in a society and thus incurring its civic obligations. But while promises and oaths are endowed with great significance in Locke's historical context—he thought them binding even on God—his treatment of the occasion is "hapless and clumsy", and it is the declaration, more often tacit or informal, that is of importance to him, and, obviously, whether it is fulfilled.[36] The real question may well reduce to the empirical one that Bayle argued throughout his career, namely, whether a society of atheists, or even one including them, is feasible.

Locke also excludes Catholics from the provisions of his theory, or at least appears to do so. In the *Epistola* he excludes those who seditiously teach that "faith need not be kept with heretics, . . . that kings excommunicated forfeit their kingdoms, . . . and that dominion is founded in grace" (ibid., 133). But Locke does not mention Catholics as such, and it is not clear that he thinks they necessarily hold such views.[37] He may be arguing only a general point about doctrines that are contingently held by Catholics at a certain historical juncture. For later in the *Epistola* he offers a *pari passu* argument that seems to apply to Catholics no less than to different Protestant sects. "Is it permissible to worship God in the Roman manner? Let it also be permissible in the Genevan. Is it allowed to speak Latin in the market place? Let those who wish speak it in church too" (141–3).

The same distinction between doctrinal intolerance and circumstantial intolerance is suggested in the earlier 'Essay on toleration'. There Locke distinguishes Catholic religious worship and speculative thought from "other doctrines absolutely destructive to the society wherein they live". Only they who mix the two should not be tolerated, and then only if tolerating the former would help to spread the latter.[38] He proceeds, however, to take a narrower view: "it being impossible . . . to make papists, whilst papists,

---

[36] See·J. Dunn, *The political thought of John Locke* (Cambridge 1969), 140–42. Dunn seems prepared to ascribe both Locke's distrust of atheists, and the extraordinary importance he accorded oaths in securing the social order, to idiosyncrasies of his personality rather than to any feature of his theory (257 n. 2). More recently, Dunn has published a very nuanced article in which he tends to emphasize the similarities between the views of Locke and Bayle on toleration and the narrowness of their applicability. That is, toleration here is essentially a religious question and not the broader one of autonomy that I have insinuated. "The right to freedom of conscience in Locke's eyes is fundamentally a right to worship God in the way one judges that God requires: a right which follows from and is barely intelligible without the duty to do just that" (J. Dunn, 'The claim to freedom of conscience', in *From persecution to toleration*, ed. O. P. Grell and others (Oxford 1991), 171–93, at 178). From this point of view, Locke's exclusion of atheists rests on principle and not on personality.

[37] Dunn apparently believes that Locke does think so: for Locke, "to worship one's God is a private 'concernment' between oneself and the deity in question. But to worship one's God in a Catholic rite in a Protestant country amounts to constructive subversion" (*Political thought of Locke*, 37).   [38] Fox Bourne, i. 183–4.

friends to your government . . . I think they ought not to enjoy the benefits of toleration". But quite apart from their allegiance to a foreign prince who has power over their conscience and the bindingness of their oaths, promises, and obligations, Locke's objection to the papists is that "where they have power, they think themselves bound to deny it to others".[39] Papists might be just those Catholics who think in this way.

IV. SOURCES AND INFLUENCE

It is tempting to look for a historical, causal connection to Bayle's work, given the thrust (viz. against Catholic oppression), language (e.g. "iron and fire" as instruments of that oppression), examples (e.g. worries about idolatry), distinctions (most notably, that between church and state), and especially the arguments[40] to be found in Locke's *Epistola*. In his review of that work, Basnage discussed Locke's answer to the objection that his conception of toleration supports not just diversity among Christians, but idolatry and paganism; Locke's answer was to grant the objection and insist that Christians do not have the right to demolish pagan temples, which "he illustrates with an example taken from the *Commentaire philosophique*". The example, according to Basnage, is of the missionary who, citing Luke 14: 23, tells the king of China that, when he is strong enough, he will destroy his temples and force the idolatrous Chinese into the Church. This view, says Basnage, would make all of Christianity into a serpent in the breast of every society in which it is in the minority, and legitimate the same treatment of Christians there that it accords idolaters in Christian Europe.[41]

Commenting on Basnage's review, Klibansky points out that Locke's *Epistola* was completed eight or nine months before the appearance of Bayle's *Commentaire philosophique*, and concludes that "there is no ground for supposing any dependence of Locke on Bayle" (*Epistola*, p. xxxiii). An unnoticed rebuttal, even stronger than the chronology, is that the example Basnage cites does not even appear in Locke's work. (Basnage is none too reliable; without discussion, he attributed the anonymous *Epistola* to Jacques Bernard.) But none of this rules out the connection. The general argument illustrated by the example certainly is to be found in Locke. "What right can be given to the magistrate to suppress an idolatrous church, which may not

---

[39] Fox Bourne, i. 187–8.

[40] For example, Locke's argument that the magistrate's power to oppress cannot be exercised on behalf of the Church, because there always remains the question as to which church, rests on a premiss insisted upon by Bayle throughout his work (cf. *Epistola*, 95–9).

[41] Henri Basnage de Beauval, *Histoire des ouvrages des sçavans*, Sept.–Nov. 1689, 23–4. The text from Luke contains the words 'Compel them to enter', on which Bayle offered his *Commentaire philosophique*.

also in its own time and place be used to ruin an orthodox one? For you must remember that the civil power is the same everywhere, and the religion of the prince is orthodox to himself" (ibid., 111–13; see also 81–3). This argument at least approximates Bayle's assertion that error has all the rights of the truth it only appears to be; and for it Locke could have turned to Bayle's *Critique générale*, which was published over two years before Locke even began the *Epistola*. There, he would have found Bayle arguing that those—Catholics and Protestants alike—who would persecute others because of their own claim to orthodoxy thereby open the gate to persecution of all by all.

Let them turn whichever way they can, they will never place any certitude in their cause if not the certitude of their persuasion, i.e. they will never show that it is certain that they have orthodoxy on their side, but only that they believe they have it, and that they have nothing more than the most ridiculous sects. If they believe as a result of their conviction that they have the right to destroy other sects, each sect must, as a result of its conviction, have the same right to destroy all those not in agreement with it.[42]

Moreover, although Bayle is known for his exclusion only of atheists, he could also have been a source for Locke's exclusion of Catholics. In the *Critique générale* he argues that "although princes have no right over conscience, they can nevertheless make more or less severe laws concerning the toleration of religion, and things may sometimes be such that it is prudent to expel a certain sect—for example, when there is reason to believe that it is conspiring against the state". Here Bayle argues against Maimbourg that Catholics are untrustworthy citizens because (1) "only French theologians do not recognize the Pope's power to absolve their oaths of loyalty to the prince"; (2) in practice, even the French often behave as if the Pope had this power; (3) the spirit of Catholicism is such that Catholics are more likely than not to recognize this power in the Pope.[43]

However, given that the essentials of Locke's view are already to be found in the 'Essay on toleration', the safest conclusion is that he did not find in Bayle a source for his views, but only moral support for them, which he might also have provided for Bayle. Even so, it is not impossible that Locke and Bayle had a common source for their argument for toleration based on the indistinguishability of the veridical from the erroneous conscience. For an earlier published version of it is to be found, however unexpectedly, in

---

[42] *Critique générale*, XIII. v: *OD* ii. 56–7. Bayle makes the same argument at, among other places, XX. v: *OD* ii. 87; and XXI. vii: *OD* ii. 94, where he uses it to overthrow the literal interpretation of Luke 14: 23, thus anticipating the *Commentaire philosophique*. We know that Locke owned Bayle's *Pensées diverses sur la comète* (in its first edition, 1681), his *Dictionnaire*, and his *Commentaire philosophique* (J. Harrison and P. Laslett, *The library of John Locke* (Oxford 1965), entries 236–237a). That he should have possessed or at least seen the *Critique générale* is far from impossible; its burning in the Place de Grève, Paris, in 1683 assured its dissemination.

[43] *Critique générale*, XXIII. iv: *OD* ii. 105–6.

Jurieu's *La Politique du clergé de France* of 1681, a truly seminal work in light of the controversy it sowed.[44] There Jurieu sets out his standard view that the prince should not tolerate religions contrary to the fundamentals of Christianity, at least to the extent that he should not allow their introduction into the realm.[45] But he also sets out the following positions. In the moral sphere, it is good for the prince to lead his subjects to the true religion, but only by means approved by that religion and not by violence and bad faith. In the political sphere, it is false that a single religion is necessary for a great, flourishing, and peaceful state. Why? First, because history shows that a multiplicity of sects yields the prince greater authority in dealing with the whole;[46] but also because otherwise the pagan emperors would have been justified in their persecution of the Christians. "There is no man who is not convinced that he is in the true religion. The Great Sultan believes himself to be on the road to salvation just as the Christian king does" (226–9).

What is to be made of this surprising convergence of views, regardless of their provenance? An obvious remark concerns the historical circumstances. Locke, Bayle, and Jurieu were Protestants at a time of Catholic persecution, and their advocacy of toleration was joined, understandably, by Basnage, Paerts, and other Protestant authors. In addition, while all three may mobilize metaphysical argument in various contexts, none is a dogmatist in the fashion of the Cartesians, for example. In particular, their metaphysics of toleration is, as it were, a non-metaphysics. The open-endedness of their arguments suggests a more specific chapter in the history of philosophy—a kind of Popperianism *avant la lettre*, on two counts. Popper has argued that espousing essences blocks enquiry. An extension of his argument may be that one needs not only to be freed from the stultification of essences, but also to be free (in the way proposed by toleration advocates) in order to pursue research in their absence. People must be free, in a way that Plato of course rejected, to follow the argument wherever it may lead.

Secondly, and specifically against Plato's anti-toleration argument, Locke, Bayle, and even Jurieu avoid doctrines of human nature. They liberate enquiry from any essence of the human being that blocks questions of what people are about, the goals that are open to them, and the means of achieving their goals. This anthropological open-endedness does not really characterize the rest of the work of Jurieu, who after all was given to historicist

---

[44] Locke possessed this work both in English translation and in an edition of 1682. Bayle, of course, knew the work, defending its view of Catholics against Maimbourg and calling Jurieu "one of our finest writers" (*Critique générale*, XXIII. i: *OD* ii. 103–4). An important point in this dispute is whether Catholics are more liable than Protestants to foreign manipulation, i.e. by the Pope, against the prince—a point that is of great interest to Locke.

[45] Once established in sufficient numbers, however, as were the Huguenots in France, minority sects could claim toleration (*La Politique du clergé de France*, 235–6).

[46] See Locke, *Epistola*, 141.

predictions based on his reading of the Bible. Nor does it fully express the spirit of Locke's views. But in ways that cannot be argued here, the indeterminancy of the human situation is at the core of Bayle, who thus anticipates Hume, pragmatism, existentialism, and even deconstruction.

Department of Philosophy
University of Western Ontario

8

PIERRE BAYLE, LIBERTINE?

DAVID WOOTTON

I

[S]ince Man after his Fall was unable to obey the exact dictates of Reason, there was nothing more necessary than to introduce Love into the World; for it cannot be conceived how Mankind could have subsisted without it. The Passions, with respect to the natural benefits of Society, are the same thing as Repentance in celestial concerns, a Plank after Shipwreck; and since Reason was to become so feeble, we could not have had recourse to a better shift than that of the Passions, of which Love is without dispute the principal one, and in some manner the Soul of the World. ('Eve' [F])[1]

Pierre Bayle was born in 1647, the son of a Huguenot minister in the south of France. At the age of twenty-one he converted briefly to Catholicism; when he reconverted to Protestantism, he was obliged to flee the country to escape the legal penalties faced by relapsed heretics, and went to complete his education in Geneva.[2] He worked first as a tutor in Switzerland and in France, under an assumed identity, and then as a professor in the Protestant college in Sedan. When that was closed in 1681 by the government, he moved to Rotterdam, where he taught and, for a time, edited a journal, *Nouvelles de la république des lettres*. In 1693 he was dismissed from his teaching position: he had increasingly come into conflict with Pierre Jurieu, a prominent Huguenot theologian and a former protector. Jurieu denied that heretics had a right to be tolerated, whereas Bayle, in his *Commentaire philosophique* of

© David Wootton 1997

[1] *The dictionary historical and critical of Mr. Peter Bayle*, 2nd edn (5 vols, 1734; repr. New York 1984). I quote from this translation (which I have checked against the French) except in the passage where I invite the reader to consult Popkin's selection. References to the articles in the *Dictionary* are followed by the letter of the remark in which the passage appears: '*in corp.*' means the passage appears in the main body of the article. When quoting from the Preface, Clarifications, etc. I give volume and page numbers of this edition. Nevertheless, the second French edition (1701) should be consulted whenever possible because it distinguishes the text of the first edition from additions made in the second.

[2] If 'Nihusius' [H] is to be read as autobiographical, Bayle was not persuaded of the superiority of Protestantism over Catholicism, but held to the sceptical opinion that one should uphold the religion in which one had been born and raised. At the time, he described himself as returning *ad paternam legem*.

1686, insisted that heretics could be wrong in good faith and therefore should not be punished.[3] For Jurieu, Louis XIV, who had revoked the Edict of Nantes in 1685 and commenced a systematic persecution of Protestants, was a tyrant who should be overthrown; Bayle, on the other hand, insisted that to allow subjects to judge their rulers was to invite anarchy. Bayle thus approved of the government of James II in Great Britain, while Jurieu supported William of Orange's invasion.

Jurieu freely charged Bayle with both heresy and atheism. In retrospect he interpreted a work Bayle had published in 1682, *Pensées diverses sur la comète*, which had argued that atheists made as good citizens and subjects as Christians, as a defence of atheism (a term which he and Bayle used to refer not to denial of the existence of any God, but to denial of divine providence). In 1697 Bayle published his *Dictionary historical and critical*. Jurieu saw the work as defending scepticism and unbelief, and found in it attacks upon Christian views of the Bible and innumerable obscenities. His judgement was in large part shared by the Church court which heard his complaints, by Protestant theologians (such as Le Clerc) who were at odds with him on most other questions, and by the eighteenth-century *philosophes*, who found in Bayle an inexhaustible source of anti-clerical arguments. The *Dictionary* remains one of the most extraordinary works of erudition and argument ever compiled; its wide influence throughout the eighteenth century has made Bayle seem the founder of the Enlightenment, and has led to his being regarded as if he were a *philosophe* of the high Enlightenment, although he died in 1706.[4]

II

Bayle's *Dictionary* is a work of enduring historical importance. But it also presents us with an immediate and extraordinary challenge. For two hundred and fifty years there was a broad consensus that Bayle was to be read as an enemy of religious faith. Although in the *Dictionary* he repeatedly denied that he intended to undermine belief, it was generally agreed these protests could be ignored, because the implications of his arguments were evident, and it could scarcely be believed that he did not understand them or that he was unprepared to accept their consequences. Notoriously, Bayle argued that an omnipotent God could not be sheltered from responsibility for Adam's fall. Even if one attributed free will to Adam (a view which was scarcely

---

[3] See A. G. Tannenbaum, *Pierre Bayle's Philosophical commentary: A modern translation and critical interpretation* (New York 1987).

[4] The classic account of the reception of the *Dictionary* is P. Rétat, *Le Dictionnaire de Bayle et la lutte philosophique au XVIIe siècle* (Paris 1971).

compatible with divine omnipotence and omniscience), God had failed to intervene, and was thus as morally responsible as a mother who allowed her daughter to go to a ball knowing she would be seduced. As a result, most men and women were damned to eternal hell fire; but even leaving aside the next world, since the Fall life in this world had been accompanied by so much pain, injustice, and distress that no sensible person would choose to be born. In Bayle's view, no coherent Christian theodicy was possible. Christians must accept God's goodness on a faith which was contrary to reason, or else consider the alternatives: materialist atheism, or Manicheism. The presumption of most readers was that Bayle had opted for one of these alternatives.

In the *Dictionary*, Bayle protested against the argument of Arnobius, the Church Father, who had denied the existence of the pagan goddess Juno because she had allowed her temple to be burnt down. Where, Bayle asked, was the God of Israel when the King of Babylon burned the temple of Solomon? Could not such arguments be used to destroy faith in any and all religions? "I do not know what the Fathers dreamed of, in some of their Arguments against the Gentiles" ('Chrysis' [A]). Most readers of Bayle assumed that he did know what he was thinking of when he attacked existing arguments for faith.

For the last thirty years this presumption has been vigorously questioned. Most of the recent work on Bayle has taken his declarations of religious faith as being literally true. More cautiously, Mme Elizabeth Labrousse, author of the most important study of Bayle's life and thought, has conceded that it is not difficult to interpret Bayle as attacking Christianity if one does not assume that he always means what he says; and that if one does interpret him literally one must often be struck by how lame his declarations of faith are. Nevertheless, she holds Bayle's arguments are entirely compatible with orthodox Christianity. If he may have often doubted his own belief, there is nothing in his presentation of the issues which represents an attack on religion.[5]

It is a strange fact that this consensus among Bayle scholars has not been systematically criticized in English or French, and yet intelligent, well-informed readers of Bayle continue to doubt it and to prefer the traditional

---

[5] E. Labrousse, *Pierre Bayle*: vol. i, *Du Pays de foix à la cité d'Erasme* (1963; 2nd rev. edn, Dordrecht 1985), 271; vol. ii, *Hétérodoxie et rigorisme* (The Hague 1964), x, 214, 239, 309, 315, 336, 343, 345, 352, 414, 415 [a remarkable argument: if Bayle were an unbeliever he would have concealed his unbelief more carefully; since he does not he is a believer!], 442, 443, 603, 608; see also ead., *Bayle* (Oxford 1983), 59–60. A brief summary of Labrousse's position is 'Reading Pierre Bayle in Paris', in *Anticipations of the Enlightenment*, ed. A. C. Kors and P. J. Korshin (Philadelphia 1987), 7–16. Apart from the works listed in the bibliography of this last volume, one may note the following recent contributions to the new orthodoxy: R. Whelan, 'The anatomy of superstition', *Studies on Voltaire and the 18th century* 259 (1989); J. Kilcullen, *Sincerity and truth* (Oxford 1988); A. C. Kors, *Atheism in France, 1650–1729* (Princeton 1990–), i. 244–62.

reading.[6] It would seem that what is at issue is how one is to interpret a text like the *Dictionary*, and that many people are unwilling to abandon a type of interpretation which at the same time they hesitate to defend. My purpose here is to defend the traditional reading of Bayle, but to do so in part by exploring an issue which has hitherto been largely ignored: the purpose of the "obscenities", to use Bayle's term, which are scattered so widely through the volumes of the *Dictionary*.[7]

Bayle uses the term 'obscenity' to cover almost all references to sexual passion and sexual activity. The central argument of the *Pensées diverses* was that base passions—pride, greed, ambition—are what govern our behaviour in society, rendering the principles we lay claim to irrelevant. Since sexual desire was in Bayle's view the most important of the passions, he was bound to give it a central place in the discussions of human motivation that run through the *Dictionary*. Bayle might have claimed that his account of the behaviour of fallen man was entirely compatible with the strictest Christian morality, but, as we shall see, he admitted that his very interest in the subject implied a tension between his own behaviour and the strictest standards. I believe we can go further and argue that Bayle's discussions of sexuality are intended to undermine Christian moral principles and defend "libertine" values.

The term 'libertine' originally meant a person freed from slavery. It was used from the mid-sixteenth century to refer to those who refused to recognize their subjection to God but thought of themselves as their own masters. Libertines were believed to deny that they were subject to the law of God and thus to recognize only practical constraints on the pursuit of pleasure.[8] A group of intellectuals have come to be termed by modern

[6] See the review essay by D. P. Walker, 'Subversive activities', *New York review of books*, 23 March 1967, 20–23; also Q. Skinner, 'Meaning and understanding in the history of ideas', *History and theory* 8 (1969), 3–53, at 33–5. There are several works in Italian defending a traditional reading of Bayle. The most important is G. Cantelli, *Teologia e ateismo: Saggio sul pensiero filosofico e religioso di Pierre Bayle* (Florence 1969), reviewed by M. Heyd, *Bibliothèque d'humanisme et renaissance* 39 (1977), 157–65. Of recent work in English one may note particularly S. O'Cathasaigh, 'Bayle and the authorship of the *Avis aux réfugiez*', *Studies on Voltaire* 219 (1983), 133–45; id., 'Bayle's *Commentaire philosophique*, 1686', ibid. 260 (1989), 159–82. Two cautious assessments of the new orthodoxy are R. Pintard, 'Les Problèmes de l'histoire du libertinage: Notes et réflexions', *Dix-septième siècle* 127 (1980), 131–61; and, in the same volume (197–211), Rétat's 'Libertinage et hétérodoxie'. Finally, I owe a considerable debt to the thesis of M. L. de Miranda, 'Pierre Bayle: Irreligious author or sincere believer?' (M.A., University of Western Ontario 1989).

[7] The only other discussion of this subject known to me is L. Weibel, *Le Savoir et le corps: Essai sur le Dictionnaire de Pierre Bayle* (Paris 1975): a work whose defects outweigh its virtues, but which provides a useful discussion of Bayle's articles on 'Héloïse' and 'Abelard', and on 'Acosta'.

[8] J. C. Margolin, 'Réflexions sur l'emploi du terme *libertin* au XVIe siècle', in M. Bataillon and others, *Aspects du libertinisme au XVIe siècle* (Paris 1974), 1–33; D. Wootton, 'Lucien Febvre and the problem of unbelief in the early modern period', *Journal of modern history* 60 (1988), 695–730, at 703–4.

scholars the *libertins érudits* because they put a formidable scholarship to the task of demonstrating the relativity of moral values.[9] Bayle, both in his scholarship and in his approach to moral and social behaviour, was in many ways the heir of these men—Naudé, Le Vayer, Patin—and of their mentors, Montaigne and Charron.[10] It is because he falls, I believe, within this intellectual tradition that Bayle may be termed a libertine. He writes as one wise in the ways of the world and prepared to tolerate behaviour others would condemn. How he came by his wisdom (other than through book-learning) we shall never know.[11] There is no good reason to believe the story that Jurieu's enmity was sparked by an affair between Bayle and his wife, though one can understand why attentive readers of the *Dictionary* may have wanted to invent a story of this sort.[12]

III

Bayle's *Dictionary* fills five folio or twenty-five quarto volumes. It was originally conceived, according to a *Project* published in 1690, as a compendium of errors to be found in other dictionaries (v. 784–96). Such a work, had it been completed, would have been an unreadable volume of eccentric erudition, outdated almost as soon as it was published. After 1693, Bayle was dependent on publishing for a living, and he received financial assistance from his publisher, Leers, for a very different work. This book, it was hoped, would sell widely, for it would contain numerous "obscenities" which were bound to attract readers, and cheek by jowl with them philosophical arguments which were likely to provoke theologians. The work was thus deliberately conceived—and advertised in the Preface (i. 6–7)—as one that would run counter to moral and religious orthodoxies. This was to be no mere compilation of facts.

Bayle's *Dictionary* is organized alphabetically, as one would expect. The thousands of entries are very largely devoted to individuals, each dealt with in a short factual article. But from these articles there spring innumerable footnotes in which Bayle quotes sources, argues over matters of fact, and discusses issues of principle. Thus, in his own words, he appears in two characters, as historian and commentator (i, p. lxxxi; v. 810). But the most

---

[9] R. Pintard, *Le Libertinage érudit dans la première moitié du XVIIe siècle* (2 vols., 1943; 2nd edn with new introduction, Geneva 1983). See also the valuable study by L. Bianchi, *Tradizione libertina e critica storica* (Milan 1988).

[10] On Charron, see T. Gregory, 'Pierre Charron's "scandalous book" ', in *Atheism from the Reformation to the Enlightenment*, ed. M. Hunter and D. Wootton (Oxford 1992), 87–109.

[11] Bayle puzzled over Mlle Scudéry, whose novels betrayed a similarly inexplicable knowledge of the sexual passions: *Oeuvres diverses* (1727), reprint, ed. E. Labrousse (4 vols, Hildesheim 1964), i. 149b–150a. [12] Labrousse, *Pierre Bayle*, i. 144–7.

striking characteristic of the *Dictionary* is that one finds in it not just these two voices of Bayle, but innumerable interlocutors. There are authorities and critics quoted at length arguing on different sides of every question. But there are also innumerable fictional voices: unnamed individuals whom Bayle claims to have heard presenting one view or another, and more complex fictions. Bayle asks himself, for example, what Simonides would say if transported through time and space and confronted with the arguments for Christianity, or how Charron might have responded to his critics.

This multiplication of voices is characteristic of Bayle's work. The *Dictionary* was the only work he published under his own name: Leers had to put the author's name on it to protect the copyright, essential if the costs of such a vast enterprise were to be recouped. At other times Bayle wrote under different guises: sometimes a Catholic, sometimes a rationalist Protestant, and sometimes a fideistical one. He published works in which he attacked his own publications, and within individual works he included letters, dialogues, and debates. How are we to explain this strange, obsessive multiplication of one author into innumerable voices? Mme Labrousse sees it as a reflection of Bayle's intellectual style. His skills were critical, not synthetic. He built positions up in order to pull them down. He loved to argue different points of view and feared to commit himself. This is almost certainly part of the explanation, but there is another possibility that should be borne in mind. For Bayle devised a whole series of stylistic techniques which enabled him to deny personal responsibility for what he wrote, displacing that responsibility on to fictional authors, quoted authorities, imaginary interlocutors. Such techniques enabled him to obtain a polemical advantage, to publish the unpublishable, and have it read by the unsuspecting. The *Pensées diverses sur la comète* is ostensibly a work by a Catholic on whether comets bring disaster in their wake. It is certainly something very different, a polemical attack on Catholicism under the guise of an assessment of pagan idolatry.[13] Bayle is certainly capable of writing one thing with the intention of conveying a quite different, unspoken message. But how many such unspoken messages may one text contain? Are the *Pensées diverses* not only an attack on Catholicism but also on Christianity?

Given Bayle's normal behaviour as an author, we are entitled to ask ourselves if the *Dictionary* has a concealed purpose. Perhaps we can learn something by looking at the topics to which Bayle addresses himself? At once Bayle's vast enterprise appears the more puzzling. The Preface promises "obscenities" drawn from Montaigne and Brantôme.[14] Eagerly (or with

---

[13] Cf. W. Rex, *Essays on Pierre Bayle and religious controversy* (The Hague 1965).

[14] An excellent discussion of Montaigne's treatment of erotic and sexual themes is to be found in J. Starobinski, *Montaigne in motion* (Chicago 1985), 185–213. The *Vies des dames galantes* by Brantôme (d. 1614) is a source for articles such as 'Joanna of Naples'.

dismay) we look for articles on these authors. There are none, nor on Aquinas, Cicero, Copernicus, Descartes, Galileo, Gassendi, Horace, Naudé, Plato, Richelieu, Vanini, to name only individuals to whom Bayle frequently refers. At the same time, there are articles on innumerable people we would never think to ask about: Francis Barbarus, Jean Fernel, Armand de Gontaut, Pierre Jarige, the Parthenai women, Charles de Quellenec, James Golius, Mark Zuerius Boxhornius are treated at length. Nor can one predict what one will find in an article: 'Rorarius' contains a lengthy discussion of whether animals have souls, while, as we shall see, 'Quellenec' is about impotence, 'Patin' about abortion.[15] Most subjects, however, Bayle does not deal with and dismiss; rather, he recurs to them. Thus 'Francis of Assisi' discusses how Francis rolled in the snow to quench the fires of lust. Do the temptations of the celibate interest you? Then Bayle's marginal cross-references will lead you from one article to another, from 'Francis', through 'Fontevraud', 'Guillelma', 'Fraticelli', 'Arodon', 'Democritus', and 'Brachmans', to 'Gymnosophists'. Thus each reader constructs his or her own text. The responsibility of the author is not only displaced on to innumerable voices within the text, but on to the reader. A salacious reader will be distracted from 'Francis' to a series of articles on sex and celibacy, from 'Erasmus' to an equally long series of articles on kissing; but this is the reader's choice, not (in appearance) the author's. Even within an article the same process takes place as one chooses which of the innumerable lengthy footnotes to read. In the article on Charron, one can easily read only those notes which discuss why Charron was thought to be a sceptic and an opponent of Christianity and ignore those which maintain he was a believer. Sometimes (as we shall see in 'Laïs' and 'Patin'), if one takes the trouble to read all the notes, a pattern of argument and imagery begins to appear that the casual reader, skimming quickly through the text, would never notice.

Bayle has thus produced a radically decentred text which lends itself to an infinite variety of subjective readings. Any account of the *Dictionary* needs to explain its peculiar structural features. The obvious explanation for them is, I have suggested, to displace responsibility from the author. And Bayle explicitly appeals to them for this purpose. In his reply to his critics, he protests that if his work contains errors they are innocuous precisely because his book lacks system:

But if a layman, who bears no public office, as myself, should drop amongst vast collections of History and Learning, some error in Religion or Morality, I do not see

---

[15] There was no subject index to the *Dictionary* in Bayle's lifetime: i. 14–15. Consequently, his critics were slow to locate some of the more subversive discussions. Vol. i, pp. cxxii–cxxviii, reprints the proceedings relating to the *Dictionary* before the Consistory of the Walloon Church of Rotterdam. Bayle's account of the proceedings is on lxxix–lxxxi. It is impossible not to conclude from these documents that Bayle was acting in bad faith when he promised to correct the *Dictionary* wherever the Consistory found fault with it.

any reason why any body should be concerned at it. It is not in such works as these that the reader seeks for the reformation of his faith. No man takes for his guide in this matter, an author who only speaks by the by, and occasionally; and who by his very throwing his sentiments, as pins into a meadow, sufficiently shews that he cares not to be followed. The errors of such a writer are of no consequence, nor deserve that the world should be disturbed about them. Thus the Faculties of Divinity in France dealt with Michael de Montagne's book. They left untouched all this author's maxims, who, without following any system, method, or order, heaped up and tacked together whatever his memory presented to him: but when Peter Charron, a Priest, and a Doctor of Divinity, came to vent some of Montagne's sentiments in a methodical and systematical treatise of Morality, the Divines were no longer silent. [16]

IV

Bayle thus hoped to escape censorship, like Montaigne.[17] But his main defence against his critics was that he had not advocated unbelief or sexual licence. He had described the arguments of atheists, and had noted how hard it was to reply to them. But he had always insisted that reason should be sacrificed to faith (v. 833–6), and he was entitled to be taken at his word. Those who read Bayle as a believer follow his own injunctions on how to read. One must not, he insists, assume that an author sees and accepts the consequences of his arguments; one must not assume that, because an author refutes an argument used to support a conclusion, he rejects the conclusion ('Charron' [P]; v. 825). In short, an author can only be held responsible for views he explicitly endorses ('Charron' [K]).

Following these principles, Bayle reads a whole series of authors to whom unbelief had been attributed as sincere believers, amongst them Pomponazzi, Charron, and Hobbes. On Bayle's principles, perfunctory and formal declarations of orthodoxy are to take precedence over all else. Of Charron he writes:

[I]f you object against him, that he makes some Remarks, which strike at Religion, and shew, that he was more persuaded of the Force of his Remarks, than of the Truths, at which those Remarks are levelled, he may answer you: "I should be such a one as you say, if I were directed by the weak Light of my Reason; but I do not trust such a Guide; I submit myself to GOD's Authority, I captivate my Understanding to the Obedience of Faith." ('Charron' [L])

---

[16] *Dictionary*, v. 810; see also v. 798, and 'Charron' [O].

[17] It is sometimes maintained (e.g. by K. C. Sandberg, *At the crossroads of faith and reason* (Tucson, Ariz. 1966), 99–107) that Bayle had no reason to fear censorship and persecution. An elementary refutation of this claim is to be found in 'Socinus' [K, L], and in 'Acosta' *in corp.* and [C]: Bayle could not have been clearer had he been deliberately addressing the question of his own freedom of expression. See also S. Groenveld, 'The Mecca of authors?', in *Too mighty to be free*, ed. A. C. Duke and C. A. Tamse (Zutphen 1987), 63–86.

Of course, you may object that the sort of faith-against-reason you are being asked to accept is psychologically implausible. Perhaps it is for you; but how are you to judge of what other people are capable?

At first sight, then, everything hangs together. Bayle has a view about how to read texts which involves giving primacy to their narrowly defined literal meaning. He himself reads texts that way and he asks that you should read him that way. He believes there is a need for a book which will be comparable to Naudé's defence of all the great men who have been falsely accused of magic, a book which will defend all those falsely accused of atheism ('Knuzen' [C]: Knuzen is the exception, a self-confessed atheist). He, of course, will be of that number, portrayed as a faithful Protestant. Thus Bayle has followed Charron in constructing "a Shield against all the Darts of his Enemies".

There are problems, however, with Bayle's principles. The first is the problem of the hostile reader. Bayle knew that most readers thought that Pomponazzi, Charron, and Le Vayer were not upholding orthodoxy but attacking it. To present the case against religious beliefs as strongly as they had done, and to accompany it by a weak statement of faith, might present problems for attackers, but it would not guarantee one against attack. What counted was not just the literal meaning of one's words, but the balance of the argument and the tone of the author's voice. Bayle made the point himself by pointing out the largely cosmetic changes that Charron was forced to make to the second edition of *De la Sagesse*:

From whence we may infer, that, upon several Occasions, a Man appears to be an Heretic, only by his manner of expressing himself. Take away certain Words, which seem too harsh, and make use of others, which signify the same thing, but are not so blunt, and, whereas you was [*sic*] accounted an Heretic, you will be looked upon as Orthodox. ('Charron' [O])

An author, knowing that hostile readers exist, knows that he needs to pay attention to tone and implication, as much as to literal meaning. It is sometimes maintained that to read Bayle as if he were an unbeliever is anachronistic: this is how the eighteenth century read him, but his own world was very different. The very people who make this argument also insist that the fideism they attribute to Bayle is peculiarly modern, a view which is itself, I suspect, anachronistic.[18] In any case, the *Dictionary* had hostile readers who saw in it evidence of unbelief from the very beginning, and the additions and clarifications Bayle introduced in the second edition did nothing to mollify them. He had promised to correct all passages which gave offence, but in the second edition he only added new material: he took nothing out. It is true that he wrote a revised and censored version of the

---

[18] Labrousse, ii. 443.

article 'David' which had drawn much fire. But Leers published the original article as an appendix on the ground (Bayle reports) that to drop it would be to lose sales.[19] To accept this displacement of responsibility from Bayle to Leers at face value one has to give Bayle the benefit of every doubt.

Secondly, there is the problem of the complicit reader. Mme Labrousse rejects an interpretation of Bayle which would see him as writing to be read between the lines, on the ground that in order to do this he would have had to be confident of having an audience of complicit readers. His immediate environment was that of Huguenot refugees in Holland, men and women of faith. The traditional interpretation of Bayle thus misunderstands the nature of his audience.[20] There are two problems with this line of argument. The first is the obvious one that one may write to change one's readers' minds. The second is that Bayle was certainly writing for an international and interdenominational audience. He thought that some of his contemporaries were unbelievers—Saint-Evremond and Vossius amongst them—and there is no reason why he should not have been addressing them.

Lastly, there is the problem of Bayle's own practice as a reader. In 1676 he had read Naudé and La Mothe le Vayer in the normal way, as men whose arguments undermined Christianity and who were surely aware of the fact. In the *Dictionary*, such orthodox readings threaten to recur. Thus Epicurus argued that one should worship the Gods, even though they had no interest in men. Bayle's interpretation teeters on the edge:

It may be those were not mistaken, who accused him of doing this out of Policy only, and to avoid the Punishment he would infallibly have incurred, had he overthrown the Worship of the Gods: But this Accusation would have been rash, though perhaps not without Ground: For we ought in Equity to judge of our Neighbour by his Words and Actions, and not by the secret Intentions we fancy he has. ('Epicurus' [G])

However, Bayle is well aware that one is not obliged to confine oneself to a carefully "equitable" reading. He accepts that an author's true sentiments are not always what they appear to be, and that we do not always believe everything we are told. In the case of Malherbe, the mere fact that he had said that "the religion of gentlemen was that of their prince" (a view shared by Charron) is ground for suspicion. A few such remarks must weigh heavily in the balance, and lead one to suspect that, whatever his outward show of religion,

he conformed to the common usage by way of precaution . . . he had reason to fear a real and effectual damage, by not observing the commands of an absolute obligation,

---

[19] Thus no edition of the *Dictionary* ever appeared which did not contain the original text of 'David': P. Burrell, 'Bayle's *Dictionnaire historique et critique*', in *Notable encyclopedias of the seventeenth and eighteenth centuries*, ed. F. A. Kafker, *Studies on Voltaire* 194 (1981), 83–103, at 99.   [20] Labrousse, ii. 599.

such as those of his church are, to communicate once a year, to hear mass upon holydays and Sundays. A man of parts, who wants to make his fortune, or desires to continue in his present condition, will never despense with this kind of precepts; he will so behave himself, that his neighbours, friends, and domestics shall not know, that he despises his church. . . . All the religious actions, that Malherbe performed, were so easy, and so necessary to his fortune, and to the reputation of an honest man, which he maintained in all other things

—that it is easy to discount them.[21]

Bayle seeks to bar an interpretation of his own texts in terms of the "secret Intentions we fancy he has", and we can produce no conclusive testimony from his neighbours, friends, and domestics. Faced with this seeming impasse, it may help to look at the *Dictionary*'s treatment of "obscenity": for on the one hand the theme of "obscenity" is bound to cast light on whether Bayle accepted orthodox Christian moral principles; on the other, Bayle had no need to be as cautious in discussing sex as in discussing theology. This theme presents our best hope of obtaining insight into Bayle's private opinions.

V

Bayle is in no doubt that the *Dictionary* contains obscene passages, just as it contains arguments against religion. The question, in his view, is whether he is within his rights to report the beliefs, words, and behaviour of others, and whether he should be interpreted as endorsing the things he reports. The standard view of Bayle is that he is an inflexible moral rigorist. Mme Labrousse thinks he never jokes when there is a question of morality at issue.[22] Certainly he insists that, though reason must give way to faith where questions of theology are concerned, the literal text of the Bible must be subordinated where necessary to moral principles. If the Bible appears to advocate religious persecution, or to justify immoral behaviour on the part of David and others, then it must be reinterpreted in the light of natural reason. A lie, for example, can never be justified, even to save a life. It is thus easy to assume that there was an immense gap between Bayle's moral rigorism and the *libertinism* of his disciple, Mandeville.[23]

Yet, as we have seen, readers of the *Dictionary* were promised something else. Bayle did not fail to deliver, as is clear from Popkin's selection, which is exceptional in recognizing the central importance of sex in the *Dictionary*.[24]

---

[21] 'Malherbe' [C]. Acosta resolved to behave in a similar way, but failed to maintain the pretence and paid a terrible price for his failure: 'Acosta' *in corp.*
[22] Labrousse, ii. 606.   [23] See, e.g., Wootton, 'Lucien Febvre', 723.
[24] Pierre Bayle, *Historical and critical dictionary: Selections*, ed. R. H. Popkin (Indianapolis 1965).

Turn Popkin's pages: in 'Abimelech' [E] Bayle discusses whether Isaac was wrong to have sex with Rebecca without taking care to close the window first; in 'Hall' [F] he discusses an English theologian who thought priestly celibacy impossible, and who asked, "A good swimmer may hold his breath under the water for some portion of a minute: why not for an hour? why not for more? A devout papist may fast after his breakfast till his dinner in the afternoon: therefore, why not a week? why not a month? why not as long as Eve, the maid of Meurs?" He goes on to quote an example employed by Hall: "Do not our histories tell us that during the reign of Henry Third, Robert Grosthead, the famous bishop of Lincoln, during a visitation, 'was fain to explore the virginity of their nuns, by nipping of their dugs.' *Indignum scribi,*[25] as Matthew Paris [writes]?" In 'Hipparchia' [E] he discusses those who are willing to perform the sex act in public; he seems to approve not only of Hipparchia but of Theodorus, the atheist, who replied with actions not words when he wished to refute a sophism of Hipparchia's that it was lawful to do to someone else anything that it was lawful to do to oneself: "Theodorus did not waste any time answering her as a logician. He threw himself upon her and untied her gown. Considering the manner of attire, and speaking in present-day terms, we would say that he 'raised her petticoat'. . . . This is a very gay and cavalier way of replying to a woman's sophisms. Hipparchia was not disconcerted at all." In 'Jonas' [C] he discusses how Icelanders offer their women to foreigners. In 'Mammillarians' [D] he discusses the conventions governing kissing and placing a hand on a woman's breast ("I only report these things to show that there is no subject to which the conversation of reputable people does not sometimes descend"). At other times he adopts a more directly moralistic tone. Thus he attacks the Jesuit casuist Sanchez for reporting the sexual activities to which penitents confess. It is hard to reconcile his claim that "when once vice is attested to either by history or by court record, authors have a right to mention it" [C], with the support he declares for the view that Sanchez should never have been allowed to publish reports of the sins to which people confess. If directors of conscience need such information, it should be transmitted orally or in secret manuscripts, not published abroad.

Bayle thus oscillates between a happy willingness to report those things which are *indignum scribi* and a prudish distaste for books which do as he does. Faced with this inconsistency, it is not so much what he says to which we need to pay attention, as the tone with which he says it. After all, Bayle has invited the reader to read the book in search of titillating matter; the occasional moralistic remark can be discounted if it is clear that his real intent is to encourage thoughts of bared breasts and lifted petticoats. 'Arodon' seems to me an article of this sort. Bayle praises Arodon, a Jew, for

---

[25] "It is shameful to mention it."

recommending that husband and wife not talk during love-making and have only pious thoughts, and for declaring that otherwise their children will be deformed. A Christian could not have expressed worthier sentiments, even though the medical doctors teach that "a child conceived when the mind is distracted—I mean when one's thoughts are serious, grave, and spiritual—is simple, silly, and imbecilic" ('Arodon' [A]), and even though the poets write of the murmuring that accompanies love-making. Bayle then indulges in a series of apparently irrelevant asides, beginning:

And this has led a modern writer[26] to find some proofs for an interpretation he has given to the words of a Greek poet that contain a description of the cave of the nymphs. "Concerning the agreeable murmur of which Homer speaks," he says, "this is doubtless the endearing words of lovers . . . that accompany the most favourable familiarities and that caused the most knowing of all the poets in the art of love to say:

> Her kind complaints, her melting accents hear,
> Whilst with fond sighs she wounds the listening ear." (Ovid)

In this essay, Bayle declares his support for Arodon, but he gives the poets the best of the argument. When he returns to the question again, in 'Francis' [D], it is to mock those who imagine one can or should engage in pious, restrained lovemaking (even though Montaigne is of their number). Elsewhere he similarly commits himself to a view he clearly does not support. In 'Fontevraud' he discusses Robert d'Arbrissel, an abbot who was said to go to bed with young women to test his chastity. Bayle claims not to believe the story, but leaves his reader with the impression that it is a story to be believed.[27] Bayle claims to endorse Socrates' view that "a beautiful woman is a more dangerous animal than a scorpion", but in fact he shows a good deal of sympathy for those who put themselves in the way of temptation declaring their intention to overcome it:

They advance to the combat with boldness and chearfulness . . . both parties behave themselves as if neither feared to be vanquished, and it is very probable this security is not so much founded upon a knowledge of their own strength, as upon an unwillingness to come off victorious in this conflict; and at the worst the conflict itself, whatever may be the event of it, is not without its charm: if a victory follows, it is so much gained upon nature; if they are foiled, it is so much gained for her. ('Fontevraud' [N])

It is easy to dismiss such essays as mere (if somewhat tame) pornography, but Bayle has a number of serious purposes. The first is a straightforward one: it

---

[26] Le Vayer.

[27] Bayle insists on a strict fidelity to the evidence when it comes to evidence of atheism; but he is prepared to go beyond the evidence, trusting rumour, gossip, and insinuating a presumption of guilt when it comes to questions of sexual activity: cf. Weibel, 94–5. This double standard presumably reflects the fact that Bayle had to defend himself only against the first sort of charge, not the second.

is a matter of fact that sex is important in the affairs of the world. Rulers, for example, are not governed by the inflexible laws of political self-interest, not constantly engaged in the pursuit of power. A Henry IV will happily sacrifice a military advantage for the sake of a sexual conquest, frequently prefer pleasure to power. Second, Bayle uses sex to illustrate one of his favourite themes: the fact that people's actions do not correspond to their principles. Everywhere people recommend chastity; nowhere do they practise it. This theme is linked to the larger problem of theodicy, for God has both made sexual activity pleasurable and, for the most part, forbidden it:

How is it possible that under such a Being men should be drawn to evil by a bait that is almost unsurmountable, I mean, by the sense of pleasure, and are deterred from it by the fear of remorse, infamy, or several other punishments; they spend their lives, tossed by these contrary passions, pulled sometimes one way, and sometimes another, being sometimes overcome by the sense of pleasure, and sometimes by the fear of the consequences. Manicheism probably arose from a strong meditation on this deplorable condition of man. ('Guarini' [E])

Thus Bayle constantly returns to sexual subjects because he wants to stress the central importance of sex in human experience and the problems this poses for moral theory and religion.

"A strong meditation on this deplorable state of man" involves thinking about sex both practically and morally. An example of the first is Bayle's discussion of Erasmus's claim that, although he had not always been chaste, he had never been a slave to love. Bayle thinks that Erasmus's desire to preserve his reputation would have prevented him from having recourse to prostitutes, while he wrote so many books that we can well believe that he had insufficient time for the prolonged courtships, the extended emotional turmoils that accompany affairs with respectable (married) women. Sexual abstinence must thus have been imposed on Erasmus by circumstance and by choice, not by principle. For Bayle, the problems presented by adultery seem practical, not moral.[28] Elsewhere he protests against jealousy, and advocates the community of women.

At other times, though, Bayle is quick to see an issue of principle, particularly when the principle at stake is independent of sexual ethics. 'Quellenec' is singled out by Mme Labrousse as an example of the sort of article that Bayle should have left out of the *Dictionary*. But this extensive discussion of the legal practice of ordering public sexual congress, in order to judge whether a man is impotent and a marriage should be dissolved, is intended to expose the injustice of an irrational practice whose origins Bayle is concerned to identify and whose demise he believes he can celebrate (v.

---

[28] 'Erasmus' [EE]; see also 'Scioppius' [B, T].

799).[29] Bayle sees the whole procedure as an invasion of privacy and as biased against the man. For the fact that he may not be able to perform in public does not mean he cannot perform at all. Nor is he likely to have any success if a hostile wife, seeking an annulment, offers him no co-operation. Such trials can rarely (although Bayle notes an exception) have happy outcomes. Bayle begins his essay with the report that the body of Quellenec was sought out by the women of the court after he had been killed in the massacre of St Bartholomew because they wanted to inspect his genitals: their curiosity had been aroused because he had been the defendant in a trial for impotence. They are engaged upon a grotesque assault upon his body in death; but this is no worse, we are to understand, than the humiliation of the trial itself.

My suggestion, then, is that Bayle's discussions of "obscenities" are not only intended to titillate but also to raise serious issues. In order to discuss those issues he must pretend to approve orthodox sexual morality, while often gently mocking it (as in 'Arodon') or undercutting it (as in 'Erasmus'). To support this view I shall now turn to two extensive essays which deal with central topics in any realistic analysis of sexual morality: prostitution and abortion.

VI

'Laïs' is an article that Bayle himself draws to the reader's attention in his 'Clarification' on obscenity. In it he provides an account of the life of the most famous courtesan of ancient Greece. Laïs was particularly attractive to orators and philosophers: Demosthenes travelled far to see her but could not afford her; Aristippus purchased her services frequently; while to Diogenes the Cynic she gave herself free. However, she was unable to tempt Xenocrates, into whose bed she climbed. In general, Bayle appears to admire Laïs. He describes her as having the better of an encounter with Euripides, who had attacked prostitutes, by quoting against him his own line: "Nothing is filthy but thinking makes it so" ('Laïs' [S]). (He then tells us he is sure the story is apocryphal.) When he criticizes her, it is for turning down a paying client.

In the course of this lengthy article, there are, I think, two moments that best enable us to judge his views. The first is when he sets out to describe the attitude of Aristippus, who was teased by his associates because he had to pay for what Diogenes got free. He replied that he paid Laïs so that he could have her, not so that others could not. To Diogenes, he compared sharing a prostitute with someone else to staying in a guest house or being one

---

[29] A modern work covering some of the same ground is P. Darmon, *Le Tribunal de l'impuissance* (Paris 1979), of which there is an unsatisfactory translation (London 1985).

passenger amongst others on a boat: one had no need of exclusive possession in such circumstances. Told that Laïs evidently loved Diogenes, not him, he replied that he did not expect the food he ate to love him but to give him pleasure. It was he who took Laïs, he said, not she who took him. What does Bayle encourage us to think of Aristippus? It is hard not to get the impression that he thinks him a better philosopher than Xenocrates, who mutilated his member in order to associate it with pain: so successfully that Laïs could dismiss him as not a man but a statue.

What strengthens this view is that Bayle himself adopts Aristippus' outlook in a gratuitous aside on the same page. He is discussing how Laïs is said, like other courtesans, to have become a procuress in old age. Thus she continued in the service of Venus:

This puts me in mind of the invalids or disabled soldiers, who have been sometimes mentioned in our Gazettes. When they can no longer bear arms, they are sent upon the coasts to exercise the militia. If you would have another comparison, consider the mule spoken of by a Greek historian. Having done long services to the people of Athens, she was exempted from labour, with permission to go and pasture where she pleased; but that she might not be useless, she went and placed herself before the waggons, and in some measure incouraged the beasts of burthen that drew them. For which reason it was ordered, that she should be kept all her life at the public expence. (I)

Thus, like an old soldier, or a faithful mule, Laïs has performed useful service to the public. We are by now prepared for Bayle's treatment of the varying stories of her death. Some say she was stoned to death in the temple of Venus by jealous women; others that she choked on an olive stone. But Bayle prefers to think she died making love: "Which to one, who had devoted herself to the service of the goddess Venus, was a glorious death; she died in the bed of honour, and in signalizing her fidelity; just as when a warrior is killed in a battle." [L]

The only sensible reading of 'Laïs' is to see that in it Bayle has chosen to adopt a pagan, not a Christian, attitude to sex. We are invited to admire, not to condemn, Laïs and Aristippus. This is not to say that Bayle thinks we should imitate them. The old are fortunate to experience the philosophical detachment that comes with having their sexual drive diminish. But their attitude to sex, like that ascribed to Erasmus, is practical, not moralistic or sentimental, and it is only on such a basis that one can hope to bring principle and practice into line.

Such an interpretation may seem surprising, given Bayle's reputation for moral strictness, but fortunately we can confirm it by comparing the implicit argument of 'Laïs' with the explicit argument of letter seventeen of the *Nouvelles lettres critiques sur l'histoire du Calvinisme* (1685), which is concerned with sexual jealousy. There he argues that it is rational that human beings should establish rights of property in scarce resources, in land for example, while sharing in common inexhaustible resources, such as the air, the sea, fresh water. But since women are an inexhaustible source of sexual pleasure, and since there are enough of them to go round, there is no rational reason for men to establish private property in women. In short, there are no rational grounds for one person to lay claim to an exclusive sexual property in another. Marriage is the product of an entirely irrational jealousy, but a wise man, Bayle makes clear, will adopt the attitudes of Aristippus. We ought to be as willing to lend our wives to others as our books, and we ought to prefer sexually experienced women to inexperienced ones. Both divine providence and mere jealousy may have driven men to institute marriage, but secular reason suggests that society would have been better off had they not done so. Here, then, there is a clear conflict between natural law as it is established by reason and the moral code taught by religion. Bayle always argued that one must obey one's conscience, but it is far from clear that he thought that there was a conscientious obligation to sexual fidelity.[30]

Bayle does not deny that sexual jealousy may have had some beneficent consequences, for by encouraging courtship it has encouraged sophistication and delicacy. But he also makes clear the contradictory character of any benefits that derive from jealousy. For women to civilize society, they must participate in social life; but if husbands are to be secure, they must keep their wives in captivity: "presque tous les peuples du monde . . . tiennent les femmes dans une espèce de captivité".[31] Bayle alternately appears to approve and condemn this state of affairs, but a careful reader would be bound to conclude that such paradoxes and inconsistencies are the necessary consequence of an irrational moral code. Nor is it clear that he was convinced that jealousy was an inescapable natural instinct which, however irrational, must be accepted as inevitable. In *Nouvelles de la république des lettres* he had reported that a very different set of conventions governed relations between the sexes in Malabar. There "les enfans ne peuvent être Nobles que du côté de leurs mères, parce qu'il est libre aux femmes de prendre autant de maris qu'il leur plaît, et de les quitter quand bon leur semble".[32] The evidence would suggest that Bayle thought this to be the best way of managing sexual relations.

In another lengthy article in the *Dictionary*, 'Patin', Bayle seems in effect to approve a similarly pagan attitude to abortion and infanticide. For the real

---

[30] I am not, therefore, persuaded that Bayle was convinced that Christian morality and natural reason always coincided, despite Labrousse, ii. 280–83. Locke seems to have been conscious of similar difficulties when it comes to grounding sexual morality in natural law: "Thus for a man to cohabit and have children by one or more women, who are at their own disposal, and, when they think fit, to part again, I see not how it can be condemned as a vice, since nobody is harmed, supposing it done amongst persons considered as separate from the rest of mankind." ('Virtus', in John Locke, *Political writings*, ed. D. Wootton (Harmondsworth 1993), 240–42).   [31] *Oeuvres diverses*, ii. 284b.   [32] Ibid., i. 259b.

subject of 'Patin' is Patin's description of Paris as, in Bayle's words, "infected with an horrible corruption, and as filled with such creatures who having done all that was necessary to people the earth, do afterwards all that is necessary to people the Limbo" (*in corp.*). Just as 'Quellenec' begins with a victim's body, so Bayle begins his discussion in 'Patin' with the death of Mlle de Guerchi, apparently as the result of a botched abortion. The dead woman had been refused burial in holy ground and her body thrown into a lime pit; the midwife is soon to be tortured; later we learn that she has been executed. We then learn that De Guerchi had wanted to have the child: the abortion had been forced on her by the father, the duc de Vitry. De Guerchi's mistake, we soon discover, was to hesitate. Had she sought an early abortion her life would not have been in danger.

Bayle then explains that, since 1557, women who obtain abortions have been punished more severely than any other criminals; nevertheless, this was the most common of all crimes, for fear of public opinion, of disgrace, is more powerful than the pangs of conscience and the terror of the scaffold. As Bayle remarks, this is confirmation of the argument of the *Pensées diverses sur la comète* that social sanctions are more effective than religion or the state in maintaining order and shaping behaviour. Religion teaches that infanticide is worse than the murder of a stranger;[33] moreover, Catholics believe the victims are denied access to heaven, since they die unbaptised, being confined to limbo. Yet innumerable women scarcely hesitate to commit this crime. They turn to abortion to hide the fact that they are pregnant. "It is in vain to say, that the art of abortion is not far from it's perfection; and that if you except the art of curing Venereal distempers, there is none which an unhappy industry, occasioned by the wants of an infinite number of people, has improved more than this", for abortions nevertheless sometimes fail, and infanticide when successful is sometimes discovered ('Patin' [C]).

Bayle then raises the question of whether it is right that women should be tortured by fear of public disgrace to the point that they are forced to run such risks. Would not children's lives be saved if the disgrace attached to illegitimate pregnancy was reduced? Abortion is much rarer where female chastity is less valorized. Bayle presents the view that the effect of the fear of disgrace is to make women act contrary to their consciences and their religious beliefs. Does he not expect us to conclude that social pressure should reinforce, not undermine, moral behaviour? And that if in this case it does not, it must be because society does not really want to regard infanticide as a worse crime than promiscuity? This view will be reinforced when Bayle on the next page quotes Henri Estienne as reporting that infanticide is much

---

[33] Bayle moves back and forth between what we would term *infanticide* and what we would term *abortion*; though he raises the question of whether they are morally identical, he avoids answering it.

rarer in nunneries now that nuns are sometimes allowed to leave the cloister, marry, and keep the child.

Bayle goes on to argue that perhaps only one foetus in three survives to baptism, so many miscarry, are aborted, are stillborn, killed at birth, or die before they can receive the sacrament (throughout, we may note, Bayle adopts the fiction of the truth of Catholicism, thereby distancing himself from the authorial voice). Abortion, in particular, has been common in all societies, even though it was not in the past as safe as it is now. At this point one might feel that Bayle's discussion of abortion was finely balanced between recommending that it be treated as a crime and arguing that certainly illegitimate pregnancy, and perhaps even abortion, should be less severely censured than they are. Two further details tip his argument decisively in this second direction: he points out that the law treats women who conceal their pregnancy and whose children are born dead as if they were guilty of infanticide, despite the fact that many of them may have had no intention of killing their children, planning only to raise them in secret. Thus the law negates the presumption of innocence. Secondly, Estienne is called to testify that it is only servant girls who are ever convicted (here Bayle gives a cross-reference to a whole article devoted to the double-standard which allows masters to seduce their servants). Clearly the present state of affairs is indefensible, and what is in question is not the morality of women, but the standards of society.

Bayle's discussion of abortion ends with a poem, the 'Ballade à Mademoiselle D***', which emphasizes that women, not men, pay the price for, as Bayle puts it, allowing the cat to get at the cream. The poem's refrain is "Then of the rose the thorn alone is thine"; but before we are invited to enjoy its plangent treatment of sex and abortion, we are reminded once again of the sharpness of the spine, for Bayle introduces us to another cadaver. Estienne is accused of misinterpreting a passage in Ovid, whose true meaning can be gathered if one reads a book by G. Lamy in which he reports an autopsy on a woman who had had children. How could one know that she had had children before opening her up? By the stretch marks on her stomach? But these can be caused by past obesity. Then the midwife present shows Lamy and those with him the incontrovertible proof, a tear in her perineum: "she showed me, and all the company". This woman's body is about to be cut open, and Bayle makes the exposure of her pudenda to the public gaze seem in itself a form of assault. Bayle's discussion of abortion thus begins with a cadaver and a woman about to die, a tragedy as he terms it; it ends with another cadaver, followed by a further execution and by the ballad to Mlle D: "De rose alors ne reste que l'épine". Where are our sympathies at this point supposed to lie? There seems to me only one answer possible, although I find it a surprising one. The answer, surely, is with the women who are tortured, executed, denied decent burial, subjected to medical examination. By the end, what Bayle has done is present abortion from the woman's point of view (that is to say, the point of view of women who resort to it), ending with a poem by a woman to a woman about abortion. And despite his equivocations, one comes away with two clear conclusions: early abortion is better than late; and it is the double standard which valorizes female chastity which is primarily responsible for infanticide.

Bayle's Preface promises to titillate. But Bayle uses "obscenity" for a purpose: to advocate pagan rather than Christian values, and to attack the hypocrisy underlying the double standard. Of course he does not do this consistently. His own views may have been confused; even if they were not, he could scarcely have mounted a systematic attack on conventional and orthodox morality. But just as in 'Patin' the orthodox and conventional expressions of opinion seem to be subordinated to the radical rethinking of the question, so elsewhere, he seems to be more concerned to take with his left hand than to give with his right. In his article on Joanna, Queen of Naples, for example, he maintains it is much worse for a queen to have lovers than for a king to have mistresses; but he provides a convenient cross-reference to an article on one of her lovers in which he develops at length the point that the relationship between a queen and her courtiers is like that between men and their mistresses: the reversal of the relations of power entails a reversal of the sex roles, so that courtiers no more dare avow their sexual desire for their queen than women dare avow their desire for men. The reversal of roles that comes with a change in relations of power (Bayle explicitly uses military metaphors to make this point) is nicely dramatized by the fact that Joanna seduces her young man by exploiting the fact that he has an effeminate fear of mice, frightening him into bed. Thus the argument of the one article is undercut by the other, and the crucial difference is shown to be not that between men and women, but that between the powerful and the weak.

Bayle the feminist (which is the interpretation I am proposing here) is an even more remarkable idea than Bayle the atheist, but any reconsideration of what constitutes "obscenity" is bound to cast in doubt established values, and it is worth noting that Bayle held that the psychological (and even some of the physical) differences between men and women were the result of nurture, not nature. He had no difficulty believing that women could make good soldiers, and he wrote favourably of educated women. In contemporary society women were, he believed, brought up with attitudes and values designed to facilitate their subordination to men.[34] Indeed, Bayle's willingness to insist

---

[34] Labrousse, i. 113–14, ii. 77–8; Bayle, *Oeuvres diverses*, i. 73b–74a, 149b–150a, 275ab, 341b. For Bayle's knowledge of feminist literature, see *Dictionary*, 'Marinella'. Mandeville shared Bayle's feminism: see M. M. Goldsmith, *Private vices, public benefits* (Cambridge 1985), 156.

on the fundamental equality of women and men extended to the point of defending the view that women could be appointed priests and could administer the sacraments. He went so far as to argue that there were good grounds for opening the priesthood to the female sex. Queen Elizabeth (whom Bayle admired) would have been well within her rights had she appointed herself Archbishop of Canterbury.[35]

VII

What was Bayle's response to the charge that he had published obscenities and undermined orthodox morality? The longest of his Clarifications is given over to this subject (v. 837–58).[36] The claim I want now to make is that, if one reads the whole of that essay, one is bound to recognize that the position Bayle adopts involves a plea of guilty to the charge as most people would understand it, although he insists he is not guilty of the charge as he chooses to define it. Bayle's first move is to define nine types of obscenity: (1) when an author describes his own debauchery in positive terms and invites others to imitate him; (2) when he writes stories which make sex seem attractive; (3) when he writes lewdly about particular circumstances and particular people; (4) when he attacks licence but describes it too vividly; (5) when in the course of a scientific discussion he writes frankly about reproduction; (6) when he writes a commentary on Roman love poetry; (7) when he writes a historical report of improper behaviour; (8) when he discusses improper behaviour in the context of an analysis of cases of conscience; (9) when he quotes other people speaking freely, or retails information given him by others, in the process never explicitly or implicitly approving of impurity, but censuring it.

Bayle concedes that authors in the first category should be punished, and that there is room for dispute about how one should regard those in categories two to eight; but he maintains that he himself is in category nine, against which no objection can be made. Now it is obvious that category nine is a specious category. Bayle is claiming that an author is in no way responsible for what he chooses to repeat from his sources; yet in his essay on "defamatory libels" (v. 743–65) he insists that those who circulate, even those who read, libels are every bit as guilty as those who write them. If one applies Bayle's own logic to Bayle, then he lies in what he admits to be the disputable categories, 2–8.

Bayle's second move is to appeal to past practice. Authors have always written about sex and, though some have disapproved, freedom of expression in this area has always been defended. Indeed, pillars of the community have

---

[35] *Oeuvres diverses*, iii. 1037a–1040a.
[36] It should be compared with *Oeuvres diverses*, ii. 291a–294a.

felt free to write commentaries on Ovid or medical treatises on reproduction. His third argument is that, even if such works are morally suspect, that does not make them illegal. Nobody can be required to live all the time according to the moral standards of the Gospel. Moreover, one should not judge a man's life by his writings: criticism of the book should not extend to criticism of its author.

Bayle next outlines his own practice: he has not himself used obscene words, even if he has quoted others doing so; he has left indecent passages in Latin, not translated them; he has quoted indecent passages only from books which are already well known, not those which are obscure. (Bayle's definition of a well-known book is surely offered tongue-in-cheek; he knows perfectly well that the whole point of his *Dictionary* is the obscurity of many of the sources he draws upon.) Of course, the whole definition of what terms one may employ is at issue. How far should one use euphemisms? Bayle attacks a view with which we are likely to have little sympathy: one which holds one should never use words such as 'adultery', 'bottom', 'castrate', 'pregnant', or 'prostitute'.[37] His response is that euphemisms are often just as suggestive as blunt speech, since everybody still knows perfectly well what is being discussed. Indeed, since euphemisms and indirect expressions require the reader to put his imagination to work, they may be more, not less, dangerous; they can seduce an incautious reader where blunt speech would put him (or rather her) on guard. If he has been at fault in this matter, his crime is in any case merely a breach of good taste. If some people are offended, this is not the author's responsibility, and authors are not obliged to stay always within the bounds that they would respect if talking in polite, mixed company; nor can an obscenity in a book be a personal offence to an anonymous reader in the way that an obscenity in conversation is an insult to the actual audience. Women blush in company, not when they are reading in private. Indeed, women who have read novels will find nothing shocking in his articles on Héloïse and Abelard (in which, as it happens, Bayle discusses flagellation, and seems to take a peculiar, Protestant satisfaction in the fact that Abelard would beat Héloïse if she was reluctant to have sex with him on holy days). The Bible is full of blunt speech and wicked behaviour; historians and moralists have always felt free to describe immoral acts.

---

[37] See also *Oeuvres diverses*, i. 69a–b. Eighteenth-century French usage was evidently more prudish than English. In 1750 Mandeville's French translator could not bring himself to translate this couplet:

> How firm her pouting Breasts, that white as Snow,
> On th'ample Chest at mighty distance grow.

"Ceux qui entendent l'Anglois", he wrote, "s'appercevront aisément, pourquoi je me suis dispensé de les traduire. J'ai été obligé pour la même raison d'adoucir quantité d'expressions qui auroient pu faire de la peine aux personnes chastes" (B. Mandeville, *The fable of the bees*, ed. F. B. Kaye (2 vols, Oxford 1924), i. 69), despite having translated Mandeville's view (derived from Bayle) that women do not blush when reading bawdy in private.

Bayle's defence thus comes down to the following claims: (1) one should be free to report the words and deeds of others; (2) one should be free to use plain language; (3) since everybody always talks about sex authors should be free to write about it, and since other authors have had a large measure of freedom in this respect that freedom should be extended to him as well. These are admirable arguments, and represent an important defence of principles of freedom of expression. But they do not deal with the real issue, which lies in Bayle's claim that authors cannot be required to live up to the moral principles of the Gospel. Not everyone can pray and do acts of charity all day long. It is not by these Gospel standards that one decides whether someone is an *honnête homme*, an *homme d'honneur*. An *honnête femme* may go to the theatre (which Bayle later attacks as indefensibly obscene, and falling into his first category), or make an effort to dress fashionably. Such behaviour does not make one a *femme galante*. By Gospel standards, we are all to be condemned; in everyday life other standards have to be employed: those of Pliny, for example, who defended his own poetry on the ground that many reputable men had written obscene poems.[38]

The issue here is whether Bayle does not stand on the brink of rejecting Gospel standards and embracing worldly ones. And this is the issue that is consistently raised by the "obscene" passages in the *Dictionary*. The question is whether he is not an author who belongs in category 4: one who condemns vice, but describes it in such a way as to make it seem attractive and to make the condemnation seem irrelevant. The fundamental issue is one of tone (a question which is, of course, inseparable from questions of vocabulary and style, as Bayle himself well knows). And that issue can only be settled by studying Bayle's literary technique—his aside on the hard-working donkey in 'Laïs', his recurring references to mutilated bodies in 'Patin', his use of military imagery in 'Laïs', in 'Francis', in 'Joan'. Such a study leaves one in no doubt that Bayle wants to defend what many people do (visit prostitutes, obtain abortions), not uphold the principles that Christian moralists have always sought to maintain. The *Dictionary* is, quite deliberately, a "libertine" text, and there is nothing in Bayle's Clarification to counter this impression.

VIII

A study of the "obscenities" in the *Dictionary* serves, I believe, to reinforce the traditional view that Bayle is a writer who does not always directly say what he thinks. We have seen that instead he uses poems to counter arguments, images to convey opinions, symbols to suggest values. If the text of the *Dictionary* is seen as a literary *tour de force* and not merely an

[38] *Dictionary*, v. 839–40; see also 797–8.

achievement of scholarship and philosophical argument, it at once becomes easier to recognize how Bayle achieves his effects. But the "obscenities" are not only interesting as a case study in Bayle's literary technique. For if I am right in my reading of them, they at once put Bayle outside the range of orthodox Christianity. Bayle does not merely have a prurient interest in the vices of monks or the sexual practices of foreign nations. His intent is to question a Christian hierarchy of values, just as two of his favourite authors, Montaigne and La Mothe le Vayer, had done before him. The "obscenities" in the *Dictionary* place it firmly in the tradition of the *libertins érudits* as that tradition was conventionally interpreted. Had Bayle written an article on Montaigne he might have felt obliged to discuss whether Montaigne's "obscenities" are evidence that should be placed in the balance when weighing his claims to faith. By insisting that almost all the atheists he discussed were men of conventional virtue (Bayle's praise of the moral character of Epicurus and Spinoza caused much offence), by going so far as to claim that it was a peculiar aspect of God's providence that only men of good character were attracted to atheism (v. 813), Bayle nearly evaded the question of how one might interpret an obscene fideist. The absence of an article on Montaigne makes Bayle's discussion of interpretation incomplete. What Bayle offers us instead is an article on Le Vayer.

As far as obscenity is concerned, Bayle treats Le Vayer's case as if it were strictly comparable to his own (rather, one might say, than to Montaigne's). Here is a man who wrote obscenities but did not practise them. It is quite wrong to judge his morals on the basis of his works, and he defended his obscenities in terms that Bayle adopts as his own. But what of the charge that was also levelled against Le Vayer, of irreligion?

It is likely this suspicion was grounded on some dialogues which he wrote, and which appeared under the name of Orasius Tubero, and on his discovering generally in his works too great a prepossession in favour of Scepticism or the Pyrrhonian principles. It is certain that there is a great deal of looseness [*libertinage*] in the dialogues of Orasius Tubero; but he that should conclude from thence that the author had no religion, would render himself guilty of a very rash judgment: for there is a vast difference betwixt writing freely what may be objected against faith, and believing it to be really true. ('Vayer' *in corp.*)

Thus Bayle tries to assimilate the gap between expression and belief to the gap between words and actions. Le Vayer wrote obscenities but did not practise them. Why should he not also have attacked religion but continued to believe? Bayle's discussion of Le Vayer's putative faith is exceptional, for he quotes no evidence, cites no sources. Le Vayer's faith is at the degree zero of interpretative charity. Bayle does not, as in 'Charron', defend the text, only the man. And even then, the defence is only one of form.

In the next footnote he accepts the hypothesis that Le Vayer had no faith. Le Vayer was made preceptor to the Duke of Anjou but not to the young

Louis XIV, and it had been suggested, wrongly in Bayle's view, that this was because he was suspected of unbelief:

For since it was judged that so wise a man would carefully avoid instilling the Libertinism of Orasius Tubero into the young duke, it was more reasonable to conclude that he never durst presume to inspire it into the young monarch. Cardinal Mazarin was too well acquainted with mankind not to know that a Philosopher, who, by I know not what train of arguments, is led to Pyrrhonism in religion, is a man of a quite different character from a man who becomes impious out of brutality and debauchery. Such a Philosopher, in all particulars like la Mothe le Vayer, would be very uneasy, that persons liable to make an ill use of his opinions should ever imbibe them. He would always be so discreet as to keep them from youth, and much more from a prince whose solid piety may extremely contribute to the public happiness. [C]

Le Vayer is thus "in all particulars" like a discreet unbeliever, and it hardly seems "a very rash judgment" to suspect him of being one, and by the end of the essay it is perhaps not "a very rash judgment" to think that Bayle shares the judgements he quotes Marville as attributing to "the French Academy" and to "the world": "The French Academy considered him as one of their best members; but the world looked on him as a capricious humourist, who lived according to his fancy, and as a Sceptic Philosopher" (*in corp.*).

IX

I want to conclude by turning directly to Bayle's discussion of Christianity. We will look at two articles which invite an anti-Christian interpretation, and then discuss the crucial silence at the heart of the *Dictionary*, the missing article which leaves Bayle's attacks on religion incomplete and thus preserves for him the possibility of a defence against his critics.

Bayle reports that the poet Simonides was asked by a ruler to define God. He failed to do so, reporting: "the more I consider the matter, the more obscure it appears to me" ('Simonides' [F]). Thus Simonides was a sceptic. Bayle comments, "Simonides might easily have answered, had he been contented with popular notions, and those lively impressions which are now called inward proofs", but he was right not to be. This comment shows Bayle distancing himself not only from tradition and education as sources of knowledge of God, but also from Cartesian philosophy, which he generally appeals to as presenting unanswerable difficulties for materialism and atheism. Bayle then outlines an orthodox Christian reply to the question, taking an example from Tertullian, and imagines how Simonides would have set about showing that the answer was unsatisfactory. He proceeds to launch an attack of his own upon Tertullian, supported yet again by an imaginary Simonides, now speaking on behalf of a gathering of pagan sages and pressing

Bayle's own favourite problems in theodicy. Finally, Simonides refutes an imaginary contemporary theologian, at which point Bayle can conclude that Christianity provides no certain knowledge of God's nature. Christians "are beholden for their great knowledge, only to their having the happiness of being educated in a Church, where they obtained an historical, and even sometimes a justifying faith of revealed truths. This convinces them of the existence of several things which they do not comprehend". Thus Bayle places on one side reason, on the other tradition, faith, and revelation. How would Simonides have chosen between them?

[T]hough Simonides should have had the opportunity of consulting and examining the scriptures, without the influence either of education or grace, he would not have got out of his labyrinth and silence. Reason would forbid him to deny the facts contained in the scripture, and make him perceive something supernatural in the connection and order of these facts; but this would not have been sufficient to bring him to a determination. The powers of reason, and Philosophical examination, go no farther than to hold us in suspence, and to keep us in fear of erring, whether we affirm, or whether we deny. Either the Grace of GOD, or education must necessarily come in to their assistance. And carefully observe, that there is not any system against which reason affords more objections than that of the Gospel

—as a consequence of doctrines such as those of the Trinity and of eternal damnation.

Bayle asks whether the philosophical advances represented by Cartesianism have made it easier to understand the nature of God. Cartesians have sharply separated spirit and matter, and denied that spirit can have extension. The result is intellectually coherent, but the price is that we end up with no idea of what spirit is. It thus gets us no further towards an understanding of the nature of God. Bayle concludes by producing a series of authors—ancient and modern, Catholic and Protestant—who have recognized that God is incomprehensible, including La Mothe le Vayer and (in a quotation that runs to some twelve hundred words) Charron [G].

The argument of 'Simonides' is unambiguous in that it insists there can be no rational grounds for faith and that Christianity provides no defensible knowledge of God's nature. It is ambiguous in that Bayle insists that recognition of this fact is compatible (as a result of education or grace) with faith. But what sort of faith? Bayle praises Charron's "sublime genius", and it is Charron who says, "God, Deity, Eternity, Omnipotence, Infinity, are only words, and nothing more to us". Of course, people seek to invent an idea of God for themselves, but this bears no relationship to any real object. The balance of the argument (finely balanced as it is) comes down, both in Charron and in Bayle, on the side of unbelief.

In 'Simonides' Bayle took it as given that there were grounds for accepting the Scriptures as the revealed word of God. In 'Xenophanes' he returns to his favourite subject, the problem of evil, and sets out to show that any sensible reading of the Bible would lead one to recognize that through the long course of history it is the Devil who has been victorious, not God. Bayle treats the Bible as if it were the product of a government news agency, in which defeats are misrepresented as victories, insignificant gains passed off as major triumphs. On the facts reported in the Bible, the Devil, from the moment he began his rebellion against God, has suffered few defeats, and those of little importance. Through the temptation of Eve he became master of mankind. The sacrifice of Christ upon the Cross had little impact.

Now in history we find but very few triumphs of JESUS CHRIST . . . and we every where meet with the triumphs of the Devil. The war between these two parties is a continual, or almost continual, train of successes on the Devil's side; and if the rebellious party made annals of their exploits, there is not one day in the year, but what would be there marked with some ample subject for bonfires, songs of triumph, and such other signs of victory. The Annalist would have no occasion for hyperboles and flattery, to shew the superiority of that faction. ('Xenophanes' [E])

At the end of the first 1656 years of human history, only eight people could be saved by God from the deluge. The history of the Jews is a history of betrayals of God, and the Jews were in any case a tiny and insignificant people, while the rest of the world belonged to the Devil. The birth of Jesus Christ led to temporary victories, but true religion soon succumbed in the face of heresy, superstition, and vice (now, of course, it suits Bayle's purpose to write as a Protestant). The Reformation may have improved doctrine, but it did little to improve morals or end such plagues as war. All Christians agree "that for one man saved, there are perhaps a million damned. Now the war which the Devil wages with God, is about the conquest of souls; and therefore it is certain that the victory is on the Devil's side". Bayle complains of Christians who report only God's victories and ignore the Devil's: "This is like a man who seeing people gaming, should only take an account of the losses: it would appear by such a computation that he who had won the most had lost all his money."

Thus accept the truth of Revelation, and you must also accept that on the Christians' own account they are on the losing side. Bayle finishes with a necessary self-exculpation:

Observe, that all I have been saying is every day preached, and that without any design of derogating from the almighty power of Jesus Christ. No more is meant by it than (what is also my opinion) that man is naturally so prone to evil, that except the small number of the elect, all other men live and die in the service of the evil spirit, and render the paternal love of God to remedy their wickedness, or bring them to repentance, of no effect.

But this merely restates and does not solve the problem. What Bayle has shown is that, even if we accept that the Bible is true, this gives us no grounds to have confidence in God. The big battalions are and always have been on the Devil's side; Christian faith is for the most part futile, impractical, ineffectual. If the Bible is history, then the news is bad.

But is the Bible history? Bayle's defence to his critics was to insist that he had merely shown that faith was contrary to philosophic reason, but this was of no importance as long as one could show that the Bible was the revealed word of God:

The only dispute therefore that Christians can enter upon with Philosophers, is on this matter of fact; Whether the Scripture was written by inspired authors? If the arguments the Christians alledge on this subject, do not convince the Philosophers, they ought to break off the dispute; for it would be to no purpose to enter into the particular discussion of the Trinity, &c. with people who disown the divine inspiration of the Scriptures, the sole and only way to judge who is in the right, or wrong in such controversies. (v. 830)

Jurieu protested that Bayle

fait semblant de se vouloir appuyer sur la révélation, mais le malheureux a ruiné l'authorité de la révélation par mille moyens, premièrement, en rendant méprisables et même odieux les autheurs sacrés, 2° en tournant en ridicule cent endroits de la révélation, 3° et enfin en prouvant directement et sans détour que l'on ne peut trouver la vérité par la voye de l'examen de l'Ecriture à cause de ses contradictions et obscurités.[39]

This seems to me a reasonably accurate assessment of Bayle's procedure. Of course, Bayle dare not openly combine his philosophical attacks on Christianity with a direct attack on the text of the Bible, since he is not prepared to acknowledge his unbelief openly. But he repeatedly points out that the text of the Bible may be defective. In 'David' [C] he wonders why Saul was unable to recognize David when he met him after the killing of Goliath, for the two should have been well acquainted. If this was a history book, we would conclude we were dealing with a corrupt text. In 'Abimelech' [C] he points out that Josephus regularly disagrees with the Old Testament narrative. Does he, a Jew, not understand that the revealed word must be accepted as accurate history? In 'Socinus'—to Mme Labrousse's amazement— he points out that, on a Socinian reading of the New Testament, the apostles when they spoke of Jesus were rather like Catholic theologians when they write of Mary: they exaggerated his merits superstitiously.[40] In 'Schomber' [A] he reports Celsus' view that Christ's father was a soldier called Panther, and in 'Phlegon' [D] he precedes Gibbon in casting doubt on the Gospels' reports of the darkness that fell as Christ died.[41] But much the most

---

[39] Labrousse, ii. 445.   [40] 'Socinus', *in corp.*; Labrousse, ii. 343.
[41] On Bayle's interpretation of the New Testament, see M.-H. Cotoni, 'L'Exégèse du Nouveau Testament dans la philosophie française du dix-huitième siècle', *Studies on Voltaire* 220 (1984), 37–43.

dangerous text, it seems to me, is Bayle's discussion of St Francis, for, as he stresses, Franciscans regularly compared Francis to Christ. Francis provokes Bayle's scorn, for his miracles are ridiculous, his behaviour foolish. Yet reports of his life are gathered together in a work that Bayle is happy to call the Koran of the Franciscans: a Holy Book full of fraud and idiocy. Finally, the Franciscans develop a whole "theology" of St Francis in which his deeds and miracles have an eschatological significance comparable to those of Christ. In attacking St Francis, Bayle thus attacks a symbol that can stand for Christ; in mocking the Franciscan Koran, he mocks a text comparable to the New Testament. There is nothing in the text which obliges us to read it in this way, but at the same time nothing which prevents us from so doing, if we are "complicit" or "hostile" readers. The article on St Francis thus stands in place of the article required to turn the *Dictionary* into a complete textbook of unbelief: an article on Christ and his apostles.

Now the sceptical reader will of course protest that this is to read too much into the text, to mistake Bayle's attack on Catholicism for an attack on Christianity. By the time he came to write the Clarifications, Bayle had every reason to know that his texts were open to such misinterpretation, and yet he produced a text which was yet another study in ambiguity. When he outlined the type of argument he was going to put forward—an appeal to a fideistic faith in the Bible text—a friend replied:

cela ne fera pas un bon effet dans le monde et l'on ne croira jamais que vous parliez sincèrement en cette occasion. Car enfin, un homme qui a de l'esprit et du discernement peut-il goûter un principe d'où il s'ensuit qu'on ne peut être véritablement Chrétien sans une espèce d'enthousiasme ou de fanatisme? En serez-vous réduit à recourir à cette ridicule opinion de l'homme que vous combatez le plus? . . . tout le monde croira que vous aurez voulu rire et faire voir qu'on ne peut être convaincu de la vérité de la religion par une raisonnement clair et convainquant.[42]

Mme Labrousse sees in this statement an expression of a naive faith in rationalism that Bayle could scarcely be expected to share. But it was Bayle, after all, who seemed to write as a man of discernment, who, in Leibniz's happy phrase, told reason to be silent after allowing it to speak too much.[43] Le Vassor seems to me to have had a good sense of Bayle's sense of humour and of his intransigent commitment to evidence and logic, to have understood exactly what he was trying to do.

Even if we could agree on the reading of the *Dictionary*, there would remain problems to solve. When did Bayle lose his faith? In 1668, when he abandoned Catholicism to return to "the religion of his fathers"? In 1676, when reading Naudé, La Mothe le Vayer, Hobbes, and Spinoza? When writing the *Pensées diverses*, with their defence of atheism? After the death in

---

[42] Letter of Le Vassor, quoted in Labrousse, ii. 311.
[43] Labrousse, ii. 310.

1684 of his brother Jacob, imprisoned for refusing to abjure his faith? After this event Bayle never again appealed to a benevolent providence.[44] To answer these questions we would need to have an insight into Bayle's private thoughts, and this, as he repeatedly insisted, is something readers cannot gain from texts. All we can do is concentrate on the texts themselves. Contemporaries saw that they were open to a variety of interpretations. But the challenges the revisionists of the last thirty years have yet to face are these: How can one explain the *content* of the *Dictionary* (for example, the obscenities) if Bayle was a man of faith, or, at the least, committed to upholding an orthodox Christianity? How can one explain the *form* of the *Dictionary*, unless one sees it as a device to shift responsibility from the author to his sources and his readers? Finally, if the content and the form of the *Dictionary* were innocent, why did Bayle not find a way of defending them which was not every bit as ambiguous as the *Dictionary* itself had been? The only satisfactory answer to these questions, I submit, is to recognize that the *Dictionary* only makes sense if one reads Bayle as the last and the greatest of the *libertins érudits*.

Faculty of Arts
Brunel University

[44] Labrousse, i. 199.

INDEX

3 5282 00428 1724